C. L. R. James and the Study of Culture

C. L. R. James and the Study of Culture

Andrew Smith
University of Glasgow, UK

palgrave
macmillan

First published 2010 by
PALGRAVE MACMILLAN

Palgrave Macmillan in the UK is an imprint of Macmillan Publishers Limited, registered in England, company number 785998, of Houndmills, Basingstoke, Hampshire RG21 6XS.

Palgrave Macmillan in the US is a division of St Martin's Press LLC, 175 Fifth Avenue, New York, NY 10010.

Palgrave Macmillan is the global academic imprint of the above companies and has companies and representatives throughout the world.

Palgrave® and Macmillan® are registered trademarks in the United States, the United Kingdom, Europe and other countries.

ISBN 978–0–230–22021–8 hardback

This book is printed on paper suitable for recycling and made from fully managed and sustained forest sources. Logging, pulping and manufacturing processes are expected to conform to the environmental regulations of the country of origin.

A catalogue record for this book is available from the British Library.

A catalog record for this book is available from the Library of Congress.

10 9 8 7 6 5 4 3 2 1
19 18 17 16 15 14 13 12 11 10

Transferred to Digital Printing in 2014

Contents

Acknowledgements vi

The Cover Image vii

Introduction 1

1 Forms 20

2 Contexts 49

3 Crowds 82

4 Players 108

5 Uses 135

Conclusion 158

References 162

Index 171

Acknowledgements

Parts of this study have been developed from arguments and accounts first proposed in other contexts. I am very grateful, therefore, to the relevant publishers and editors for permission to reproduce material produced for the following journals: *Cultural Sociology*; *The International Journal of the History of Sport*; *Theory, Culture and Society* (further details of these publications are given in the reference list). I have benefited from the often shrewd comments of peer-reviewers who assessed the work I submitted to those journals, and from suggestions provided by the editors of the journals themselves.

I have also benefited very much from discussions with many colleagues and friends, not all of whom I have the space to list here. Particular mention is due, however, to Professor John Bale (Keele University), Professor Neil Lazarus (University of Warwick) and to Professor Satnam Virdee (University of Glasgow), all of whom have been very generous with their time and their ideas in relation to various pieces of work on James which I have shown them. Professor Brian Stoddart (La Trobe University) was especially supportive, reading and commenting on a first draft of the book.

I owe a particular debt of gratitude to *The Sociological Review*, and to the writing fellowship supported by the journal, of which I was recipient in 2003–4, and in the context of which I first began working systematically on James. I am also grateful to Professor Bridget Fowler, who has been an unstinting source of support and advice. She was also the person who first pushed me to consider writing a longer study of James, and took the time to read and comment on that study when it was finally drafted.

Thanks also to my Mum and Dad, to my brother Phil, and to my own family, for all their love and encouragement. James Young recalls a story about the elderly C. L. R. James in Brixton, telling the child of visiting friends that in the new society which he hoped they would live to see, every child would have a chocolate biscuit in one hand, and a chocolate biscuit in the other. The preparation and writing of this book coincided with the birth and the first years of life of my sons Sam and Laurie, who have brought amazing joy and fun with them. They would certainly share this particular Jamesian vision of the future. Finally, this book is dedicated to Emma Purvis; a very insufficient thank-you for all of her love, her critical good sense, and her brusque dismissals of intellectual posturing.

The Cover Image

The cover image is one of the huge number of photographic studies produced by Eadweard Muybridge at the University of Pennsylvania, building on the method he pioneeringly developed in California from 1872, and published in a vast compendium called *Animal Locomotion* in 1884–5 (Hill 2001). The model for his particular series, as for accompanying series in which a cricket ball is bowled or caught, was apparently 'the best all-round cricketer' from the University (Muybridge 1901). It seems a fitting image for the cover of a book about C. L. R. James. After all, James himself had long planned, but never completed, a book which would contain photographs of great cricketers alongside examples of classical athleticism; a visual demonstration, as it were, of the relationship he often discussed between modern and ancient popular sporting practices. It can be fairly guessed that whether or not James knew Muybridge's work, he would have appreciated the decidedly Greek framing of many of these sporting studies. He would have appreciated also, though, the way in which past aesthetic virtues were being to made to move, were becoming part of a new way of representing human beings. James, the great lover of film and its ability to capture the dynamism, the sheer rush of human beings, would surely have taken some pleasure in the way in which Athens, cricket and the first flickerings of cinema come together here.

Introduction

I

Recent years have seen a much deserved, if somewhat belated, development of interest in the work of the West Indian historian, novelist, critic and activist, C. L. R. James. James' reputation has long been secure as the author of a ground-breaking historical work – *The Black Jacobins* – and of *Beyond a Boundary*, an equally ground-breaking work of social and cultural criticism. Recent years, however, have seen a growing recognition of the extraordinary breadth of James' interests and writings. In the period just before James' death in 1989, and since, a three-volume collection of selected works have been published, along with a number of anthologies (following in the successful footsteps of a *Radical America* selection from 1970), as well as many previously unavailable texts of various lengths. At the same time, the number of critical introductions and studies devoted to aspects of James' life and work has proliferated. Scholars in a wide range of disciplines are increasingly acknowledging the importance of James' analyses for anyone interested in making sense of the development of modern society and culture, and his work has even begun to make an appearance in that inner sanctum represented by the edited volume of readings in social theory (for example, Lemert 2004: 413–22). Moreover, James' wider public profile has continued to develop as it did in the later years of his life and as befits someone who was wary of academic seclusion. Certainly in the British context, it is notable how often James' name crops up in the broadcast and print media, although we can perhaps imagine how he would have responded to the posthumous attention lavished on him by not one, but two, 'New Labour' ministers (see Høgsbjerg 2006).

Despite all of this, there is as yet no full-length study dedicated to the central claims that underlie James' analysis of culture, although both Nielsen (1997) and Grimshaw (1991) have written at length about these issues. This is surprising, because James' work has a great deal to offer anyone interested in seeking to make sense of modern culture in all its diversity of forms. James was an astute critic of literature and art, writing with real verve on a dizzying array of subjects from Flemish art to the American abolitionists to postcolonial African and Caribbean novelists. More than this, however, he was one of the few critics of his time to treat seriously popular culture, writing with insight about (among other things) sport, soap opera, carnival and film. James' personal experience of popular culture's political charge in colonial Trinidad, allied to a real mastery of the European high cultural tradition, gave him a breadth and generosity of vision that stands out among twentieth-century intellectuals. Even those who most obviously invite comparison, such as Raymond Williams, are more limited than James in some respects, having less to say about the experiences of colonisation and of racism in the shaping of the modern world.

In all of his very varied writings on these subjects James displays a remarkably consistent and rigorous but also highly original approach to understanding culture. Dismissing all judgements based around supposedly timeless literary or artistic qualities, James insists on understanding cultural forms and practices in and through their social and historical context. 'For me', he wrote in 1953, 'social criticism and literary criticism are indistinguishable [...] I strive for a social criticism which will illuminate the text' (1992: 232–4). At the same time, however, he equally rejected what he saw as a 'Stalinist' interpretation of culture, that is to say, the assumption that aesthetic or artistic achievements could somehow be read as the automatic expression of a specific class consciousness. James was always alert to the subtleties, nuances and ambiguities of cultural expression and he insisted on a careful reading of texts on their own terms as the first principle of any properly historical analysis of culture.

This study is written in the belief, then, that James offers to anyone interested in the analysis of culture a series of lessons and provocations, as well as a distinctive method, all of which warrant systematic consideration. What follows is, of course, expository in some respects, but I have tried also to draw out some of the many challenges of his approach for contemporary readers. It seems a fittingly 'Jamesian' way of approaching things to ask not just what something means but also: what can be done with it, where does it get us?

II

There are at least five biographies of James currently available (Buhle 1988; Worcester 1996; Young 1999; Dhondy 2001; Renton 2007), as well as James' published autobiographical memories in *Beyond a Boundary* and in his letters to Constance Webb. It is not my intention, then, to provide a detailed account of his life here, but a short sketch (drawing largely on these sources) may be helpful for those to whom he is a new name. James was born in 1901 in Trinidad, within the small and relatively precarious black middle class. His father was a local school teacher. It was, however, his mother who was the more significant influence on him, and who would later provide significant emotional support for his writerly ambitions. From her James acquired a habit of voracious reading and it was this, along with his family's Puritanism and the wider surroundings of a popular cricketing culture that defined his early life. He won at a young age, as his family expected, one of the rare scholarships available to support attendance at the island's prestigious Queen's Royal College. What his family did not expect, however, was that their son would refuse the trajectory which was thus opened up to him: an overseas education followed by a political or professional career. Instead, James gave himself over to cricket, at which he was more than adept and – sceptical already of authorised voices or programmes – to reading whatever his intellectual curiosity led him to.

James graduated in 1918 and moved to a teaching position, later returning to work in the college itself. Unlike some of his contemporaries, then, he did not immediately become a member of the Caribbean diaspora in the universities or other institutions of the metropolitan world, and this affected his perspective in important respects. Apart from anything else, this was a period of ferment in the Caribbean in which, especially after the First World War, trade-unionism and anti-colonialist sentiment was growing. The Garvey movement, on the one hand, and the writings of W. E. B du Bois, on the other, both suggested some relationship between these local political rumblings and events beyond the region. James himself, it seems, was not closely involved, or at least not vocally involved, in these developments and although he had links to the populist leader Captain Cipriani, such things were filtered in and through his emerging literary ambitions. The early series of short stories that he wrote in this period, for example, show already an astute eye for popular cultural practices, and a sympathetic understanding of the struggle to establish some sense of control over daily experience which lay at the heart of many such practices. These stories emerged into a small but energetic cultural scene, centred for a while around *The Beacon* magazine, whose literary hallmark came to be a brand of social realism tinged with romanticism and which prided itself on its success in scandalising the prim moralities of the local elites. There was also, amid these circles, an increasingly confident questioning of imperial assumptions. James himself contributed 'A Defence of the Intelligence of the Negro' to *The Beacon* in 1931, in reply to a typical example of expatriate racism. It might be argued, in this respect, that the fact that James spent his entire early adulthood in Trinidad (not unlike du Bois' New England upbringing) prevented him from internalising a sense of himself as racially inferior. Drafted towards the end of this period, although only published on his arrival in England, was the book which James no doubt planned as the first salvo of a literary career, but which proved to be his only full-length work of fiction: *Minty Alley*.

James had continued to play cricket throughout his time in Trinidad, with and against some of the island's very best players. And it was at the request of one of these, Learie Constantine, that James moved to Britain in 1932, initially in order to act as a ghost-writer on the former's biography. Initially, James spent time in London, as befitted the aspiring British intellectual, but he subsequently joined Constantine in the Lancashire village of Nelson. Both Constantine and Nelson's radical traditions were important in challenging some of James' complacencies about the values proclaimed within British culture, and about the supposed superiority of that culture. Experiences of English racism no doubt also played their part, but there is no real suggestion that these forced an existential crisis on James, as they did famously for Frantz Fanon. More typical of James' perspective at the point of his arrival in Britain is the altogether ambivalent comment in the preface to his *Life of Captain Cipriani*, which was published in 1932: James appeals to the readers of this book to send him 'anything which would be useful in the effort to rid ourselves of the weight we have carried so long that some of us scarcely realise that we are carrying it' (1932b: n.p.). Very quickly, however, such hesitance was left behind. Indicative, in some respects, was James' decision to fillet his original text in order to form a more polemical pamphlet, *The Case for West-Indian Self Government*, which was published in the following year. At the same time James became politically active among both the Independent Labour Party, and in various other organisations of the non-Communist left, as well as in groups campaigning among the colonial diaspora in London, particularly in the context of the invasion of Abyssinia by Italian forces in 1935.

There followed a period of extraordinary productivity on James' part. Alongside his work as a cricket correspondent for *The Manchester Guardian* and, later, *The Glasgow Herald*, he wrote a huge amount in a very short space of time. Quite apart from the rapid-fire polemics expected of someone quickly becoming established as a significant voice in political debate, James wrote and starred in a play, *Toussaint Louverture*, opposite Paul Robeson. He also produced a significant, critical account of the Communist International, entitled *World Revolution*, and translated Boris Souvarine's anti-Stalinist biography of Stalin. Most significantly, perhaps, he researched and published his acclaimed study of the Haitian revolution, *The Black Jacobins*, alongside a shorter, popular work called *A History of Negro Revolt*. The former has become an established classic of black (or, perhaps, red) Atlantic historiography, focused as it is around the way in which the struggles of the enslaved at the 'periphery' of the colonial world were both catalysed by and subsequently came to defend the principles proclaimed by the French revolution. Equally central to the book is a penetrating account of the interplay of conceptions of 'race' and class, and in this respect it invites comparison with du Bois' similarly epoch-making work, *Black Reconstruction*.

Many things that would come to typify James' intellectual production begin to emerge here. Not the least of these was his love of working within (and often starring in) small political groupings. Yet James' attachments were remarkably pluralist and the list of those he worked with or influenced in a variety of formal or informal contexts is amazingly broad, and includes many of the central figures in the history of the movements for decolonisation alongside the leading lights of the Bloomsbury set and of the independent left in Britain. An important general point thus emerges: James, who was by now describing himself as a Marxist, was nevertheless always generous in respecting the particular shapes and histories of different political or social struggles. It was, in a sense, this question which led him to leave Britain in 1938, when he headed first for a speaking tour of America and later for Mexico and discussions with Trotsky over the organisational and theoretical approach of socialist movements to 'Negro' politics.

In a sense, James' time in America is both the most intriguing and the most opaque period of his life. Much of his work from this long decade was conducted under the cover of pseudonyms in various journals and papers, as he and his close-knit group of collaborators (most prominently, Raya Dunayevskaya, who first persuaded James to remain in America, and Grace Lee) worked in and around the fragmented anti-Communist left in the country. Recently, thanks to the assiduous work of a number of scholars, many of James' shorter political writings from his time in America have become publicly available, although it is likely that there may well be more to be discovered. James' role in this context was very much that of the engaged intellectual and he came, with his group of associates, to define a series of distinctive positions on a number of significant issues, of which two are particularly noteworthy. The first relates to the question of black politics which had brought James to America in the first place. In the course of a long series of interventions James and his colleagues argued for the importance of recognising the specific historical and experiential grounds from which anti-racist struggles emerged, and insisted that such struggles had their own parameters and that they led, therefore, to their own conclusions about what socialism might look like. James was thus wary of any attempt to treat the 'Negro question' as simply an annex of class struggle. He was equally wary, however, of a black politics which ended up hamstrung by its own limited intent: he was wary, in other words, of the idea of blackness being erected as some kind of ethical or political good in itself. This is an entirely typical position: James was consistent in giving due recognition to the particular historical contexts out of which, or against which, social movements emerge, but insistent also that such movements need, in the end, to open outwards into something wider, lest they end up walling themselves in.

Such considerations tied into the second set of emerging arguments in the work of James and the group of which he was part. The debates here are entangled ones but, broadly speaking, through a series of publications, some of which began as internal discussion papers within various party contexts, James and his collaborators came to develop an increasingly pluralist, decentralised view of political organisation, with a strong emphasis on the degree to which popular struggles might involve their own forms of autonomous organisation. The texts of this period (which include *Notes on Dialectics*, *State Capitalism and World Revolution* and significant essays such as 'Dialectical Materialism and the Fate of Humanity') contain a marked scepticism with regard to bureaucratic structures that comes close, in later works, to an anarchist position. There is scepticism also of the tendency in Marxism to assume that events are determined by an abstract historical logic, the code to which is entrusted to a privileged few. By contrast, James and his collaborators called for a more attentive reading of historically changing social relationships and structures of production, and for a correspondingly more flexible approach to political organisation.

On the face of it, James' literary ambitions, whether as novelist or historical writer, seem to have been put aside in this period. Yet this is only partly accurate. America was the place where James came face-to-face with proliferating forms of mass entertainment on a new scale – the Hollywood film industry, the radio serial, the comic book, the pulp thriller – and understanding these cultural phenomena, and understanding their audiences no less, was central to his work during these years. As, indeed, was his determination to understand, historically, America's distinctive literary tradition. Moreover, James fitted easily into the vibrant cultural scene in and around Harlem, and he became a supporter and friend of many of the most significant members of a new wave of young black writers: Richard Wright, Ralph Ellison and James Baldwin, among others. It was, all the same, only towards the end of his time in America that such concerns and interests became incorporated openly into his public writing. In the later of the political statements mentioned above, for example, James insists with increasing vehemence on the lessons to be learned from a careful consideration of the changing forms of American mass culture. Indeed, a lack of concern for these questions was one among a number of reasons why James and those around him finally ended up breaking with Trotskyism. Later, under the threat of deportation, James would produce a full-length study of Herman Melville as part of a campaign to be allowed to remain in the country. This was itself extracted and expanded from a longer historical study of American culture for which James carried out the groundwork in this period, but which remained unpublished at the time.

Politically, these were turbulent but invigorating times for James. They were turbulent but invigorating times personally as well. He had left his first wife Juanita in Trinidad when he first embarked for Britain and in most of the existing accounts of James' life she is an all but invisible figure, appearing only in order to facilitate her disappearance from the story; that is to say, only as the distant party from whom James sought a divorce in Reno in 1948. He did so in order to allow him to marry Constance Webb, a young actress he had met during his first speaking tour of America, and to whom he poured out an extraordinary series of letters, many of which have subsequently been published. As Farrukh Dhondy notes, there are times when James' letters to Webb appear to be addressed to an imaginary or impossible subject, and it does seem as if he saw their hoped-for relationship as a kind of world historical romance in which the torn parts of Atlantic modernity would be symbolically recomposed. There is more to it than that, though, as I argue below: James' correspondence with Webb reveals a longing also for a politics in which the subjective, the emotional or the personal, is no longer seen as suspicious. In the comparative seclusion of those letters he reveals also the extent to which reflections on literary and creative endeavour continued to be an integral part of his thinking at this time.

In order to avoid deportation, James left America in 1953, returning in the first instance to Britain. His relationship with Webb had already broken down, crushed in part by the pressure of James' political commitments but also, perhaps, by the pressure of all that James had projected on to her and on to them. James' political relationships were also strained by the gap that now separated him from his collaborators, although there was theoretical as well as geographical distance at stake in the various splits which eventually took place. This was not immediate, however, and for a while collaborations continued in various forms. This led, among other things, to the publication of *Facing Reality*, a collective response to the Hungarian uprisings in 1956 which appeared in many respects – as would events in Poland later – to vindicate an emphasis on self-organised popular resistance. James, meanwhile, had remarried, this time to Selma Weinstein, who was and remains, a significant writer and campaigner around the intersecting issues of gender, class and 'race'.

She and James moved to Trinidad in 1958 at the behest of Eric Williams, leader of the People's National Movement and on the cusp of becoming the first leader of a formally independent Trinidad. This move marked a further shift in James' concerns, towards a more concerted focus on the colonised world, and on the kinds of troubled regime which would succeed colonial rule. The signs of that trouble were obvious enough from early on. Williams had once been James' pupil in Queen's Royal College, and James had long seen him as a protégé: the former's doctoral thesis, later published as *Capitalism and Slavery* (1944), was based on an initial suggestion of James', and there are stories of the older man chaperoning Williams around the pubs of London with a copy of Jane Austen in his pocket. In Trinidad, however, it quickly became clear that Williams saw a threat in James' insistently progressive and anti-imperialist politics. In the end James was dismissed from his post as editor of the party's newspaper on a fabricated fraud charge, although not before he had played a pivotal role in the campaign which secured a significant symbolic victory: the appointment of Frank Worrell as the first black captain of the West Indian cricket team.

These disillusioning experiences were to be repeated, to some extent, in Ghana where another figure who had received support from James,

Kwame Nkrumah, would follow Williams' path into autocracy and reaction. They were compounded in the case of Trinidad when James returned in 1965 in an attempt to establish a new popular party with a base among the workers in the oil industry, an attempt which failed more or less completely and which perhaps suggests that James misjudged the degree to which his cosmopolitanism and his intellectualism were seen as alienating factors by ordinary Trinidadians. James himself, however, kept faith in the ability of working men and women to grapple with, to understand and to lay claim to, the best of the heritage of Western civilisation, and he laid out his own vision of that heritage in a series of panoramic public talks in Trinidad in 1960 that were subsequently published as *Modern Politics*.

Whatever the losses that resulted from James' departure from America, there were some advantages. In both the Caribbean and in Britain between times, James immersed himself afresh in cricket. Whatever his doubts regarding the prospects for the independence of the colonised nations, he had the pleasure of watching as the popular optimism and confidence of that period was reflected in the performances of an extraordinary generation and more of West Indian players of the game. In Britain James returned to sports journalism, and wrote a number of significant longer articles, some generic and others focused around particular individuals. More importantly, however, he completed and published what can probably be said to be his last major work, *Beyond a Boundary*, in 1963. This is, in company with *The Black Jacobins*, the book on which James' current reputation most obviously rests. It is also one of those books which can be appropriately called a one-off, certainly in terms of its arguments, but also in its extraordinary stylistic synthesis of autobiography, critical analysis, history and polemic.

In the last decades of his life James spent time variously in Africa, the Caribbean, North America – to which he returned, thanks, in part, to a cricket loving member of the American consulate – and in Europe. After years spent in relative obscurity, James became someone whose opinion mattered, consulted by political figures such Walter Rodney and Maurice Bishop, and sought out by young writers such as Ngugi wa Thiong'o. His own writing, however, became a little more fragmented and marked at times by a newly reflective tone. Indeed, towards the very end of his life James sought on a number of occasions, always unsuccessfully, to write an autobiography. To some extent such changes were due to James' growing infirmity. He had struggled, for much of his life, with illnesses of various kinds and had been severely injured in a car crash in 1962 which left him more fragile, and more short of energy, than he had once been. To some extent also, perhaps, there was some measure of defeat here: his one-time comrade Grace Lee Boggs suggests that James either chose to escape, or no longer lived in a situation which allowed, the kind of immersion in popular culture and in ordinary working lives which had once energised his politics (Boggs 1993). Be this as it may, James' capacity for critical insight never left him and even late in his life, as he was adopted as a pioneer figure by the black power movement on both sides of the Atlantic, he remained at best sceptically sympathetic so far as that movement's presuppositions were concerned. James died in Brixton, in 1989.

III

It is perhaps needless to say, after this, that one remarkable strength of James' work, practical as well as intellectual, was his ability to see or to seek the relationships between what are usually treated as distinct 'kinds' of experience, politics or culture. James unquestionably widens the horizons of his readers in this respect: it is hard to imagine another twentieth-century thinker who would so instinctively have brought Heidegger to a reading of Wilson Harris (James 1980: chapter 12) or memories of cricket's 'bodyline' controversy to the interpretation of *Moby Dick* (Gair 2002). And as this second example makes clear, James brought popular and 'high' culture together in a single analysis just as often as he brought together perspectives from different historical contexts. It is tempting, in this respect, to call James a 'contrapuntal' thinker, in Edward Said's phrase, and James was certainly one of the exemplars that Said had in mind when he called for thinking across and between conventional cultural or national boundaries (for example, Said 1993: 312). I say 'tempting', however, because to some extent Said's call has been swept up and hollowed out by a tidal wave of recent theoretical discussions of migrancy, displacement, diaspora and so forth, not all of which have bothered to retain the marked emphasis, in both Said and James, on recognising the specificity of local experiences, of local political and historical circumstances. There is an inspiring synoptic reach in James' work, but there is also an insistent focus on our 'sitedness' and on the importance of grasping the economic and social relationships that have come to characterise particular contexts. There is some muddy bathwater to be thrown out here, for sure: the idea of an uncontaminated or self-contained national history, for example, deserves the drain, as does any idea of a racially or ethnically defined intellectual heritage. But we need to be careful not to throw out, along with this conservative claptrap, the importance of understanding our emplacement, the degree to which we are part of legal, political and economic orders that often determine a great deal about what is possible or impossible for us. James, in many ways, provides us with a model of what it means to work across many of modernity's given boundaries, without ever losing sight of our groundedness, of the social, material and historical determinations of our lives.

There is a second sense in which James' work often involves a bringing together of things which are conventionally kept apart, and this is his characteristic insistence on thinking about the different parts of social experience (economic, cultural, political, personal and so forth) as wholly interrelated. Obviously this does not mean that James was unable to recognise the difference between a sonnet and a strike ballot. Nevertheless, it seems clear to me, as I will argue at greater length at various places in this study, that James was sceptical of any political struggle which, in the name of that struggle, sought to insist that there were parts of human life which could be discounted as secondary or weightless or as distractions from what really mattered. Convalescing beside the Atlantic in 1943 from an illness brought on in part by the tensions of his clandestine existence in America, and in part by his more or less total submergence in political activism, James wrote a letter to Constance Webb. It is one of the very few pieces of James' writing from that frenetic period of his life in which can be found some sense of peace, some sense of his managing to be what, in many ways, he continually sought to be: the still centre around which many centrifugal histories could fall into pattern. 'I am political', writes James, and political work consumes 'my every activity'. And yet, he says, that political longing cannot be thought of as something separable from the most personal longing: 'to sit on the platform with Constance and watch the evening sun go down'. He continues: 'The connection may seem monstrous. It isn't. Somehow the intensity of a personal experience, even at this distance, the sense of beauty and companionship, which are so very rare, such things when exercised in the imagination and over a continent's distance, seem to give a personal meaning and significance to the great struggles opening up' (1992: 130). This seems to me to be an image worth holding on to, and one that might serve as a reminder that for James there was no useful line to be drawn between our political and personal lives. Moreover, that a lasting politics requires the effort to bring the scattered parts of our experience together.

This position plays out in a number of ways in James' writing. It is noticeable how often, for example, his conclusions in political or historical debates are pre-empted by, or recapitulated in, his approach to cultural or artistic matters. A short example might be useful here. When James and his colleagues broke from the mainstream of the Trotskyist movement they did so partly because they believed that this mainstream had become dogmatic and unhistorical in its approach to political organisation. That, in other words, Trotskyism had fallen into what James called, in various places, 'synthetic cognition' (1986 [1950]: 133), which I take to mean a failure to treat the forms of things – in this case, the existing organisational forms and practices of the left – not as givens, nor as done-and-dusted solutions, but as creative responses to specific historical circumstances – responses, therefore, which may no longer be tenable or appropriate in a changed situation. There is obviously a debate to be had here about whether James was right with regard to this particular question of political practice, and the fact that he left America when he did makes it hard to answer such a question definitively either way. A generous reader of these debates might well give credit to James and his collaborators for appreciating ahead of time the importance of those more improvisational and decentralised forms of political activity which, in fact, did emerge in the sixties and afterwards. More critical readers have accused him, in his emphasis on spontaneous political action, of a descent into mere wishful thinking. In any case, what is noticeable is that this conclusion with regard to a strictly political question – the importance of understanding particular forms of practice as historically specific and the need not to be trapped in a rigid defence of such existing forms – is exactly the same general claim that lies at the heart of James' analysis of cultural practices, from his writings on changing cricketing style to those on the shifts in film-making technique. When James talks about cultural forms, about how those forms can be seen to express the contentions of their historical context, and about how new forms of practice emerge as older ones become entangled in contradictions (in themselves, and in relation to the world of which they are part) – when he makes these arguments he clearly draws on an approach which is born of his political thinking. Conversely, he arrives at political conclusions with regard to these questions, in part at least, because he had struggled for a similarly historical understanding of human creativity in its wider sense.

I am, in this respect, unconvinced by the fact that the story of James' intellectual life is often told as one in which a period of fierce political engagement is followed by a retreat into more ethereal cultural matters. In fact, it seems to me, James' most interesting and important writings about culture come directly out of those periods of his life when he was most concertedly involved in political work. This can certainly be claimed of his studies of American popular culture and of Herman Melville, which are inseparable from James' period of underground activism in America. But it is true also of *Beyond a Boundary*, the central arguments of which were already emerging during James' first period in Britain in the 1930s and which were concluded amidst the struggles and tensions of decolonisation in the Caribbean. There are no convincing grounds, it seems to me, for talking about a 'cultural turn' on James' behalf. Rather, throughout his life, cultural creativity and political struggle were treated as part of each other, however much bourgeois aesthetes, on the one hand, and leftist ideologues, on the other, sought to tear them apart.

In the writing of this study, I have tried to be true to James' own practice in a number of ways. The first of these follows from what has just been said: I have tried, at various points, to make clear how James' approach to cultural questions, his treatment of the idea of artistic individualism, for example, or his emphasis on the critical role of the crowd, are inseparable from his thinking in other areas and from his thinking about popular political struggles in particular. Although this is a book dedicated to his cultural writing, it would offer an odd and amputated vision of James if that was all it were about.

IV

There is a second sense in which I have tried, in writing this account, to be true to James' own practice. Wherever possible, I have sought to limit my use of theoretical jargon, and to avoid references to debates in the academic literature, except in a fairly general sense. At one or two points I have compared James' position with that of other writers who have developed a historical or sociological account of culture. But I have done so, generally, only in passing and have pursued these comparisons only in so far as they have been useful in clarifying James' own position. There are a number of general studies of James available which tackle such issues in greater detail, for those who are interested in doing so. The fullest of these is probably Frank Rosengarten's recent account (2007).

It can be said, without naming names, that not all of the recent expositions of James' work have thought that this question of style was worth bothering about. This is itself indicative of a notable and unwelcome irony: much of the newer literary and cultural criticism which claims James as a founding figure (I am thinking of work in branches of cultural and postcolonial studies most obviously) has become mired in a horribly restrictive technical language, or in a jokey linguistic complexity beneath whose smoke and mirrors there seems to lurk a radical doubt about the usefulness of the whole enterprise. This was not a doubt that James shared. He was, in many respects, a believer in the Enlightenment ideal of the public intellectual, at least in a qualified sense. Qualified because, for James, there were always publics in the plural to be considered and he never lost the ability to raise awkward questions for a particular audience by bringing the experiences of another context to bear (as, for example, in that questioning engagement with the black power movement which I mentioned above (see James 1980: chapter 15; 1984: chapter 15)). Qualified also because James consistently refused to accept that the word of the specialist was final and, as I argue later in this study, his own intellectual production was marked by his openness, not just to the experiences of ordinary men and women, but to their own often insightful and critical interrogations of those experiences. And this is, of course, the point. James had no time for cabalistic intellectual discussions not simply because of what would be lost to a wider audience through such parochialism, but also because of what would be lost to the discussants themselves. An emphasis on the role of the audience in shaping cultural production was a hallmark of his position, and it is an emphasis which he extended to his accounts of the production of intellectuals, just as much as to the work of musicians or actors. This emphasis in James has, moreover, a significant effect: it puts a great deal of intellectual position-taking and the rarefied language in which it is couched into perspective, making clear the extent to which intellectual work is itself carried out within particular structures, within its own conditions of production, which inevitably bear upon what is produced. Another way of saying this is that James' emphasis on the popular audience allowed him also to reflect consciously on the specific conditions of his own writing, his own work as a cultural producer. His emphasis on the popular audience gave him a sense of the often self-serving nature of existing intellectual debates and he was, as a consequence, never likely to be dragged into a practice where florid theorisation became the symbolic price to be paid in order to hold down a place as a recognised 'intellectual' (Kauppi 2005).

I have tried to write this study, then, in such a way that it will be open to non-specialist or non-academic readers of James, of whom there are many. I have done so not just in an attempt to produce something that is in keeping with the practice of James himself. I have done so also, and more importantly, in an attempt to think consciously, as James seems to me always to have done, about my own position in a structure of production, and in an attempt to realise how much one may lose as a result of what appears to be, at first glance, the privileged nature of that position.

Stylistic aspiration is, of course, not necessarily the same as stylistic achievement. But James, at least, gives us much to aspire to. Whether or not one agrees with his interpretation of Hegel in *Notes on Dialectics* (1980 [1948]), for example, and opinions differ markedly about the philosophical conclusions of the book, it strikes me as a model for anyone looking to set about the business of summarising and synthesising challenging ideas in an uncomplicated and non-patronising way. A model also in the sheer sense of fun that it brings to intellectual inquiry, for which the increasingly workmanlike wordplay of critical writing post-Derrida is no substitute. James' own literary style is not the least of his legacies and offers us, unquestionably, something to aim at.

V

A few final comments. In general, in what follows, I have acted as proponent for James. I do so in the firm belief that his work is not just of historical interest, but also that he has much to offer which is peculiarly relevant for readers at the start of the twenty-first century. In a sense it is the wider job of this study to substantiate that claim, but I would point at the outset to some of James' characteristic positions: his sceptical defence of the Enlightenment project, for example; his supple, creative and humanist Marxism; the glint of utopianism in much of what he wrote. This last point, above all, perhaps, is significant: James provides us with the kind of resources of hope that David Harvey describes (2000: chapter 9), but of a hope based in a fierce critical-mindedness. James may have been an optimist, but we should not forget that his optimism never betrayed him, as it did some significant others on the left, into underestimating the awfulness of the Soviet system, or into a belief in its possible regeneration.

In any case, I have sought here to make a strong case for the enduring usefulness of James' work generally, and his cultural analysis in particular, and to draw out from what are often fairly diverse and occasionally scrappy sources, those claims or arguments which seem to me to form the heart of James' approach. In one or two places I have noted some of the limits of James' arguments, and some of their contradictions, but in general I have been concerned to present what seems helpful, challenging and provocative in his work, rather than what seems problematic. There *are* problems, of course. James' thesis about the representative significance of great sports players, for example, does not pause to ask about the degree to which such symbolism has generally come in a very gendered form in the modern world, and therefore tends to overlook the limits which may nestle in the heart of the very practices deployed in the name of 'freedom' (on this see Gregg 2000). And this applies, perhaps, not just to the question of gender. As has been variously pointed out (Ross 1996; Dworkin 2007) James' forward-looking account of American modernity leaves surprisingly little space for the historical experiences of indigenous Americans, just as his perspective on post-colonial nationalism in the Caribbean skips over rather easily the particular historical experiences of those of Indian origin in the region.

Others have suggested that the tensions or stresses that followed from James' peripatetic life led him into contradictions as often as they led him to new insights. Or, perhaps, that the contradictions were the price James paid for occupying a space where certain kinds of insight fell within reach. For Brett St. Louis (1999, 2007), for example, James' work is often marked by a 'bad faith' in these respects. James, he argues, is inconsistent in his description of human identity or selfhood. In his American writings, this appears as something relatively undefined, an open process, an unresolved 'becoming'. In other contexts, however, especially during his political involvement in the Caribbean, he was willing to appeal to an idea of identity as defined by birth or by place or by nation. Personally, I do not find this criticism particularly helpful and one of the claims that I want to make in what follows is that James' work has at its heart the always open tension, present in the best of Marxism, between an understanding of our historically and socially constituted selves, and a recognition of our capacity for change. Moreover, it seems to me that James was often concerned to get past a sterile face-off between ideas of 'being' versus those of 'becoming' in order to insist on the more challenging question: if we are capable of changing ourselves and our world, as he clearly believed we are, what should such change look like?

Such criticisms relate, however, to a broader issue, which is the particular tension created by the fact that James so often operated as both critic and defender of what he called 'Western civilisation'. He was, as we will see, insistent on recognising the violence and the limitations that have routinely accompanied that civilisation and the actions undertaken in its defence. Yet he was also someone who considered the values expressed in the tradition of the Enlightenment to contain an as-yet-unredeemed promise. Nowhere, perhaps, has the tussle over James' legacy been fiercer than with regard to this issue, although it has sometimes proceeded in rather covert fashion. Anthony Bogues' study of James' early political thought (1997), for example, is an important text and it certainly opens up some of the ground which I wish to consider here (as in his provocative but unelaborated suggestion, for example, that cricket was part of what rescued James from a dogmatic, mechanistic Marxism). All the same, Bogues is surely a little too confident in claiming James as a member of a black radical tradition whose insights were owed, above all, to his Caribbean origin. When, for example, he attributes James' bold political manoeuvrings in America to his 'Caribbean audacity' (56), it is impossible not to recall James' own scathing response to similar judgements regarding West Indian cricketers. On the other hand, Farrukh Dhondy, in his biography of James, responds to moves of this sort with an overstatement of his own: 'The distinguishing fact of his intellectual legacy was that it owed nothing to Africa nor to any tradition apart from the one which began with the Greeks' (2001: 67; see also his comment that James' 'constant and probably only source of pride in Trinidad and the Caribbean' (162) was the region's writers). To take such statements seriously one would need to discount not only *The Black Jacobins* but James' whole repeated thesis regarding the way in which historical experiences in the Caribbean were peculiarly representative of modern dilemmas as such. James, in short, is not well served by simplification. Above all, he thought of himself as a dialectical thinker, as one of many who worked by taking and turning the historical weapons of Western modernity against itself, interrogating it from the point of view of those experiences it disqualified or overlooked, but doing so precisely in the name of the supposedly universal ideals which it had proclaimed.

For the most part, in any case, this study is not addressed explicitly to such debates over James' legacy, nor to the various, more specific critiques of James that exist. Rather it aims to provide a clear account of James' approach to the various practices and products of human creativity, of what gets called 'culture' with a small 'c' (as opposed to the more encompassing way in which the word is used by anthropologists). Even this fairly limited aim faces some difficulties in relation to someone like James, whose thinking was so instinctively comparative and relational, and for whom the habit of placing things in sealed intellectual compartments was anathema. Studies such as this one, however, need some boxes to work with and these are the boxes I have used for the purposes of what follows: I begin, in Chapter 1, by emphasising James' concern with the question of 'form'. I start here primarily because this is where James himself started, because he repeatedly argued that we could understand cultural practices and their historical or other kinds of significance only once we had adequately got to grips with what they meant in their own terms, as symbolic practices operating according to their own criteria of success and failure. This is followed by a second, counterpart chapter that looks at the way in which James situates cultural forms and practices historically, at their changing historical expressions, and at their relationships to particular social contexts and conflicts. Chapter 3 considers James' intriguing and pioneering emphasis on the role of audiences in determining the meanings of games, films, texts and so forth, while Chapter 4 looks at his approach to the creative artist as an individual. The latter question is one of the many occasions where James' position challenges established assumptions in the social scientific discussion of such things, and I have tried to draw out some of these challenges. Here, as in other places, I have also sought to offer some account of James' own historical situation, and of the way in which his reflections on the experiences of colonised populations, for example, or on the experiences of ordinary working men and women, help explain how he arrived at some of his provocative positions. Chapter 5 is more general, and seeks to get a sense of what it was, in the end, that James found in the best of culture which meant that it mattered as much as it did, to him and to many others.

James being James, the walls between these thematic divisions are rather porous. To some extent, for example, discussion of culture's historical meaningfulness pre-empts a discussion of the role of the audience, just as discussion of the great artist necessarily starts to suggest what James saw as the importance of great cultural innovations or achievements more generally. Here, undoubtedly, I fall well short of James' own characteristic style which is so often marked by an absence of such plodding divisions, and by the corresponding and exciting sense – familiar to any of his readers – that for James, writing about one thing was implicitly writing about everything. Or that, at least, writing about one thing (a novel, say, or a riot) always opened out into many other wider questions and connections.

A final comment. Aldon Lynn Nielsen notes wryly at the start of his own critical study that everyone seems to make their own James. This is, of course, the case and Nielsen does so himself, constructing a James whose primary concern is with 'the revolutionary capacities of the written word' (1997: xx), and the possibilities for both conformity and disruption inherent in language. There is no denying, of course, that James was a writer by inclination and by long practice. Nevertheless, James was certainly not only concerned with the question of the written word. It seems to me important, in this respect, not to lose sight of James' no less explicit concern with other, more performative kinds of culture: music, for example, dance, oratory and, perhaps above all, sport. And above all sports, cricket. I have tried in what follows to draw my examples from across the wide fields of James' cultural writings and, indeed, from the body of his published work as a whole. For what it is worth, however, I should admit that 'my' James is particularly the cricket-loving James. This is partly because I share his love of the game, of course, but there is something else to be said as well. James' close reading of cricketing forms often seems to me to be better – fuller, more alert to detail, more intuitive and even more convincing – than his close reading of some other kinds of cultural production, such as film. James argued, as I suggest towards the end of this study, that different kinds of creative practice could provide us with particular ways of seeing the world. To a significant extent James saw the world in and through cricket. This, not exclusively, but often, is the James that I am interested in describing in what follows.

1
Forms

Introduction

In 1968, C. L. R. James published his only public statement on the so-called D'Oliveira affair. The affair, which in many ways typifies the complicated entanglements of racism, class, imperial politics and cricket, revolved around the initial failure of the MCC, English cricket's decision-making body, to select Basil D'Oliveira for the English touring party due to leave for South Africa in that year. The significance of their decision hinged on the fact that D'Oliveira was himself born in South Africa and was designated by the regime as 'coloured', and therefore barred from participation in the first-class form of the game. He had moved to England in 1960, serving a qualification period and proving his abilities as a player at both league and county levels before being selected as a member of the English test side. The inclusion of D'Oliveira in the touring squad would have placed the South African government in a politically impossible position, requiring them to acknowledge both the presence and the talent of a player previously disqualified from the national stage on 'racial' grounds. Although the selection committee's decision was defended publicly as a purely cricketing one, this defence was met with widespread incredulity. This was the case, not least, because at the end of the preceding season D'Oliveira had scored a famous century against the touring Australian side, a performance that most commentators assumed would guarantee his selection. Peter Oborne's (2004; see also Gemmell 2004: chapter 9) account of the events makes clear the many shabby complicities that underpinned the actions of the MCC. Key members of English cricket's establishment were certainly more than keen to maintain cordial relations with Vorster's apartheid regime.

James' only response to these events was made in the pages of the African literary studies journal *Transition* (itself the context for a number of other important debates over culture and politics, for example: Okara 1963; Wali 1963; Chinweizu et al. 1975; Soyinka 1975). What is striking, but absolutely typical, about his response is that James begins his analysis *not* with a discussion of apartheid, nor of sport's political potential, but by stating unequivocally: 'The first and most important thing is to prove [D'Oliveira's] status on the field of play' (1968: 37). James follows this with a long and equally typical tunnelling through the relevant cricketing statistics, analysing D'Oliveira's performances in detail and focusing on the character of his play, central to which is James' sense that he has proved himself 'the man to seize an occasion' (37). Only having done this, only having spent the majority of the article getting to grips with D'Oliveira's form (both in the sense of a record of achievement and in the sense of a distinctive style) does James move to the conclusion that his non-selection is unjustified and therefore 'a political demonstration [...] equivalent to an endorsement of the South African regime' (38). He ends by calling for the resignation of the selectors involved.

On the face of it, the fact that James begins by so assertively putting aside the non-cricketing aspects of this controversy seems surprising. After all, if he is associated with anything as a writer and thinker, it is with his famous rhetorical question in *Beyond a Boundary*: 'what do they know of cricket, who only cricket know'? James is thought of, first and foremost, as someone who was concerned to understand the social and political ramifications of popular cultural practices such as sport. It is his insistence on looking beyond the boundary to the wider meanings and uses of the games people play, the films they watch and the music they dance to, that has made him an increasingly well-regarded figure among sociologists and historians of culture. Indeed, it is that concern in James that motivates me to write this book. Yet if we are to do justice to that aspect of James' thought we have to begin where he begins, which is, almost always, exactly where he begins his article on D'Oliveira: by paying scrupulously close attention to the particular text or game or image that is at hand.

In fact, we can have few excuses here, because this is a practice that James repeatedly enjoins his readers to follow. It is, in other words, a central and constitutive part of his whole approach to making sense of culture, and to learn something from James about doing the latter requires us to start by understanding why he is so insistent about the former. The example of the D'Oliveira affair is a particularly striking one, of course, because even for readers who are not interested in thinking about sport as anything other than entertainment, there is no avoiding the degree to which these events were saturated with politics. In that respect James' pointed focus on 'the field of play' seems remarkable, perhaps even contrary. One could, however, cite any number of similar examples from James' wider writings in order to demonstrate that his approach to D'Oliveira was in keeping with his approach more generally. Take this, for instance, the opening to his appreciation of another great cricketer, Rohan Kanhai:

> The investigation [... of ...] any great cricketer should deal with his actual cricket, the way he bats and bowls and fields, does all or any of these. You may wander far from where you started, but unless you have your eyes constantly on the ball, in fact never take your eyes off it, you are soon writing not about cricket, but about yourself (or other people) and psychological or literary responses to the game. This can be and has been done quite brilliantly, adding a little something to literature but practically nothing to cricket, as little as the story of Jack and the Beanstalk (a great tale) adds to our knowledge of agriculture. (1984: 165)

Nor was this a practice that James maintained only in relation to sport. Here he is writing about the poet Walt Whitman in *American Civilization*, the draft of an unfinished study of American modernity which he wrote in the fifties, but which was only published towards the end of his life: 'we have to ignore all the things Whitman said about himself *and depend entirely upon the literature as literature. We shall have to watch that and by watching that, we shall be able to reconstruct the real Whitman*' (1993: 51, my italics). James' reading of Whitman's form, at least of the long, liturgical lists of *Salut au Monde*, treats his poetry as a failure. Whitman's repetitive hailing of the wider world reveals, he says, a thwarted longing, the desire to reconcile a romantic individualism with the extraordinary possibilities for social and productive cooperation that were emerging in America. This was, in many respects, what James saw as the essential contradiction of American modernity. But James arrives at this broader conclusion only because he first interprets *Salut au Monde* as a failure in its own terms: it is the fact that it is 'ridiculous as poetry' (56) which provides the thread that ties the poem to its social and historical context.

What, then, are we to make of this? Anna Grimshaw, who worked with James in his last years and who was instrumental in making available to a wider public *American Civilization* and many of his other writings, tells us in her introduction to the *C. L. R. James Reader* that although he struggled with the question of artistic form for much of his life 'the commitment James made to a political career meant that he never acknowledged publicly, until much later, the central place of this project in his life's work' (1992: 4). One understands his hesitance. A concern with 'literature as literature' can easily be presented as the antithesis to meaningful political engagement. From this point of view, to get too caught up in analysing the form of a novel, its language, its plot construction, its style, can be seen as a naïve mistake, the sort of navel-gazing best confined to the ivory towers inhabited by a certain kind of otherworldly literary critic. Indeed, to call someone a formalist can be to charge them with something worse than naïvety; it can imply, at best, a blinkered commitment to art for its own sake and, at worst, a wilful disregard for politics or history. Such claims were certainly thrown James' way during his lifetime. When, for example, 'J. R. Johnson' (James' pseudonym in the socialist press) and his closest collaborators left the Socialist Workers Party in 1940, Joseph Hansen, in a score-settling article in *Fourth International*, specifically attacked James' interest in art and literature as a petty-bourgeois indulgence that fed his 'flights of high school essay writing' (1940: 165). Hansen went on to picture those same interests as a kind of decorative bandage, designed to conceal James' political misunderstandings, which 'jut out from [his] copious references to ancient history, to literature and to esthetics like unlanced boils' (165). He capped off his attack with the damning verdict that Johnson/James was an 'unconscious empiricist and formalist' (1940: 166; compare Renton 2007: 165–6). Further weight was lent to this judgement, in his account, by the fact that Hansen could report at first hand that Leon Trotsky had arrived at a similar conclusion after he and Johnson/James had met at Coyoacan, Mexico in April 1939 in order to discuss, among other things, the question of the relationship between 'Negro' and socialist politics in the United States.

What I want to consider in this chapter, then, is why it should be that James, despite his awareness of the ways in which this claim might be perceived, continued to emphasise the integrity of forms of culture and consistently underscored the need to make sense of such forms on their own terms before one could begin to ask other kinds of question about them. There are, it seems to me, both theoretical and historical issues involved in answering this question. Later on, I also want to reflect on the challenges that James' view holds for anyone interested in trying to think about culture in sociological or historical terms.

I

Hansen is not the only one of James' interlocutors, then or since, to find in his respectful treatment of cultural forms evidence of a failure of critical imagination. Take, for example, some of the more recent responses to *Beyond a Boundary*, James' famous study of colonial politics, sport and his own life. It is this book, along with *The Black Jacobins*, which has been central in securing James' reputation, and it has certainly won him his widest readership. At the same time, however, it has been the cause of no little bemused and occasionally censorious judgement on the part of subsequent commentators. The key note of such responses is pained surprise: surprise that C. L. R. James (of all people) should reveal himself to be a proponent of cricket (of all sports). Cricket, after all, is surely the cultural practice most indelibly tainted by its association with British imperialism. The game had undergone, in the Victorian period, what Sandiford calls a 'mummification' (1994: 24); the stripping away of the rambunctious gambling and drinking culture which surrounded Georgian matches. Cleaned up and reimagined as a pastoral idyll, cricket became the perfect expression of the Victorian elite's view of the world: anti-commercial, celebratory of bodily prowess, rule bound and hierarchical. Consequently, the game became a key vehicle for instilling the physical and mental disciplines that were transmitted by the reformed public schools to which that elite sent their sons. For the same reason, it came to feature in the curricula of the educational systems established domestically for the working classes (Bateman 2003: 41–4) and in the schools established to train the elites of the colonial world (Mangan 1998; Birley 1999: chapter 9; Sandiford and Stoddart 1995). For those 'gentleman imperialists' (Cain and Hopkins 1993a, 1993b) who were the primary movers and shakers of the British Empire, it was cricket that most obviously expressed their sense of what was admirable, and through which, in many ways, they conceived of the whole great 'game' of imperial authority. Hence, for instance, the image of the stalwart servant of Empire commanding 'his hundred wind-baked ruffians', in some distant outpost, 'as if they were the Second Eleven and he their captain' (*The Standard*, 1907, cited in Mangan 1998: 64). Hence, as Cain and Hopkins point out, the emphasis placed on field sports such as cricket in consolidating a shared corporate ideology among the staff of significant imperial institutions such as the Hong Kong and Shanghai Bank (1993a: 439).

What is unsettling about *Beyond a Boundary*, then, even for some of his sympathetic critics, is not simply the fact that James expresses such undisguised affection for this game, with its dubious historical associations, nor even that he focuses so much of his energy on a loving and detailed consideration of the respective styles of its great players. Rather it is the fact that, throughout the book, James openly defends what he calls 'the ancestral creed' (1983 [1963]: 247). That is to say, precisely the old public school ideal of cricket as something to be played for its own sake and in adherence to an unwritten 'spirit' which guides the conduct of players and marks out the cricketing field as sacrosanct, a space apart from the political, racial and economic inequalities of social life more generally. The final chapter ends, after all, with James hoping that the book will help his son, who lives in America, understand what it means to say that 'it is not cricket' to throw a game for money, and that it might encourage him to recognise that such a code 'may be of some use' (ibid.). The epilogue which follows goes even further. James, reflecting on the West Indian tour of Australia in 1961, says of the West Indian captain, in the very last words of the text: 'Thomas Arnold, Thomas Hughes and the Old Master himself would have recognized Frank Worrell as their boy' (252). In the sentence immediately prior to this he has presented the 1961 tour as a watershed, played out against the backdrop provided by the greater watershed of West Indian federation: 'Clearing their way with bat and ball, West Indians at that moment had made a public entry into the comity of nations' (252). Yet in the last breath of his most famous work James seems to turn all the energy and optimism of this moment of decolonisation inside out, finding in it a historical vindication of the Victorian games ethos and its iconic figures: Thomas Arnold, the pioneering rector of Rugby school; Thomas Hughes, author of *Tom Brown's School Days*; and W. G. Grace.

No wonder that some of his readers have looked askance. Might this not be, in fact, proof positive of James' formalism, of a faltering political nerve when it came to the sport in which he had invested so much of himself? Allan Guttmann certainly thinks so, accusing James of a 'typically liberal fixation on the rules of play' (1994: 27). Or, more accurately, but no less ironically, of an abiding respect for the uncodified 'spirit of the game'. This argument is echoed by Douglas Hartmann in his reconsideration of *Beyond a Boundary* (2003) in which he argues that, despite the many important lessons that James still holds for contemporary readers, he imagined the sport he loved to be far more neutral than it actually was. James, Hartmann suggests, failed to interrogate the way in which expectations placed on players of the game (unquestioning acceptance of the authority of umpires and officials; the image of the cricket field as a place of formal equality) replicate the presumptions required of citizens in a model liberal democracy. James failed, in short, to recognise why it was that the game was such a crucial pedagogical tool of Empire.

Guttmann and Hartmann are not alone in their views. James Young, author of an otherwise enthusiastic biography, suggests that 'at a deep psychological and cultural level', C. L. R. James 'never succeeded in throwing off the cultural imperialism to which he had been subjected during his formative years' (1999: 301). Cricket, of course, was weapon of choice in the ideological armoury of that imperialism. By implication, the sport is one of those 'English achievements' about which James was always 'somewhat romantic' (ibid.), even if he was aware of the racial and class politics that surrounded the game in the Caribbean. Brian Stoddart, the pioneering historian of cricket in the West Indies and elsewhere, as well as a long-standing and generous expositor of James' work, arrives at a similarly qualified conclusion. The social and political contradictions of cricket in the colonial world, he says, are 'nowhere [...] better described than in James, the Marxist who loved a game which, theoretically, represented much of what he wanted to eliminate and, so, had to find a resistance strain within it' (1998: 84). The inference invited by Stoddart's wording is clear: James' account of cricket not only grapples with a contradiction, it comes perilously close to falling into one. His submission to the moral code of cricket, in other words, is in conflict with his overt political position and *Beyond a Boundary* is a brilliant but never completely successful attempt to wriggle out of this conflict. It is thus, as Grant Farred puts it, 'a text of last resort' (1996a: 176), a somewhat desperate attempt to reconcile the worlds of Marxism and cricket that had been so influential in James' life. Helen Tiffin is less nuanced, and far more condemnatory, of the author's failure to question the fundamentally '*English* moral standards' (1995 [1981]: 364) which, she claims, underlie the sport. Of all of his explorations into the relationship between British institutions and colonial experience, Tiffin argues, it is in regard to cricket that James' critical insight is most obviously misled. 'Nowhere', she argues, 'does James really confront the meaning of English cricket with its uncomfortable West Indian reality' (364). Because he is overly concerned to justify his claim that the sport is an art in its own right, James simply sidelines this 'uncomfortable' reality, which is 'that in cricket the colonial simply proves he can abide by the rules and the morality of the British game. He does not and has not in any significant sense altered the assumptions behind it' (367; compare Gregg 2000).

It would be foolhardy to suggest that there are no 'inner contradictions' to be found in James' work. However, his defence of cricket's ethic of disinterested participation, his deeply felt desire to preserve the integrity of the cricket field is not, in my opinion, one of them. E. P. Thompson's much-quoted phrase seems to me to be far more acute: 'the clue to everything lies in [James'] proper appreciation of the game of cricket' (Buhle 1986: 249). By understanding why James insisted on defending cricketing 'form' we can start to understand his reading of cultural forms more generally. More particularly, we can begin to understand why it was that he insisted so frequently that no road opens out onto the politics of culture that does not first pass through a sensitive interpretation of cultural practices in their own terms.

Apart from anything else, what seems to pass unrecognised in the criticisms I have described is that *Beyond a Boundary* is a book in which James is himself interrogating exactly this issue. Moreover, he is interrogating *himself* and his own responses to this issue. It helps to remember, in this respect, that the key themes of *Beyond a Boundary* (the insistence on reading cricket as an art-form; the emphasis on the role of the audience; the relation of sporting styles to a wider zeitgeist) had all been worked out by James at least three decades before the book was finally published. It is possible to trace their emergence and evolution, for example, in the reports that James produced for both the *Manchester Guardian* and the *Glasgow Herald* in the late 1930s (Smith 2006a). Many things intervened in James' life between then and the final completion of *Beyond a Boundary* in the early 1960s, but one event above all: his invigorating and turbulent time in America. And what that period in America opened up for James, immersing him as it did in a popular culture which approached activities like sport in a very different way, was a space for reflection on his own relationship to cricket and its 'English' ethos.

James is at pains to make this clear. In a well-known section towards the end of the aptly titled chapter 'Old School-tie', he situates the themes of the book precisely in relation to his experiences in America. It was there, he tells us, sitting amid the 'unaccustomed' hostility of rival American baseball fans, that he realised just how deeply the 'code' of cricketing practice had been ingrained in him, despite the fact that he thought he had 'said good-bye to all that' (1983 [1963]: 51) on leaving Britain. He goes on to describe his own shocked response to the discovery that American sports fans were largely nonchalant about basketball stars who took money to deliberately underperform. The point of his story is not that the fans were wrong, but that it was in light of their responses that he came to look at himself and his own reactions anew. The realisation that his political comrades shrugged their shoulders along with the fans drives the point home:

> When the discussions began they looked at me a little strangely. I, a colonial born and bred, a Marxist, a declared enemy of British imperialism and all its ways and works, was the last person they had expected that sort of thing from. By the time we had discussed for some little while I was looking at myself a little strangely. (54)

In other words, far from presenting some unconscious defence of an imperial 'games ethic', *Beyond a Boundary* is the work of someone driven to reflect, by a kind of culture shock, on what might or might not be at stake in the defence of cricket's peculiar boundaries.

Something else can be noted here as well. If cricket's supposed ideological lesson was that of deference to authority in a general sense, or even authority within the limited confines of a school, it was extraordinarily ineffective. James is explicit about this, insisting that within the classroom of his childhood 'we lied and cheated without any sense of shame' (1963 [1983]: 34). Indeed, he deliberately points out the irony of the fact that the code of behaviour to which he and his classmates adhered so rigorously on the cricket field was one whose precepts they blithely ignored in order to enter that field. For the young James, expected to study hard and to secure a profession, cricket was illicit, a forbidden distraction. Hence: 'in order to acquire this code I was driven to evasions, disobedience, open rebelliousness, continuous lies and even stealing' (36). James is talking here in an autobiographical vein about his own struggle against familial and communal expectations but the statement serves to underline, at the outset of *Beyond a Boundary*, what the book will continually reiterate: cricket, however much the later Victorian educationalists treated it as an instantiation of their world-view, has no one-to-one relationship, no necessary carry over, to a more general moral or political outlook. This confessional beginning to *Beyond a Boundary* is mirrored by a confessional ending in which James discusses the campaign, of which he was chief orchestrator, to halt years of racial discrimination and see Frank Worrell instated as West Indian captain. His point in this latter instance is exactly the same as his point in the former: an adherence to the code of cricketing conduct is not automatically translated into political quietism. 'According to the colonial version of the game, you were to show yourself a "true sport" by not making a fuss about the most barefaced discrimination because it wasn't cricket. Not me any longer. To that I had said, was saying, my final good-bye' (232–3). All of which problematises the idea that cricket is a game in which certain values, protocols of conduct and bodily practices coalesced in such a way that it became a quasi-magical means of turning out deferential colonial subjects. James' shock at finding basketball players selling out and his disappointment at his friends' laissez-faire response to this, cannot be dismissed as simply a knee-jerk puritanism on his part. Something else was clearly at stake.

For James, growing up amid the unavoidable racial and class inequalities of colonial Trinidad, it was precisely the integrity of the cricket field, the fact that events which took place on that field operated according to a distinctive criterion of meaning and success, which mattered and which gave the sport its live political significance. Of course he knew very well that the history of cricket in the Caribbean had been that of a particularly conservative institution, embraced early on as a symbolic marker of loyalty to 'race' and class among the white elite and wielded by subsequent elites as the symbolic evidence of social consensus, even as it served to re-enforce all kinds of chauvinisms and dispossessions (Stoddart 1995). James' account of the class rivalries that structured the formation of different black clubs on the island, for example (1983 [1963]: chapter 4), makes absolutely clear his awareness of the game's relationship to the inequalities of wider society. In the same way, his orchestration of the campaign to have Worrell installed as West Indian captain was a public response to the enduring racism which assumed that even the most talented black performers required the cerebral presence of a white leader. James knew that cricket was never just cricket. But precisely because the cricketing field had its own *formal autonomy* it could become the space in which insurgent political energies and sympathies were expressed. The cricketing code of disinterested participation was, in many respects, a lie. But it was a lie which created its own precarious, charmed circle. And in that respect, as he ends the book by suggesting gently to his son's generation, it was 'of some use'. It was on this field that a great deal was made possible, politically and personally, that had not been possible elsewhere for the vast majority of Caribbean society.

On the most obvious level, what this means is that there was political potential in West Indian cricket because the equality which was meant, 'in principle', to obtain during the game, threw into relief the absence of any, even notional, equality outside of the game. This 'contrast between the ideal and the real' says James, 'tore at my insides' (1983 [1963]: 72). By definition, this contrast could only be seen to exist because of the very fact that cricketing relations and their meanings were symbolically marked off and distinct from quotidian social relations. Writing about the lower middle-class club Shannon, he famously describes how the way in which members of the team played expressed a sense of social antagonism: 'Where [this] appeared was in the actual cricket, the strokes, the length and the catches [...] It was not mere skill. They played as if they knew that their club represented the great mass of black people in the island' (60–1). He goes on to say, in words that have been much repeated: 'As clearly as if it were written across the sky, their play said: Here, on the cricket field if nowhere else, all men in the island are equal' (61). Abbreviated in this way (which is, it is worth noting, the version of the sentence that the UK's Channel Four adopted in promoting their coverage of the English cricket team's 2003 tour of the West Indies), James' statement *does* sound as if he were just another starry-eyed adherent of the Victorian field sports ideal. But, of course, James does not end his statement there but, instead, with the stinging rider: '... and we are the best men in the island' (61). There is political potential in cricket *only* because the cricketing field is what Ashis Nandy has called 'a protected domain' (1989: 3), a space which operated, in principle, outside of the surrounding modes of racial and class power which structured life and delimited opportunities in the Caribbean and elsewhere. In *The Black Jacobins* (1980 [1938]) James had argued that it was the revolting slaves of San Domingo who sought most urgently to substantiate the principles of equality proclaimed in the Declaration of the Rights of Man and Citizen. In exactly the same way here, if in a lesser key, James points out that it was the team who represented the black masses who in their play sought to realise cricket's formal principle that once upon the field, all men were equal. But in doing so, of course, they staged a form of symbolic revenge whose repercussions resounded far beyond the boundaries of the cricket field itself. James, a passionate lover of the game, certainly did believe in the code that defined its autonomous form of practice. His experiences in America made clear to him how heartfelt was his acceptance of those articles of cricketing faith. But James was too astute, too self-aware an observer, and from a context where the sport was too obviously politicised, for him not to recognise that it was the game's own world of meanings which allowed it to throw wider social relations into relief: 'social and political passions, denied normal outlets, expressed themselves so fiercely in cricket (and other games) *precisely because they were games*' (1983 [1963]: 72, my italics).

This, it seems to me, is where James' so-called formalism, his concern with the integrity of cultural practices in their own right, begins. It is not the preciousness of the aficionado, nor is it the blinkered tub-thumping of the fan. It is certainly not the unconscious acquiescence of the colonial who has not properly decolonised his mind. Rather it begins with a serious sociological lesson about culture which James was astute enough and self-critical enough to learn. Like Pierre Bourdieu (1993a, 1996; see also Smith 2006b), James understood that the games of culture were not 'fair games'. He recognised that in ways both open and surreptitious, social inequalities do make themselves felt in sport, literature, art. Nevertheless, like Bourdieu, he recognised that 'precisely because they were games' these cultural practices left open a space in which those social inequalities could become newly visible and even contested (on this, see Bateman 2009). Precisely because entry into these fields is defined by the assumption that they operate according to their own rules they present a space in which the rulers of the wider social world are deprived of recourse to their usual means of asserting authority. Moreover, because they are fields organised around their own meanings and values they can cast the political and economic orthodoxies of the social world into an unfamiliar and unflattering light.

In the end, through a mixture of circumstance, contrivance and public pressure, Basil D'Oliveira *was* selected for the touring side destined to depart for South Africa in 1968. Vorster's government made it clear that it was not willing to accept his presence and as a result, despite the MCC's shamefully desperate efforts to broker a compromise, the tour was cancelled. These events led directly to the sporting boycott of South Africa, which played its own part in the eventual dismantling of apartheid. James knew what he was about when he insisted that the 'first and most important thing is to prove [D'Oliveira's] status on the field of play'. This might be taken as credulous acceptance of the MCC's disingenuous claim that the debate over D'Oliveira should take place on purely cricketing ground. James was, indeed, happy for such contests to take place on purely cricketing ground, but not because he was credulous. The affair did not need politicising; after all, the politics were there already. What James recognised was that cultural practices have the ability to make the forces of social power pause at the edge of the 'field of play', to compel them to justify themselves in terms of what is taken as valuable in or on that field. This is the lesson that James had learned from his youthful experience of cricket amid the rigid stratifications and racism of colonial Trinidad. It is the same lesson that underpinned his lifelong concern with reading cultural forms, firstly, in terms of the rules, expectations and values which they themselves establish and sustain.

II

James' willingness to work through the detail of cultural practices, therefore, is not conservative. If he spends time, as he often does, closely examining changes in bowling technique, verse form or film editing, it is not because he venerates culture for its own sake in some romantic way. In the incomplete 'Preface to Criticism' that he began during, or soon after, his time in America, he specifically distinguishes his approach from that of a contemporary criticism which responded to any socially or politically inclined reading of culture by turning cultural products into magical objects, objects possessed of a unique potency or aura. James is wonderfully dismissive of the secular priesthood that claims guardianship over these fetishes: 'the magists, the textualists, the metaphoricals, the cultists of ambiguity and the whole formalist school' (1992: 258).

On the other hand, we should be wary that this recognition does not lead us into an opposite, but equally mistaken, interpretation. James' attentiveness to cultural practices in their own terms is not something undertaken for cynical reasons either, it is not mere strategy any more than it is mere formalism. James had no interest in refining culture as a weapon in the service of politics. In this respect the 'Preface to Criticism' lays out the lines of engagement for a war on *two* fronts, because he begins by explicitly distinguishing his approach to culture from that which marches 'under the banner of Stalin/Zdhanov/Mao-tse-tung' (257) for which literature, for example, becomes merely 'a vehicle for the propagation of economic and political programme [sic]' and the audience 'a receptacle into which to pour advanced ideas' (ibid.). Both approaches, James suggests, are equally destructive of those pleasures and possibilities which draw people to games or films or art in the first place. If the latter, reactionary, response suffocates what matters in culture – '[i]n seeking [...] to defend the work itself from all alien influences, they isolate it from the social movement and they end up destroying it' (ibid.) – the former treats it parasitically, as nothing more than a 'vehicle' or a means to an end.

Here, as so often, James' position on culture is indistinguishable from his politics more generally. For the most part, it seems to me, he was exemplary in remaining alert to that danger of which both Max Weber (1978a) and Hannah Arendt (1969) have warned: that political means can quickly usurp their supposed ends, becoming ends in themselves. Soviet Russia, of course, stood as a bloody testament to this danger throughout James' career, and it was largely in response to the Kremlin's political manipulations – including, notably, Communist Party manipulations of black insurgency in America – that he and his colleagues developed their critique of the politics of the vanguard party, seeking to develop in its place a more democratic model which refused to turn popular struggle into a 'vehicle' by which a leadership might ride to power (among the landmark texts of this developing critique are James 1986 [1950] and James, Lee and Chaulieu 1974 [1958]). In exactly the same way, although in relation to a slightly different question, James agreed with Frantz Fanon that anti-colonial nationalism was perilous, and that it might easily become reactionary rather than liberating. He recognised that the patriotic ideal of the nation as an end in itself could easily be used to justify postcolonial repressions (compare, for example, James 1980: 227 and Fanon 1967a: chapter 3). There were, of course, his own bitter experiences with Kwame Nkrumah and Eric Williams to reflect upon in this respect: James had given private intellectual support and public political endorsement to both, only to watch them become increasingly autocratic and self-serving leaders in Ghana and Trinidad respectively.

A key achievement of James', thus, is that he persistently asked what political struggle was for. As I will argue more fully in Chapter 3, his typical way of asking this question was to interpose the wants and longings of the popular crowd against those political forces that claimed to speak on the crowd's behalf. The question which he makes central to *Beyond a Boundary* – what is it that men live by? – is meant to prick the self-certainty of any politics that claims to have the answers in advance. And it is his willingness to keep this same question in mind which leads him to dismiss the idea that books, films and sport matter only in terms of some final political goal to which they are contributing or from which they are seen as distracting. In the chapter that bears the title 'What Do Men Live By?' in *Beyond a Boundary*, James makes this absolutely clear. He begins, as so often, by watching the popular audience: 'A glance at the world showed that when the common people were not at work, one thing they wanted was organised sports and games. They wanted them greedily, passionately' (1983 [1963]: 150). From this James opens out a wider historical point. The great waves of popular struggle that secured democratic advances in Europe and America, he notices, coincided with the rise of organised sports and games. The 'same public that wanted sports and games so eagerly wanted popular democracy too [...] The conjunction hit me as it would have hit few of the students of society and culture in the international organization to which I belonged' (151). The conjunction hit James particularly hard, of course, precisely because he already knew it, having been witness to exactly the same relationship between an emerging popular politics and a popular audience passionate for sports and games in the Caribbean.

It is important to see the precision of James' point here: sports and games (he argues the same elsewhere about other forms of culture) are popularly desired *in the same way* that a more genuinely democratic society is popularly desired. In other words, they are not a means to something higher than themselves and nor are they, as some of his comrades in that international organisation had argued, a deflection from something higher. If there is anything of value in what we call culture, it is valuable in its own right, not in respect of some other purpose or end that lies beyond it. Indeed, were they to be made subservient to an external purpose beyond themselves, cultural practices would lose whatever distinctive and particular value they once had. On the other hand, the best of cultural activity speaks to the same desire for a fuller and better human existence that energises popular struggle; it glimpses an 'end' of politics without simply becoming a political 'means'.

There is, in other words, a deep-rooted unity between James' insistence that the struggle for socialism meant something more than a merely quantitative increase in the standard of living, something more than a few extra points on the scale of per capita income, and his insistence on treating the forms of culture as valuable in their own right. For James, the Stalinist 'stand and deliver theory of culture' (1980: 112) as he derisively called it (that is to say, the approach to cultural activities which saw in them either childish distractions or which reduced culture to a direct expression, conscious or unconscious, of a class position) was one symptom of that dehumanised, bureaucratic view of the world which defined 'good' only in terms of an 'increased use of goods' (James 1973 [1960]: 104), and in whose 'Plans' human kind figured as 'pigs to be fattened' (105) or worse. Yet James says this not because he wishes to preserve the stuff of culture in aspic, sealing it off from the wider realities of social life. He says it, rather, precisely because he finds in the best of culture some sense of the longed-for freedoms and possibilities of human kind that motivate progressive popular struggle in the first place. Hence, for example, his very clear statement in the introduction to *American Civilization*, where he insists that any attempt to understand contemporary American society 'demands that men be not treated or analyzed as economic statistics' (1993: 31). It is for this reason, James goes on to claim, that he is justified in devoting one of the book's chapters, 'dealing with early concepts of freedom, individuality, etc. of America [...] exclusively to an analysis of the writings of Herman Melville and Walt Whitman' (ibid.). It is in such writings, he says, 'that both the past of America and the indications of the future were given' (ibid.).

For the most part when James makes such comments he is consciously distancing himself from what he saw as the culture-as-propaganda instrumentalism of the Communist Party. This is, of course, as would be expected given that for much of his active political life he was embroiled in the attempt to establish a humanist Marxism against the dogmas of the Kremlin. Nevertheless, his defence of the integrity of cultural practices, and his willingness to judge those practices first and foremost in terms of their own, autonomous criteria of value was an absolutely consistent one. He was no less staunch in challenging the high-minded bourgeois professors who saw culture as a means to improve the masses, or in cautioning against the tendency of both 'negritudist' and 'black power' critics to value texts simply on the basis of their author's perceived 'race' (see, for example, 'Black Studies and the Contemporary Student' in James 1984: chapter 15; also Dhondy 2001: chapter 19). In the same way he criticises Richard Wright, for example, for granting one of his characters in *Native Son* a 'long, bad and tiresome speech' (James 1996a: 57) in order to explicate the theme of his novel. By so doing, James notes, Wright treats literary form in precisely this instrumental fashion: as simply the container of a political meaning. He threatens thereby to spoil what the 'book had already very clearly and powerfully said' (ibid.).

For anyone interested in trying to understand culture in sociological terms there are, it seems to me, at least two principles to be learned here from James. The first is that such an understanding can only begin with *what is*, from the cultural objects which are there in front of us: there can be no pre-emptive interpretation of culture and no collapsing of text into context. The crass assumption that there is some necessary or true alignment between art and class location and the comparable dismissal of mass culture by elitist critics are equally indicted in this respect. But so, potentially, is *any* approach to culture which comes heavy-handed with theory and which forgets to remain open to the surprises of human creativity, the challenges to the critic's self-assurance which are revealed when one rigorously keeps one's eyes on the ball. The lesson, to put it colloquially, is not to lose sight of what matters.

The second lesson is entangled with the first. With any attempt to understand books or films, art or sport, in terms of their relationship to political struggles or processes of historical change, comes the danger that the true and only 'meaning' of those things is discovered to lie outside of themselves. James, of course, was deeply interested in the relationship of cultural form to social context, but he was also alert to the threat that such accounts might make shadowy or thin the very things which they claimed to be explaining, destroying a sense of the intrinsic symbolic life of cultural objects and practices. That they might therefore minimise the very qualities which draw crowds to games and readers to books in the first place. One could put this another way. As Robert Pinksy suggests in his commentary on form (in relation to his own wonderful poem 'The Want Bone'): 'it is the *un*likeness that delights and illuminates' (1996: 298). It is the *un*likeness of cultural forms in relation to other practices and acts which allows them to reveal things about the latter. We can learn sociological truths from culture because its translates those truths into other forms for us. A cultural object formally identical to something else – culture perfected as politics say – is unimaginable precisely because such an object would disappear into that with which it was identical. Worse, indeed, than unimaginable, it would be unimaginably boring. A world in which 'all day long form keeps droning on that X = X' as Pinksy puts it (ibid.). This is what James understood only too well. It is the basis of his careful demonstration of the ways in which cultural forms are able to illuminate social experience not despite, but because of, their degree of 'unlikeness' to that experience. Don't lose sight of what matters, and don't lose sight of why it matters.

III

For many of his readers, I suspect, including those who are very much drawn to his political or historical interpretations of cultural practices, it is this painstaking emphasis on such practices in their own terms – his insistence that this is the 'first and most important thing' – which makes James' writing something that is so cherished. Or, to put it more accurately: what one cherishes is James' ability to explain culture without explaining it away; to explain it in ways that deepen and broaden our understanding of it and its meanings without giving the sense that he murders to dissect. One rarely feels, reading him, that a sociological account of culture is somehow opposed to, or destructive of, the joys and pleasures of human creativity. Rather, and this is of course the whole point, his writings are vibrant with the sense that the social and political meanings of culture are inextricable from its joys and pleasures or, indeed, its frustrations and missed opportunities.

At the most straightforward level, there is a cautionary note to be heeded here. The caution is that thinking sociologically about culture is a discipline, not a free pass: it requires that we strive to be more dedicated, more attentive or more scrupulous readers and viewers. Anyone can bodge together some 'sociological gossip', as he once called it, about a book or painting or sports-player. The result, as James makes clear in the quote given earlier from his essay on Rohan Kanhai, may tell us something about the person who is doing the gossiping, but very little about the book, painting or player in question, and even less about the social world of which it is a part. And there is a lurking theoretical point here which deserves to be made explicit as well. Any investigation into the social or political meanings of a cultural object or practice is both enabled by, but also constrained by, the shape and parameters of that object or practice itself. Of course there is a wide leeway here for debate and dispute, for differences in interpretation. James, as we will discuss in Chapter 3, was ever aware of the audience's role in making culture, and therefore of the possibility that different audiences might respond to the same cover drive, or the same movie, in very different ways. The stuff of culture is symbolic and expressive and precisely not, as we have seen him claim, something that can be read off like a table of 'economic statistics'. Nevertheless, James' emphasis on the respectful understanding of cultural forms in themselves is definitely a refutation of an 'anything goes' approach in which all interpretations of a Shakespearian tragedy, for instance, are equally valid. He would certainly have poured scorn on such a claim, as indeed, he poured scorn on many of the celebrated contemporary readings of *Lear* or *Hamlet* (for example, 1992: 243–6). This is the case – some readings are more valid or more convincing than others – not simply because they take into account a better or wider range of social and historical evidence, but also because the thing that is read necessarily delimits what can plausibly said about it and about what lies outside of itself. It is firstly in respect of the text itself that some readings ring true while others sound dud.

James, in short, places a much more concerted emphasis on understanding the specific, intrinsic qualities of cultural practices than have most writers in the sociology of culture or, for that matter, most Marxists (although James perhaps owes more of a debt here to Trotsky than he sometimes admitted: compare Trotsky 1991 [1925]). In any case, to a large extent social and historical interpretations of culture have entered the lists precisely as challengers to the idea of literary or artistic quality as something which is simply inherent in certain objects. There are good reasons for mounting this challenge, to be sure. Not the least of these is the degree to which such a view serves to present our cultural canons, in all their parochialism and elitism, as the inevitable ascension of the 'best which has been thought and said'. In this regard it has been and it remains important to recognise the degree to which ideas of literary or artistic value are socially formed, being the products of long historical struggle involving men and women who often have extremely unequal access to the material and symbolic resources which might secure for them the elusive prize of cultural 'consecration'. Nevertheless, there are times – reading Pierre Bourdieu, for example, whose term this is – when one gets a sense that cultural practices in all their variety and specificity have somehow been flattened so that they appear to be merely shadows thrown onto the wall by ongoing political or social struggles. Bourdieu is, of course, scrupulous in recognising that events in the 'field of cultural production' take place on their own specific terms. Nevertheless, in his model the practices and products of the cultural field come to figure primarily on account of what is done *with them*: which is to say, how they are used to take possession of or to contest positions in that field itself (see the sympathetic criticisms offered by Graeber 2001: 28–30). James' approach to culture, comparable as it is with that of Bourdieu in many respects, seems to me to call for a rather different balance to be struck. His close attention to cultural forms compels us to recognise that not everything about those forms can be explained from the outside, as it were: cultural forms and practices have important qualities of their own, and these qualities are often what draw people to them. This is not to deny that broader historical and social energies will find expression in the many symbolic and creative activities in which we take part, but it is to remember that the specific logic of those activities shapes that expression. Moreover, the particular conventions and expectations that shape the writing and reception of a piano sonata are not those that shape the playing or watching of a game of football. Different limits and different conditions of possibility apply in both cases, not just intrinsically in terms of their meaningfulness *as* piano sonatas or football matches, but also in terms of what wider social meanings they might convey and how they might convey these.

By the same token, and as we have seen already in relation to his review of *Native Son*, James recognised that the primary imperatives placed on anyone who writes a novel, acts in a film or plays a particular sport, are the imperatives due to those activities themselves. He wrote, for example, a deeply critical letter to Constance Webb about Paul Robeson's performance in Margaret Webster's 1944 Broadway version of *Othello*. Just as with his response to the D'Oliveira affair, James' account focuses rigorously on the dramatic and literary qualities of the production. And on this score, James reports, it was 'lousy' (1992: 141). Lousy, because neither Robeson nor the others on the stage mastered the cadences of Shakespeare's blank verse. Of Robeson he is particularly critical in this respect, accusing him of simply 'saying' his lines. As a result the play failed to 'ring', humanly or poetically. Without due attention to those 'rhythms and the tonal qualities' that are 'organic' to the work, he says, it becomes mere melodrama; Desdemona's undoing appearing to be the result of a soap-opera-like plot twist.

Of course the production was significant for other reasons: Robeson's presence in the play, James recognises, and the relationship between Othello and Desdemona itself, could not but serve to highlight tensions in America over 'the Negro question'. To this degree the staging was a politically important 'event'. But precisely in so far as the play was seen to be important as an 'event', it was liable to be a failure as a play. Had it been successful as a dramatic work, had it brought to life Shakespeare's writing and the human characters at the heart of the action, the production would have 'lifted off the roof' (142), by which one assumes he means something more than just an enthusiastic reception on the night. In any case, James says all of this because he is clear that 'Shakespeare was a dramatist, no sociologist' (ibid.). His dramatic works are concerned with characters and their relationships, and are produced in a stylised language which brings with it specific qualities of resonance and depth. It is precisely in these ways, in and through the qualities which are specific to dramatic writing as such, that the play could have grabbed its contemporary audience by the throat, forcing on their attention urgent social dilemmas which Shakespeare grasped at the outset of the modern era, and which remain – James says – unsolved in mid-twentieth-century America:

> Every man looking at [the characters of the play] today can see them not only in individual but in social terms. [...] today we see these plays and in them is mirrored the life of society. The artist therefore can stage them with a penetration and breadth that comes from 300 years of social experience [...] today we look at Shakespeare but we have not solved the problems he posed and we can see them as he never could. And in this period of world-shaking crisis they are all around us, insisting on solution as never before. (142–3)

The incendiary possibilities of the play exist in what it is as a work of dramatic art; it is as this – not as an overt political event – that it could have spoken in a startling way to contemporary audiences about some of modernity's enduring dilemmas.

Conclusion

At the start of an essay on Frank Worrell, James makes the same point in language which reveals one of the most profound influences on his mature thought. Worrell, he says,

> lifted West Indies cricket to the highest peak possible and everybody knew that he had done it. [...] But this is the obvious, the accepted, that no one will argue about. That, however, is only the appearance of things, and a great logician, one of the greatest, has clarified the difference between the appearance of things and the essence. (1986: 255)

From here one might well expect James to sally forth into 'the essential', into the wider historical significance of Worrell's captaincy, something about which he knew a great deal at first hand. But, typically, he has something else to say:

> The appearance is not a mere superficial obviousness, that everybody can see; what our logician disdainfully calls a mere *show*. The appearance is a vital category. Because it is only by means of the appearance that the essence can manifest itself. (ibid.)

James' reading of Hegel is complicated and, so far as this study is concerned, too far off the beaten track to be followed for long. However, it seems clear that what he is suggesting here is *not* some baroque rewording of a hackneyed old story in which 'superstructure' straightforwardly reflects 'base', or 'ideas' reflect 'material reality'. It is, rather, characteristic of his whole approach to culture that he insists on recognising a more complicated entanglement between what we know and how we know it. Culture is not a 'mere show'; it makes manifest things which are bigger than itself. It throws into relief contradictions and forces which are, in important respects, definitive of the society of which we are part. But it does so only in and through its own 'vital categories', which we disdain, or treat lazily or 'superficially', at our peril. These appearances, as he put it in his *Notes on Dialectics*, are 'the *only* way in which in the present complex of conditions Essence can shine forth' (1980 [1948]: 110). One wonders, in passing, if there has ever been another contribution to a popular sports book which has begun by taking a lesson, albeit an unnamed lesson, from Hegel.

At the very end of the same essay James says something which is repeated more than once in his public and private writings. 'After you have analysed to the last comma, there is always something that defies analysis' (1986: 270). He is talking in this particular instance about an issue that we will deal with more closely in Chapter 4: the uniqueness of individual human beings and their particular capabilities. But nearly three decades before this he had already written to Constance Webb, making much the same point in a more general sense: 'the more I study things the more I see that reason, analysis, etc. go a long way but ultimately you reach a stage where something fundamental in everything defies analysis' (James 1996b: 103). There are no doubt critics who would find in such a comment proof that James never shook off a kind of residual romanticism, not to say mysticism, in his thinking. For me, however, this admission of the 'something that defies analysis' recalls much of what is most attractive in his work: it represents, for example, the James who came to reject a determinist view of history in favour of a more open-ended account, one that emphasised the fact that human beings, acting singly or collectively, can change the circumstances in which they act (for example 1980: chapter 4). That sliver of the inexplicable is thus a way of leaving a space for the contingency represented by the not wholly predictable possibilities of human action. It is not, for one moment, a denial of the fact that a fuller and richer understanding of society or history is possible and something worth fighting for. But it is a recognition of the fact that such understanding develops by considering the actions of human beings in all their complexity rather than by being imposed upon that complexity. 'Defies analysis', in this respect, means not 'defeats' or 'confounds' but something more like 'challenges' or 'confronts'. A call for a certain kind of humility then, and a refutation – much like that made by W. E. B. du Bois (1995 [1903]: 130) – of claims to know *a priori* the truth about society, about historical change, and about the human beings who make up these things. Social life wrestles our analysis of it and any analysis worth the time and energy wrestles back. And in relation to his understanding of culture particularly it seems to me helpful to take this idea of the defiance in the thing that is analysed as a standing reminder that we cannot treat cultural forms as sociologically 'see through', as windows that open transparently onto social truth. Of course, the various forms of culture *are* part of what we 'see' society 'through', but only by learning to see them, in their own terms, more clearly and by carefully taking into account the kinds of vision they make possible for us.

Coda: driving off the back foot

James' close reading of cultural forms is perhaps the aspect of his work that has received least critical consideration. Indeed writing, especially writing about sport, which cites or deploys James has often used him as a means of cutting straight to the sociological chase: that is to say, straight to speculation about the historical or political significance of an event or an individual without paying the objects in question the kind of careful attention that James saw as the prerequisite of any wider interpretation. There are, of course, honourable exceptions: Qadri Ismail's account of the Sri Lankan batsman Arjuna Ranatunga, for example (1999) as well as many of Chris Searle's articles for *Race and Class* (such as that on Muttiah Muralitharan: 2001). I want to end, in any case, by offering a short 'reading' of a single shot by the great West Indian batsman Brian Lara which, I hope, will help substantiate the account of James that I have offered in this chapter, and might also serve as a segue into the next chapter, which deals more directly with the relationship between cultural forms and historical contexts in James' writing.

The moment I want to discuss took place at the end of the summer of 1995 when Brian Lara was batting at the Oval in the final match of a six-test series against England. The series, at the time, stood at two games each. Although Lara had already scored fifty, and looked well set on what was a placid pitch, he was being tested by the quick bowling of Devon Malcolm. Malcolm himself was born, of course, in Jamaica and was thus representative *not*, I would argue, of a late twentieth-century turbulence in identities, but of the criss-crossed history which has defined the modernity of the Atlantic world from its outset (Gilroy 1993; Roach 1996; Linebaugh and Rediker 2000). Malcolm, in any case, was bowling short: that is to say, he was banging the ball into the pitch so that it flew through at chest or head height, forcing the batsman backwards. It was a tactic that other fast bowlers around the world had already tried on Lara, who was rumoured to have a technical weakness against 'the short stuff'. Moreover, as many of those watching the game would have recognised, Malcolm was setting up his opponent for a sucker-punch. Quick bowlers will often submit a batsman to a barrage of quick bouncers and then follow these deliveries with an equally quick ball pitched much further up, aimed at the stumps or legs. A batsman who has been cowed by this display of aggression, and who – for reasons of self-preservation as much as anything else – has their weight resting on their back foot, is always likely to be vulnerable against such a delivery.

Without a concerted stride forward to negate the late lateral movement of the ball in the air or off the pitch, they raise the chances of being bowled or offering a catch to the slip cordon.

This sucker-punch was indeed delivered. Malcolm pitched a subsequent delivery well up to Lara, and in the perfect place: just outside the line of the stumps, swinging slightly inwards. Moreover, the tactic worked. Lara was caught entirely out of position, with his weight backwards, leaning away from the delivery, when it should have been forwards, leaning into it. And yet, in a moment of extraordinary improvisation, he simply opened up his body by stepping his right leg out of the way, waited, and then drove the ball back past the bowler and up into the boundary boards. On the television footage one can see Devon Malcolm standing mid-pitch, breathing hard, with a look of blank resignation on his face. In the event, he was to get Lara out, but not before the latter had scored a thundering 179, ensuring that the match and series would be drawn.

A year earlier, Lara had broken the world record for the highest number of runs in an individual innings of an international match when he scored 375 against England at the Recreation Ground in Antigua. Searle, in an appropriately Jamesian phrase, described it as the moment when a scattered nation found its centre (1995: 32). He went on to quote the Antiguan radical Tim Hector who saw in Lara 'the beginning of something new' (34; see also Henry 1992). In retrospect, however, this seems to be only half of the truth. With the benefit of hindsight Lara seems to represent, not so much something new but rather one of those figures – like Aeschylus, Shakespeare or Hazlitt – who fascinated James because they appeared at, and grappled with the possibilities of, a moment of historical transition (see, for example, his essay on the artist in the Caribbean (1977a: chapter 14)). In one respect, of course, much about Lara's career does look forward to a new kind of cricket: glamorised, highly paid, mass-mediated and spectacular. The kind of cricket, one might say, appropriate to the era of globalisation and which finds its apotheosis in the highly commodified twenty-over version of the game and the celebrity culture that surrounds it. Yet this is only part of the story. The crash-bang cricketers of the Indian Premier League, for example, use bats like tree trunks and aim largely at brute-force feats of six-hitting. The roots of Lara's style were laid in an entirely different era. He used a remarkably light bat, and in general he avoided hitting the ball in the air: his first world record innings included forty-five fours but not a single six. There was unquestionably something joyful about his run scoring, but it relied more on placement and clarity of shot than it did on power. It was a style, it seems to me, which looked backwards no less than forwards, back above all to the man whose record he broke in Antigua, Gary Sobers, of whom James said, in words that could be equally applied to Lara: he was 'orthodoxy carried to the penultimate degree when orthodoxy itself disappears in the absolute' (1986: 221).

James described Sobers as the 'consummation' of a whole tradition of cricket in the West Indies. Which meant, of course, the consummation of much more than just a tradition of cricket; his play encompassed, for James, an entire history of political struggle and popular creativity in the Caribbean. Much is thus crammed into the few words when he says of Sobers: 'he is one of us. We are some of him' (227). And it is precisely this connection to a kind of popular energy which helped make it possible for Sobers, from a region seen as being peripheral, if not 'backward', to rescue cricket from the stagnation into which it had fallen in the supposed heartlands of England and Australia, where it had come to be dominated by what James referred to as 'the welfare state of mind': risk-avoidant, mechanical, cynical. The same, it seems to me, could be said with equal justice of Brian Lara who, like Sobers, grew up honing his skills in games played on the waste ground and side streets of the West Indies. And who, equally, brought a flair and élan to the game which was entirely at odds with the kind of remorseless industry that characterised Allan Border's Australian side of the time, or Graham Gooch's England. As one correspondent astutely noted:

> Once the pain of their repeated thrashings has subsided, the cricketers of England will be grateful to Brian Lara. Until this smiling, energetic young man burst into world cricket, the accumulation of masses of runs – of even a solitary Test century – had become too grim a ritual. No more. Not the least of Lara's astonishing gifts is the obvious [...] excitement he pours into virtually every innings. (Johnson in Scovell 2007: 90)

In these respects, Lara was unquestionably a product of the West Indian tradition. Had James had the chance to see him play, he would no doubt have nodded with recognition and said: he is one of us, and we are some of him. And for precisely this reason he was able to achieve, as did Sobers, something that transcended the partisan; something that appealed to longings and desires that wear no parochial or national label.

Yet there is a difference. When James called Sobers a 'consummation' he did so in the immediate aftermath of that other consummation represented by the (at least partial) decolonisation of the West Indies. And although James ends by arguing that Sobers' 'command of the rising ball in the drive, his close fielding and his hurling himself into his fast bowling are a living embodiment of centuries of a tortured history' (232), the tenor of his article, written in 1969, remains cautiously celebratory. By the time Lara emerged on to the stage of world cricket there was little to celebrate, even cautiously, in West Indian cricket or in the wider West Indian society from which it sprang. The tortured history of exile, colonisation and the plantation system had found new twists in the independent Caribbean: many of the progressive movements of the region had been crushed – often by external intervention – and the neo-liberal diktats of the International Monetary Fund, abetted by self-serving local elites, were imposing desperate social costs. In Trinidad, birthplace of both James and Lara, the 'police and thieves' that Junior Murvin decried in a reggae classic were, as he predicted (and as James himself feared, see Lai 1992: 185), destroying the nation with their 'guns and ammunition', and a kind of Hobbesian ruthlessness had come to dominate political affairs. Much of this newly tortured history has been documented by, among others, James' nephew Darcus Howe. By the last decades of the twentieth century, the hopes and possibilities of independence in the Caribbean had worn thin, and defending what they might have made possible for a wider constituency had become increasingly difficult.

This history too finds an embodiment in cricket. If Lara was also, in his own way, a consummation of the West Indian tradition, it was a tradition on the brink. Lara became part of a side that had been dominant in the world game for twenty years, but whose air of invincibility was rapidly tarnishing. It was no longer the case, as it had been when Sobers was young, that in cricket 'more than anywhere else, all the different classes of the population learnt to have an interest in common' (James 1986: 225). On the one hand, the lure of American mass culture was drawing away many of those youngsters who might otherwise have become the next generation of great players from the region. On the other hand, the administration of the game was beset by the kinds of inter-regional tension, claims of nepotism and cronyism that have characterised the dilemmas of postcolonialism in many parts of the world. Indeed, when he was first chosen for the team, senior players muttered darkly about Lara's relationship with the selector Joey Carew, whom he had known since he was a boy (Lara 1995: 44). The West Indies came into the 1995 series against England only five days after having been beaten by Australia (and therefore having lost the trophy named in honour of

Frank Worrell) for the first time since 1978. Moreover, there was bitter infighting within the camp over the captaincy, as well as simmering disputes over wages and tour commitments, all of which seemed to echo uncannily the fragmentation in West Indian society more widely. In the aftermath of a particularly heated team-meeting Lara had threatened to quit, stung by accusations that his interest in the game was largely a pecuniary one (Scovell 2007: chapter 13). On the field, the team were relying far too heavily for comfort on the bowling of their two ageing masters of the art, Curtly Ambrose and Courtney Walsh and – as they would for much of the next decade – on Lara's imperious batting.

For James, one of cricket's peculiar formal qualities was that it was a game structured around a series of individual encounters between batsman and bowler which became meaningful by virtue of being part of something bigger than themselves (see 1983 [1963]: chapter 16). Thus each encounter, James noted, was framed by the whole cumulative course of a match up until that point, so that the game was forever recalling the relationship between the detail and the larger pattern, incident and history, which is a feature of human meaning-making as such. Moreover, each delivery, and the response it elicits, contains the possibility of a change in the trajectory of the match, or series of matches, of which it is a moment: cricket was not the least of the contexts in which James learned his disdain for determinist accounts of history. At the same time, the encounter between batsman and bowler also extends beyond itself in other ways. Not only are both players individuals in their own right, bringing to that encounter a specific quality that might be called character, but also and simultaneously they are representatives of their respective teams. Thus, at the heart of the game, there is what one might call a relationship of synecdoche: that relationship between the part and the whole, the individual and the group, which James chewed over in many other contexts, especially with regard to the leadership of social movements. It is the same relationship, of course, that he believed illuminated the great works of dramatic fiction, whose achievement was to express in an individual character or in a series of limited human encounters, wider social contradictions. Precisely the relationship which Webster and Robeson's *Othello* so pointedly failed to bring to life.

The ball that Devon Malcolm bowled to Brian Lara, and Lara's response, open out into wider meanings in just this sense. It is necessary to understand that Lara was beaten, as might be said in the cricketing vernacular. And where he was in that moment is exactly where West Indian cricket was, indeed where the idea of 'West Indian' itself was: out of position, on the defensive, seemingly hopeless. This is not a claim that rests on merely a neat symbolic parallel. At that moment Lara *was* the representative of West Indian cricket, and West Indian cricket was still deeply entangled with and emblematic of whatever sense of shared identity and possible collective destiny existed in the region. These social meanings were there in that moment, not as metaphors that might be imposed from the outside, but integral to the cricketing form itself for those who watched or listened in, in the Caribbean or elsewhere. And what happened next, of course, is pure dialectic: Lara took that imminent defeat and turned it inside out. He turned the conditions of probable defeat into an image of enduring freedom and creative possibility. In its own much smaller way, the same revelation that James had written about in *The Black Jacobins* in which those who were consigned to history are revealed to make history of their own.

This was something that Lara would do time and again throughout his career, nowhere more brilliantly than in the 1999 home series against Australia when, in the second Test match, he walked out to a chorus of boos and catcalls from the Jamaican crowd, having led the team to one of their heaviest ever defeats in the preceding game. Reportedly, he said to the pugnacious Australian captain Steve Waugh: 'This is the last time that I'm gonna have to put up with this shit.' Waugh interpreted the comment as a sign that Lara was mentally exhausted and ready to surrender the leadership of the side. But he was wrong. Lara eventually took guard on the second day of the game with the West Indian batting already in tatters. Precisely when it seemed that nothing could lie ahead but defeat succeeding defeat, he played an innings of startling brilliance, eventually scoring 213 and leading, in the end, to a dramatic series-levelling victory. 'On one fantastic, sunny, windy Sunday' wrote a commentator in *Wisden*, 'Lara seduced the people of a bankrupt nation, resurrected his career as a batsman of rare gifts and reignited cricket throughout the Caribbean.' When he reached his two hundred, many of the watching crowd flooded onto the field in what James would certainly have taken as 'proof of the pudding': that is, proof of how much more than cricket was at stake in each and every delivery, each and every shot.

James interrupts his essay on Sobers to cite one of his most beloved texts: Wordsworth's preface to the *Lyrical Ballads*, in which the poet describes the effort that he and Coleridge had embarked upon to develop a newly popular poetic medium as part of a response to the terrible degradation of the rising cities and the furious restlessness of the market. With a characteristic willingness to bring the potential of popular culture to the impasses of high-brow art, James writes: '[O]f all those who go forth the world over to maintain and develop the beauty and dignity of the human mind which Wordsworth was so certain would survive all challenges, cricketers are not the least' (1986: 227). What Sobers achieved, he argues – an achievement that became universal in its scope – was to open out, to expand the imagination and the prospective vision of those who watched him; to pose in other form those questions that James himself continually posed: what might people want and what might they be capable of? '[T]his is the enlargement of our historical past and the savannahs of our future which this young man now impels into our vision of ourselves' (ibid.). Again, the words might have been written for Lara. Among those who leapt the barriers to celebrate his double century at Sabina Park there was, as if in recognition of some kind of benediction, a man clutching a baby. There can be no way of quantifying, of course, what enlargement of the savannahs of the future Brian Lara's batting opened up for his many crowds. But enlarge he certainly did, even though to understand this fully we have to understand first exactly what the play itself says; what it means to be on the back foot and out of position and yet still to send the ball racing back across the outfield, with head level, and right arm held classically high.

2
Contexts

Introduction

In March 1932 *The Times* published a number of short elegiac pieces in response to the recent death of Lord Harris, the Eton-educated aristocrat who had, in accordance with the seemingly effortless progression to high-ranking public posts assumed to be natural for a person of his class, served as both a Conservative government minister and as colonial Governor in Bombay. Harris had also been, in what no doubt appeared to be an equally natural progression, one of the earliest captains of the English cricket team and was a lifelong organiser and proselytizer on the game's behalf. Harris was certainly a proponent of the idea of cricket as the 'umbilical cord of empire', in J. A. Mangan's phrase (1998: 153), although the empire that mattered to him, in this respect, was primarily one comprised of the white expatriate or settler communities in India, Australia and the Caribbean. His reputation as the father of Indian cricket, for example, is misplaced. As Ramachandra Guha's (2002) historical account makes clear, the enthusiastic adoption of cricket in India was treated with cool indifference by the British, including Harris, so long as such indifference remained possible. It was only after local cricketers had put their talents and determination unavoidably on display with victories over the elite expatriate gymkhanas, and subsequently against touring teams, that the game was found to have been, all along, one of the many fruits of Britain's supposedly benign civilising mission.

One of these responses to Harris' death, in any case, for which the author is given only as 'a correspondent', begins as follows: 'The late Lord Harris will be regretted in many places, not least in the West Indies, where he was born. He always had a warm spot in his heart for the land of his birth.' It goes on to recall a visit by Harris to Trinidad, late in his life, during which he 'met a negro septuagenarian who had been his playmate in childhood'. Later, during the same visit or a subsequent one, the correspondent reports that Harris was prevailed upon 'to put on the pads' and that he faced the bowling of some of the island's better (white) players. 'Even on the uncertain matting wicket, and encumbered by coat and waistcoat, Lord Harris showed good form, playing forward with the left foot to the ball in the old style', the correspondent recalls.

This unnamed correspondent is, of course, C. L. R. James, who had disembarked in Plymouth less than a fortnight previously from the *M.S. Colombia* (Laughlin in James 2003: xxx) and who, as this submission to *The Times* suggests, clearly possessed remarkable self-assurance regarding his own future trajectory. An assurance that seems in retrospect to have almost a touch of the aristocrat about it and which was certainly not in keeping with what one might expect of a first-time visitor from the colonies who had just travelled third class from Barbados. James himself, recalling this period of his life in *Beyond a Boundary*, famously describes his sense at the time that he was 'about to enter the arena where I was to play the role for which I had prepared myself. The British intellectual was going to Britain' (1983 [1963]: 114). And this, indeed, is exactly the feeling that one gets from his first, short publication in England, with its sure-footed mixture of deference and self-confidence. A sympathetic and critically minded modern reader might argue that the reference to Harris' encounter with his childhood playmate has a kind of bathetic, levelling effect and that this serves to throw into relief the racism and class prejudice that were written into the structures of Empire. There is also, perhaps, a subtle impertinence in the very fact that Harris' West Indian birth is posthumously recalled. Harris had, after all, opposed the selection of the Indian-born K. S. Ranjitsinhji by England on the breathtakingly hypocritical grounds that only 'native-born' Englishmen should be eligible for the side (Guha 2002: 94). But, in all honesty, there is little in this snippet to suggest the prominent anti-imperial campaigner that James was to become, nor much evidence of the influence of that tradition of Trinidadian radicalism that Selwyn Cudjoe claims played a formative role in his intellectual development (Cudjoe 1992, 1997; see also Singham 1990; Bogues 1997). Which is not to say, of course, that this influence was not there; some intellectual heritage clearly allowed James to walk dauntless into metropolitan life, sending off dispatches to *The Times* within days of his arrival, before going on to cross swords with Edith Sitwell at Bloomsbury literary functions (James 2003: chapter 2). All the same, what seems most characteristically Jamesian in these few lines is that aspect of his writing which was discussed in the previous chapter: his eager remembering of the old man's 'form', of the way in which he stood at the crease and met the bowling.

James loved nothing more than the chance to watch the game's old masters at play. In this respect his few sentences on Harris are part of a kind of mini-genre in his early cricket writing which is made up of pieces in which he offers a close reading of the style and technique of players who are near to retirement (for example: James 1938b), or who have retired and whom he encounters as they make a guest appearance in a one-off 'scratch' game or in some Sunday afternoon friendly (for example: James 1937a). The very next piece of cricket writing that he produced, in fact, a few months later, was what he called an 'impressionist sketch' of S. F. Barnes, the great professional bowler from Staffordshire who James saw playing for the village of Rawtenstall against Learie Constantine's Nelson in the Lancashire League. Barnes was, at the time, fifty-nine. As in much of his writing about cricketers, James is on the look out for 'character', for the way in which cricket's peculiar dynamic of individual and collective effort allowed some sense of the personalities of those involved to emerge. He had, in this respect, a keen eye for what Bourdieu would call 'bodily hexis': the subtle ways in which carriage and movement, pose and poise, express something of a person and their life. And, as can be seen here, it is clear that even at this stage of his career James refused to think of 'character' as the unique preserve of the great and the good of public life such as Harris. In this, the effect of a Caribbean populism on his thinking is far more evident. After all, the same insistence on a dignifying treatment of ordinary men and women had already characterised the fictional writing he had produced in Trinidad, the most sustained example of which is his great and only novel, *Minty Alley* (1971 [1936]; see Ramchand 1970: chapter 5). Of Barnes, in any case, he writes:

> You can almost hear the old bones creaking. He is tall and thin, well over six feet, with strong features. It is a rather remarkable face in its way, and could belong to a great lawyer or a statesman without incongruity. He holds his head well back, with the rather long chin lifted. He looks like a man who has seen as much of the world as he wants to see. (1986: 7)

He goes on to describe Barnes' now time-worn but still effective 'high and straight' bowling action, how he stood in the slips, how he suckered one of Nelson's better batsmen into a fatal misjudgement. As he left the field at the end of the first innings, having taken seven of the ten wickets to fall, 'the crowd applauded his fine bowling mightily. Barnes walked through it intent on his own affairs. He had had much of that all his life' (9).

As with the piece on Harris there is no avoiding the nostalgic note here. It is a note, of course, that is in one respect entirely in tune with that habitually struck by the self-appointed custodians of cricket, its elite officials and scribes, who have always tended to present the game as one which is possessed of a fragile timelessness. Cricket, by this account, is a ritual that makes possible an eternal return to a leafy original scene in which one can, like Matthew Arnold's Thyrsis, escape the 'great town's harsh, heart-wearying roar', escape industrial squalor, escape all of modernity's mess and its unfortunate, attendant social conflicts. Cricket escapes all of these and yet is also perpetually threatened by them, so that it can well be said that melancholy or elegy is the characteristic mood of the sport, or at least of its south of England incarnation. Not for nothing has Francis Thompson's portrayal of Lord's as a place haunted by its past become a canonical piece of cricket literature: 'For the field is full of shades as I near a shadowy coast / And a ghostly batsmen plays to the bowling of a ghost / And I look through my tears on a soundless-clapping host / As the run-stealers flicker to and fro'.

It might be argued, then, that when James chooses as he does here, and elsewhere in writing from this period, to focus on the retired or retiring player he is taking up a theme that is much in keeping with that romantic mythology in which the game is seen as having one foot outside of history. The old batsman or bowler at the crease becomes revenant, like Thompson's ghostly players, and therefore an appropriate figure for cricket's troubled relationship to the contemporary world. There is, after all, something both timeless and out-of-time about Barnes in James' account; he, like the game, has seen as much of the world as he wants to see. And of such a game, of course, it would be a *faux pas* or worse, an act of vandalism, to pose sociological or political questions. Perhaps, one might speculate, it was the degree to which James' piece chimed in with cricket's self-mythologising which impressed Neville Cardus, and which led to his securing James a post as cricket correspondent with the *Manchester Guardian*.

There is, however, more to it than that. Because at the centre of James' impressionist sketch is an account of the confrontation between Barnes and Constantine, the two professional players of their respective sides, as each takes it in turn to face the bowling of the other. Barnes, for his part, was as far from cricket's traditionalists as it was possible to be, militantly asserting the rights of the professional player against the game's grandees, and repeatedly pointing out the hypocrisy of the 'shamateurism' which allowed 'gentlemen' to play the game as if 'for its own sake', even as they received lucrative payments in expenses and fees (Searle 1997). And with Constantine too, on whose behalf James had travelled to England, and for whom he was to act as ghost writer on his book *Cricket and I*, a different note is introduced. Constantine was, after all, one of the earliest black West Indian professionals to play league cricket in England and as Jeffrey Hill has argued (1994), he brought to a small northern town such as Nelson something far removed from the hazy, pastoral image of cricket in the home counties. Nor, indeed, would the crowds at Nelson, with its history of trade-union radicalism and its 'peculiar sense of modernity' (60), have shown much appetite for the pastoral. What those crowds sought, and what Constantine represented, was thrill and exertion, New World audacity and an emerging and exciting sense of the connectedness between what was local and what was global. It is no coincidence, suggests Hill, that Constantine's performances were so often described in local press reports with the adjective 'electric'. He, like the light bulb or like cinema (which had its own important part to play in Nelson's political history; see Renton 2007: chapter 2), was a very definite symbol of the modern world, rather than of a retreat from that world.

The first encounter between the pair, with Barnes bowling and Constantine batting, ends in a stalemate; the latter cautiously watching and fencing while the former gets the ball to bite and spit off a treacherous pitch. 'The crowd sat tense', writes James. 'Was this recitative suddenly to burst into the melody of fours and sixes to all parts of the field?' (1986: 9). It was not to be: Constantine, having faced down Barnes, drops his guard too quickly against 'some insignificant trundler' and is out. When the roles are reversed Constantine goes about his bowling with distinctly unpastoral effort: 'running seventeen yards and hurling the ball violently through the air, [he] began sending back the Rawtenstall batsmen. One, two, three, wickets and bails flying every time' (ibid.). Barnes, 'older than Constantine's father', came in next and for forty minutes, James records, he obdurately defied the pace and aggression of his younger opponent, getting staunchly into line with the short pitched ball, playing forward and straight to the rest. So long as Barnes remained, writes James, his side were winning. Eventually, however, Constantine gets him out, bowled behind his back.

> He came in slowly amidst the plaudits of the Nelson crowd, applauding his innings and their satisfaction at his having been dismissed. Courtesy

> acknowledged the applause. For the rest he continued as he had begun, a man unconsciously scornful of his milieu. After he left, Rawtenstall collapsed. (10)

With this encounter, one might say, history enters James' account. There is, unquestionably, a poignancy to his portrait of Barnes but it is not that misty-eyed nostalgia that fits so well with the conservative's vision of the game. It is, rather, a much more blunt recognition of the isolating responsibility that beset the professional player. Barnes is revealed as being, ultimately, a member of the working class, and one whose chief resource is an increasingly creaky and recalcitrant body. The industrial overtones in James' earlier image of the player 'set[ting] the old machinery in motion' (7) seem suddenly apposite, and one realises sharply what was at stake that led him, even while warming up against the gentlest of bowling, to wear gloves: 'He was not going to run the risk of those precious fingers being struck by the ball' (ibid.). No wonder, given that his livelihood was, quite literally, in his own hands, and given the desperate fate that awaited many of the professional players of the period when they were forced out of the game by injury or old age (Marqusee 1994: chapter 3; Sandiford 1994: chapter 5).

In this account, then, as indeed in terms of James' wider political understanding, both Constantine and the demotic traditions of northern England play a pivotal role (James 2003: 122–5, 1983 [1963]: 116). They are among the means by which James shakes himself loose of cricket's conventional refusal of history. And with this it becomes apparent just how far Barnes' style, like Constantine's, is expressive of the specific social and historical contexts in which he learned the game and in which he played, and of the limits and possibilities that follow from these contingencies. His determination as he defends against Constantine's hostility, and his skilful but rigorous control of line and length as he bowls are no longer expressions of that 'good form in the old style' which James attributes to Lord Harris, and which seems to hark back to some eternal standard of cricketing value. Instead, Barnes' style can be seen as explicitly belonging to his time and place, and to the precarious life of the journeyman professional, even one as widely admired as he was. A question is emerging in James' cricket writing, a question that will fall into greater focus and clarity in the years that follow: might it be possible, after all, to think historically about this seemingly most ahistorical of all cultural activities? How is cricketing form, indeed, how are the forms of culture more generally, related to the social conditions in which they emerge and in which they are received? Watching old cricketers at play might seem, from one point of view, an appropriate expression of the game's timelessness, of this 'field full of shades'. From another point of view, however, such players reveal very clearly the historical nature of the game, the degree to which its styles and conventions, its changing modes of play, can only be adequately understood in relation to the world of which they are a part, and of which they provide their own specific impressionistic sketch.

Nearly six years later, in one of the very last pieces of cricketing writing that he produced before leaving for America, James returned to this theme, reflecting in this case on the career of another great player of the game who was then on the cusp of retirement: Frank Woolley (James 1938a). As he does with Barnes, James spends the majority of the article focusing assiduously on Woolley's style, describing his characteristic and often idiosyncratic shot-making and singling out in particular his wonderful capacity for 'timing' the ball, which allowed him to hit cleanly but also with an apparently effortless ease. Here, once again, is the typical Jamesian concern with form, only by now it is clear that any judgement about form, about how a given player played the game, opens out into wider questions of social and historical context; it requires that we say something about how such play became possible, about what it meant.

Later on, in *Beyond a Boundary*, James will famously describe cricket's aesthetic appeal as resting on the game's ability to provide instances of 'significant form' (1983 [1963]: 202–6): a sense of motion or shape which is not just seen but felt by its audience, something received, he says, in 'the tactile consciousness of thousands' (202). The roots of that idea lie in earlier articles such as this one, because here, just as they do in his encomium on Barnes, it is the presence of the crowd that makes itself heard. James is clear that Woolley's significance lies precisely in the fact that what he did was significant to others, to the men and women who came to watch him and who 'recognized in him something beyond the average scorer of runs, some elegance of line and harmony of movement which went beyond the figures on the score-board' (ibid.). In this respect, James is clearly suggesting, Woolley's importance is defined not simply by virtue of what he achieved in terms of the game's own calculus of victories and losses, but by what he achieved in a much wider sense: his play filled a historical need, a longing for 'some elegance of line and harmony of movement' that his popular audience found few other means of meeting.

Years before he developed the term in *Beyond a Boundary*, James had spoken of 'significant form' in another context, describing how European writers like Dostoevsky and Flaubert gave expression to essentially modern dilemmas – issues of individualism and emerging mass society – by grappling with the local and specific problems which they recognised as their own. If we now think of such writers as 'universal', James suggests, this is only because of the urgency and immediacy with which they responded to the issues of their time and place. His use of the term 'significant form' (1993: 50), in other words, points us to the way in which cultural practices become expressive of historical contradictions and social possibilities precisely because they are practices that are contingent and time-bound. Of course, the phrase draws attention to the relationship between such practices and their audiences, which is, after all, the only way in which anything cultural can be said to have significance. But it draws attention also to the fact that what matters to an audience, matters because it meets them in the specificity of when and where they are, and speaks to them in ways that they find worthy of attention. Woolley's 'timing', no doubt, was a matter of technique and practice. To describe his great skill as the ability to time the ball is, therefore, to say something about what he did in terms of the intrinsic meanings of cricket as a particular kind of human activity. But 'timing' is also, thus, about timeliness, about Woolley as a figure who meant something in a particular context, and about a relationship between him and the crowds who watched him, and who brought to their watching needs and longings that made them so obviously different from that dream audience of cricket's traditionalists: the 'soundless-clapping host'.

When James writes, therefore, that 'whatever his virtues no batsman of the modern school will ever play like Woolley, as no modern historian will ever write like Gibbon', one should not read into this a wistfulness on his part for a vanished golden age. Rather, it seems to me, James is posing the question of the relationship between artistic or cultural forms and the social conditions in which these forms are made and made use of. What does it mean to say, as he says of Woolley: 'The foundations of his style were laid in another age' (James 1938a)? Or, to put it more generally: how might we go about developing an understanding of cultural practices which pays due attention to both 'style' and 'age'; due attention both to that which is specific to those practices as symbolic activities which come with their own expectations and their own histories of development *and* to the ways in which these things are related to – and revealing of – historical developments in a more general sense? For James, it is clear, such questions can be asked of sport without embarrassment, just as they might be asked of Palladian architecture or the eighteenth-century novel. Indeed, in one regard, sport poses the issue especially starkly, in that sporting events are by definition one-offs. Although in another article from this period James urges the cricketing authorities to begin systematically storing film footage of contemporary players – 'I am certain that many things now being stored in more serious spheres are likely to be of less interest in thirty years time' (James 1937a) – each innings played by Woolley was timely in a very specific sense. Sporting practice cannot be reproduced in anything like the way that, say, a novel or a newspaper can be. Even detailed filming could not adequately capture the many small interactions between crowd and player, nor all the subtle subsidiary events that take place away from, or in the moments in-between, the confrontation between bowler and batsman, and which are themselves constitutive of the meaning of the game. A game of cricket, in important respects, only ever happens once. And if, because of this, sport can be said to escape something of that erosion of 'aura' which Walter Benjamin claimed beset the work of art in an era of mechanical reproduction (Benjamin 1968: 219–53), it poses the question of the historicity of cultural forms all the more clearly because of it.

These, then, are the issues that I am concerned with in what follows. The previous chapter sought to do justice to James' careful treatment of cultural forms in themselves, as symbolic and expressive worlds of their own. However, if we are not to fall back into that overly hasty judgement which mistakes this attentiveness in James for closet formalism, in the derogatory sense of that term, we need to tell the second half of the story; we need to recognise that for James 'style' is inextricable from 'age'. Cultural practices and objects are meaningful in particular ways, true to the peculiar symbolic rules and assumptions that they establish and maintain. But that meaningfulness is always 'timely', it is made or received in specific times and places. The meaningfulness of culture cannot but be a meaningfulness in and of a wider social and political context. As Raymond Williams noted some time ago, an analysis which seeks to pay due attention to both the intrinsic and the sociological properties of cultural practices or which, indeed, seeks out some discernible relationship between these intrinsic and sociological properties, quickly finds itself walking down some very densely tangled paths. 'The intricacies of the subsequent argument', says Williams laconically, 'are extraordinary' (1976: 139). James, it seems to me, should certainly be seen as one of those figures who has most to offer to anyone interested in trying to make something of these intricacies. And in what follows, therefore, what I will seek to do is to tease out some of the central claims that he makes regarding the relationship between what is called culture, on the one hand, and what is called history, on the other. This will mean, necessarily, saying something about his understanding of both sides of that relationship.

I

It is perhaps best to begin in negative, as it were, by clarifying what James is not arguing. After all, to approach culture in the way that he began to, at least from the middle of the 1930s, means rejecting other ways of going about the same business; ways of asking what culture means which look for an answer in places that supposedly precede or transcend the social. It is, for instance, no surprise to discover James' scepticism with regard to readings of modern literature which used psychoanalytical concepts as a master-key with which to unlock the deeper and darker secrets of the authorial heart. In a letter written to the Melville scholar Jay Leyda in 1953 he says explicitly: 'to the extent you speculate on the unconscious, and make that your main emphasis, to that extent you destroy the book the author wrote' (1992: 235). James' views on psychoanalytical method are a little elusive (see Buhle 1988: 106–19) but underlying his comments here is a more general suspicion of the very idea that a novel or painting was some kind of puzzle that awaited a once-and-for-all solution. Cultural objects and practices are meaningful, but that meaning is not a singular truth which can be arrived at through a philosophical decoding or by following the crumb trail of the author's neuroses. 'Moby Dick, the whale', James insists, 'symbolizes nothing – zero – a big fish in the sea; that's all. It is Ahab and Ishmael who make these fantastic symbolisms; and Melville is superb in the way he contrasts their fantasies with the objective realism of Moby Dick' (1992: 235). More fool them, James suggests, and more foolish still those critics who continue to hunt down the meaning of literary texts as if that meaning were a hidden bounty that could be abstracted from the work itself, or from the social context in which the work is written or read.

For James the very fact that the stuff of human creativity could be treated in this way was itself historically explicable. The fact that art could be thought about as something apart from social life, indeed something to which the connoisseur might retreat in order to escape that life was evidence of the growing division between thinking and doing which he saw as one of the most damaging consequences of capitalism. Hence the story of his somewhat irascible attendance at the Havana conference of tricontinental intellectuals in 1968, during which he consistently reminded his fellow delegates that the primary aim of their gathering should be the effort to abolish the social conditions which made possible the division between mental and manual labour, and with it the very idea of the intellectual as a type of person who might meet with others of the same type in exclusive gatherings (Worcester 1996: 201–2; Colás 1999). The assumption that the meanings of works of art were surreptitious or covert, that they were trophies to be bagged and stuffed by the cognoscenti, was one of the baleful results of that 'categorization and specialisation, that division of the human personality, which is the greatest curse of our time' (1983 [1963]: 191).

For James, to be clear, it is precisely the specialists summoned up by this curse who are its true victims. He was, of course, not naïve about the degree to which modern working practices, as well as the domestic arrangements which supported them, had the effect of stifling opportunities for imaginative and creative expression. Yet he never ceased pointing out the resilient forms of popular cultural activity that did flourish in such time and space as working men and women were able to salvage for themselves. Creativity sprang anew in the very places – the calypso tents and churches, sports fields and jazz clubs – where the highbrows rarely deigned to tread. It was the intellectual who, like Ahab cursing the carpenter of his false leg, sought to deny the 'interdebtedness of mortals' (2001 [1953]: 50) without which creativity itself would be unimaginable. And one symptom of that denial were those theories which construed works of art as ahistorical objects, as allegories concerning perennial truths about human nature, or as the purely subjective expressions of a flukish and inexplicable genius.

There is, therefore, an unapologetic claim on James' part as to what art or culture worthy of the name should be or, at least, what it could be in a world in which creative or intellectual activity was recovered as something held in common. Witness his blunt statement in the draft of his *Preface to Criticism*: 'A great work of art bears its meaning on its face' (James 1992: 258). Having made this claim James proceeds, as he did on other occasions, to contrast an exclusive view of culture with the situation which prevailed in other historical and social contexts. Often, in this respect, it was the example of Athenian drama that he reached for; here it is the example of the Elizabethan stage:

> When Shakespeare wrote his plays, and they were produced and acted, author, performers and audience understood what the play was about. They did not have to take a text home and work at it. They could disagree, but they knew what they disagreed about. (ibid.)

I do not think that what James means here is simply that the audience could understand the dialogue or follow the plot. He was no crude populist in such matters and he often championed writers, such as Wilson Harris, whose work is generally held to be dense and demanding. What James is pointing to here, as with Woolley, is Shakespeare's 'timeliness'. In other words, the degree to which his works clarified peculiarly urgent social dilemmas and could be understood by their audience as doing so, as characterising and dramatising questions that burned in their own social and political existence: around the idea of individualism, for example, or the increasingly unstable idea of monarchical authority (see Taylor 1999). Precisely because cultural practices establish their own forms of meaningfulness, it becomes possible for social contradictions and historical possibilities to be refracted in them, and therefore to become recognisable or contestable in new ways. In this sense cultural practices and objects are those things 'about' which we argue and around which we are arrayed. And it was evidence of this close engagement with creative acts, this contextual and contestational making sense of history through culture, that he routinely found in popular cultural contexts. Such creativity, no doubt, was threatened by the imperatives of the market and by a dulling standardisation in production. Such were the swords that James saw hanging over the head of a popular calypso artist such as Mighty Sparrow (1977: chapter 15). Nevertheless, there was, for James, no mistaking the urgency of popular cultural creativity; the degree to which, as with Sparrow's lyrics, that creativity sprang from the effort to grapple with social existence. The doomed and wasteful hunt for original authorial intention or for cabalistic symbolism could be left, for its part, to the various modern Ahabs.

II

Culture can, of course, be explained with an appeal to other kinds of allegedly pre-social qualities: bodily or racial qualities, for example. When James famously says of a player such as Rohan Kanhai that his play embodied 'some essence of that crowded vagueness which passes for the history of the West Indies' (1986: 165–6) he is, apart from anything else, responding to those pundits who greeted the emergence of high-profile black West Indian cricketers with *sotto voce* hints about a very different kind of 'essence', about the supposedly superior athleticism of non-European bodies. It was against the backdrop of this churlish racism that James produced much of his best cricket writing in the 1950s and 1960s, and precisely against such views, therefore, that he sought to show the degree to which that success was the result of the patiently learned skills and deliberate actions of the players involved, actions which themselves rested on and were made possible by the long historical tradition of cricketing practice within West Indian popular culture. James' insistence that these achievements were therefore historically explicable and politically meaningful, that they offered, as he puts it of Kanhai, 'a unique pointer of the West Indian quest for identity [... for ...] ways of expressing our potential bursting at every seam' (166), involved a deliberate refutation of those who saw in the same events nothing more than the inevitable playing out of a biological difference.

James fought this corner for most of his life, against all-comers, and not simply in relation to what I am calling here cultural practices. In a well-known passage from *Beyond a Boundary* he takes to task no less an authority than Don Bradman, who had described Learie Constantine's achievements in league cricket as if they represented a little light hay-making in a weekend knockabout. James disputes Bradman's view of league cricket, knowing as he did the fierce autonomy of the working-class traditions which sustained that form of the game (Searle 1997: 127–30), but he disputes even more forcefully Bradman's implication about Constantine: that he was just one more carefree imported West Indian entertainer. 'We are still', he writes, 'in the flower garden of the gay, the spontaneous, tropical West Indian. We need some astringent spray' (1983 [1963]: 131). More than a decade earlier, in two articles written for *Fourth International* (1949a, 1949b), James had challenged the account of American abolitionism provided by another authoritative figure in his particular field: the Communist Party historian Herbert Aptheker (see Nielsen 1997: chapter 2 for a discussion of these essays). James is scathing about much that Aptheker had to say, including his presentation of Fredrick Douglass as some kind of noble savage: 'a magnificent figure of a man, impregnable, incorruptible, scars on his back, African prince, majestic in his wrath' (1949b: 339). In one particularly acute passage James catches Aptheker suggesting that Fredrick Douglass 'found himself' calling for insurrection. He reaches, in response, for his astringent spray: 'The magnificent African prince could do much, but that he could stand on a platform and out of his head consciously speak of insurrection – that Aptheker simply could not stand. He makes it a visitation from on high' (1949b: 340). James accepted that no more than he accepted the suggestion that Constantine simply 'found himself' batting or bowling as he did: 'Constantine's leg-glance from outside the off-stump to long-leg was a classical stroke. It was not due to his marvellous West Indian eyes and marvellous West Indian wrists. It was due, if you must have it, to his marvellous West Indian brains' (1983 [1963]: 134).

I make the comparison between James' defence of Constantine and his defence of Douglass for two reasons. On the one hand, as I have said, it is important not to lose sight of the fact that his approach to culture was won despite, and against, a tendency to see such things through the lens of 'race'. On the other hand, James' critique of Aptheker picks up on his stereotyping primarily as a symptom of a more general fallacy. Aptheker's portrayal of Douglass is representative, for James, of the degree to which he represents black involvement in abolitionism per se as a kind of appendage, or as an incidental stimulus, to a movement whose real dynamism lay elsewhere. And this, in turn, is representative for James of the entire perspective on history and social struggle that undergirded the work of Communist Party thinkers. History, in the Stalinist account, became precisely 'a visitation from on high', a force by which groups and individuals, whatever their professed hopes or intentions, are bundled towards pre-appointed ends. James spent much of his energy in America contesting both this particular view of black politics, and the view of historical and social change which sustained it (see James 1996a and my own discussion, Smith 2010, for an introduction to the wider debates here).

With this we approach a key issue, because James' willingness to think in historical terms about cultural objects and practices was necessarily tied up with his thinking about 'history' itself. And if James defended the historical meaningfulness of culture against those accounts which made reference to ahistorical values or qualities – cricket's romantic traditionalists; the 'magist' literary critics; those who sheltered behind the concept of 'race' – it seems to me that he defended, just as insistently, the historical meaningfulness of culture against those accounts which found in cultural acts or products only meanings given to them by some super-ordinate historical logic. Which emptied them of history, as it were, in the very name of History.

James' understanding of history certainly changed over time. As in most other respects, he is not a thinker with whom it is easy to point to a 'final' or settled position here. Yet this is, in a sense, precisely the point: James himself was grappling with his world, restlessly attempting to make sense of the movements and events of which he was part. There is, it seems to me, a wilful vulnerability to his thinking in this respect, an openness to the changing lessons of historical context, which is tremendously attractive. Its price, no doubt, is absolute theoretical purity or consistency. But, he would have responded, who wishes to be paid in this false coin in any case? The modern-day gnostics who sought to think themselves out of the world simply admitted thereby the completeness of their surrender to the world. James' thinking about history, in short, is exemplified more clearly than anything else by the way in which he went about thinking *in* history (see le Blanc in McLemee and le Blanc 1994: 19–27; R. King 2006). Historical understanding, including such understanding as we achieve through the symbolic and creative acts of culture, comes through our struggle with the confinements that are before us. In this respect James developed a view of historical progress, not as a metaphysical juggernaut, but as something with which we are intimate, something which we look for in the only place that it is possible to look for it: the here-and-now. The future can be seen, as it were, as the inside-out of what is, as in the slave's evocation against their world: 'better day coming' (Douglass 1969 [1855]). Nor is this merely a passive evocation, but rather the means towards getting things done; the future is an assumption by which struggles against 'what is' are begun and carried forward. In these respects, central to what became James' understanding of history and therefore also to his claims about the historical meanings and uses of cultural practices are two things which he himself exemplified. Firstly, an increasingly clear insistence on the activity or agency of human beings as the central issue – the 'why', as it were – of any historical account. Secondly, an emphasis on the centrality of contradiction and struggle – the 'how', as it were – in historical change.

In one respect, this refusal of the self-certainty which had come to characterise some versions of European Marxism was driven by James' more general disquiet with some aspects of that Marxism: his insistence, for example, on the need to recognise the specificity of histories of racism and the need, consequently, to leave political space for distinctive forms of resistance to racism. As Cedric Robinson (1995), Anthony Bogues (1997), Sylvia Wynter (1992) and many others have made clear, he was one of many twentieth-century figures who interrogated European Marxism in the name of historical experiences which that Marxism had too often overlooked or filed away into well-thumbed conceptual boxes. However, this was a critique from inside the house of Marxism, rather than outside of it, and it involved a significant turning back to Marx's own writings. A pivotal moment in James' understanding, in this regard, was his engagement, in company with Raya Dunayevskaya and Grace Lee, with the work of Hegel and the early Marx. Particularly consequential among these encounters was their reading and re-reading of the latter's 'Economic and Philosophical Manuscripts', of which they produced the first English translations in 1947 (see James 1984: chapter 6). In these manuscripts, as well as in Marx's historical studies, James and his colleagues found an under-recognised human emphasis, one that pointed to the search for creative expression as a fundamental human need, and which therefore made it possible to see the activities of 'labour' and those of culture, not as rivals for political attention – as some of James' comrades of the time did tend to see things – but as dislocated parts of a single human longing.

Neil Lazarus was certainly right, then, in what remains one of the best introductory accounts, to regard James as one of the 'truly decisive' (1999: 144) Marxist cultural theorists of the twentieth century, but of a Marxism which pivots on the presence of the active, creative human being. If he argued that cultural forms were historical forms, he meant thereby to underscore their human provenance and human uses, rather than to offer an interpretation which transcends such provenance and use. It is precisely because the stuff of culture is born of the labours of longing, thinking human beings, and because that stuff is argued 'about' by other longing, thinking human beings, that it manifests something of the particular social contexts and contests in which it was made, and in which use is made of it. Culture, in other words, is not just stuff thrown loose by the passage of History. Such a view, for James, misconceives how social change happens but it misconceives culture also, treating its objects and practices as if they were artefacts in some Da Vinci code mystery, containing a singular and eternal meaning entrusted to them by the past. Against such a view he insisted on culture as something which is done and with which things are done. Culture, or at least the culture that mattered to James, was an integral part of that continual reach towards what he called, in a key essay: 'the positive in the negative, the affirmation that is contained in every negation, the future that is in the present' (1980: 79). It is in this sense that culture can be said to be of history; both a part of how we learn to recognise history, and a part of how history is made.

III

James, in other words, clearly rejected what might now be called a 'determinist' view of culture, a view which sees culture as merely an epiphenomenon of various social and historical events. The contrasting idea of culture as a practice – as a site of active meaning-making, rather than as an inert bearer of meaning – is well-established in contemporary critical writing (for example: Dirlik 1990). As a result, perhaps, it is easy to overlook the originality of James' approach in its time and place, and the degree to which it was hard won. It was largely because he, in common with other writers from the colonial world, was willing to reflect seriously on popular culture, and on how that culture responded to and became part of political struggles, that he was able to dismiss the various kinds of timelessness to which bourgeois intellectualism and crude materialism both, in their different ways, consigned the works and workings of human creativity.

Yet if, as I have argued, James tended to present culture as something which is actively done, and with which things are actively done, this does not mean that such activity is free-floating. Culture does not become, for James, a world unto itself; it is not unaffected by the social and economic relations or the political structures in which it develops. So although we can say that James is not a determinist, he clearly *does* argue that the changing ways in which such things as movies are made, or spin bowling played, are historically expressive. This is, as I have suggested, what he means when he says that the great work of art bears its meaning on its face. We recognise, or can come to recognise, that our games and poetry, films and paintings, reveal something about the shape of our world and its possible futures even though this is rarely what those things are overtly 'about'. The question, of course, is how to describe or understand this expressive relationship between culture and historical context without slipping back into the crass sociology of the Stalinist critics who, 'taking advantage of the confusion of bourgeois thought, continue to make the most outrageous approximations between a writer's political beliefs and his artistic creation' (James 1980. 107–8). And so, for what remains of this chapter I want to suggest something of how James went about this process himself, and to extrapolate from his own cultural analysis two possible answers to this question. The first of these answers is in a negative key – having to do with the ways in which creativity is curtailed, so to speak, by historical conditions – and the second in a positive key, having to do with the ways in which particular cultural practices or acts can be said to be 'of their time', inasmuch as they both respond to and bear within themselves the evidence of contentions or dilemmas which are in some respect historically quintessential.

Firstly, as might be expected from the discussion of his account of history, it is implicit in James' understanding that what can be convincingly achieved through creative acts depends on a historical and social context which is both enabling and limiting, which makes certain things plausible or achievable, and others less so. Although James gave due attention to the vagaries of individual artistry – much more attention, indeed, than has been usual amongst Marxist critics – he insists that cultural creation is always a social phenomenon. Any such creation is reliant on the long preceding history by which particular symbolic activities become meaningful in their own right. Moreover, any such creation takes place in a specific context which shapes what might be done in and through such activities. It is not just, in other words, the great cultural achievements which can be said to be historically expressive. So too is the flawed piece of work, the artistic misstep, the failure of nerve. In this respect James' account certainly pre-empts that of Pierre Macherey (1978), who proposed a theory of literature as a kind of shattered mirror, important not so much for its ability to reflect back that which we already know, but for its eloquent gaps and absences, for 'what it does not say' (87). James only travels part of the way down this road with Macherey because he continued to insist on the possibility of creativity introducing something positively new to the world, and to our understanding of the world, as I will discuss in more detail in Chapter 5. All the same, the very fact that James was alert to what we might call the 'negative speech' of culture was a part of his challenge to those 'outrageous approximations' of the Stalinists who read literature or art as the straightforward expression of a class position.

We can take James' 1950 review of Norman Mailer's *The Naked and the Dead* as a case in point. As with all his cultural exposition, James' reading of Mailer's famous debut novel hinges on a strictly literary judgement: the work is excellent in many respects, he says, but structurally out of kilter because the character of Sergeant Croft, in all his brutality, is so completely dominant. Croft is, James argues, the novel's only fully realised figure, and the only one who convincingly develops through the course of the narrative. Those around him, as a result, appear too slight, too subsidiary, so that 'the book falls short of genuine dramatic power' (1980: 107). Hence, James says, it is not just in 'his strengths', but also 'in his weaknesses (and he has grave weaknesses), [that] this talented writer is a profound expression of American civilization' (106). Mailer's creativity fails him most particularly when it comes to imagining how General Cummings and Croft might be opposed. Against them he is able to present 'nothing, [only] a mere mass of men' (108) says James. But this faltering of creativity is a 'profound expression' of the historical situation in which Mailer wrote precisely because it reveals the limits of the credible in that situation, because it exposes the absence of social conditions that might sustain even an imaginative transcendence of the world as it was. Or, as he puts it later in *American Civilization*, reflecting on the same novel: 'The spaces and urges which give dynamism to an artistic consciousness are lacking' (1993: 267). Repelled on the one hand by bourgeois hypocrisy, and on the other by the fallacy of Soviet Communism, Mailer finds nowhere else to turn. For James, of course, this was because America lacked any kind of deep-rooted popular movement which would make it possible to recognise the shared interest that united the majority of working men and women, and by recognition of which they might become something other than 'a mere mass'.

James goes on to contrast Mailer's novel with *The Last of the Conquerors*, by the young black writer William Gardner Smith. Smith's work, he says – another indication of his refusal to collapse political into literary judgement – is the slighter of the two, lacking Mailer's reach and ambition. All the same, writes James, what it contains, far more clearly, is an insistence on the 'perspective of freedom', and on the 'reality of revolt' (1980: 110). The main character of Smith's novel, infuriated by the racism that he experiences even while fighting for the US army, does what Mailer is unable to imagine even sympathetic characters like Red in *The Naked and the Dead* doing: fighting back. And this is the case, James argues, because for obvious historical reasons, 'understanding of revolt comes easily to the Negro writer' (110), in a way that it does not to Mailer. Between them these two novels thus show forth for James, not as political tracts but in their literary flaws, a flaw that runs through the heart of modern American society. That is to say, the failure to establish common ground and purpose between the movements born of black resistance to oppression, on the one hand, and the wider popular struggle for freedom, on the other. It was a failure, James believed, which kept the historical door open for the real-life counterparts of Mailer's fascist General Cummings (see James 1996a: chapter 7).

The comparison that James makes here between the artistic visions of Smith and Mailer provides us with a reminder of an important qualification with regard to his understanding of history. He clearly recognises the way in which social conditions may either sustain or stymie creativity. He is equally clear that it is often those from contexts which are written off as backward, who may have the most penetrating insight into the nature of those social relationships that characterise modernity, as well as the most reason to challenge the taken-for-granted quality of such relationships. Others before James had argued this, of course: du Bois' metaphor of the veil (1995 [1903]), as Charles Lemert rightly points out (2003), expresses not just the pervasiveness of segregation in the Jim Crow states, but also and crucially, the wilful blindness of the white social world to its own conditions of existence. In contrast, du Bois famously argued, it was those who were 'born with a veil' who were also 'gifted with second-sight in this American world' (1995 [1903]: 45). That is to say, that their experiences forced black men and women into a kind of sceptical detachment with regards to all that passed for normal practice or expectation in America. For James a similar argument had been long simmering, at least partly in response to his encounter with Trotsky's theory of permanent revolution (see Høgsbjerg 2006; Worcester 1996: chapter 2). It is there, for example, in his insistence that the rebellious slaves of San Domingo were the pivotal defenders of modernity's promises of liberty and equality. It is there, likewise, in much of his early writing on black politics in America, in which he insisted that those who had been subject to the brutalities of racism were more likely to maintain a critical distance with regard to the lures of the welfare settlement (James 1996a: 134–7) or in relation to nationalist drum-beating in the lead up to America's entry into the Second World War (James 1996a: 17–22; see also James 1939a).

Such were specific instances of what James called, with his tongue somewhat in his cheek, 'the law of historical compensation' (1980 [1948]: 136). He had been struck by a small piece of marginalia left by Lenin in his notebook on Hegel's *Science of Logic*. The comment reads only: 'Leap. Leap. Leap. Leap'. This, for James, was the most inspiring shorthand for that understanding, which I have described, that 'the ideal' is discernible as a 'concrete negation' of what already is. In his own words: the ideal is 'in such close connection with the real that you cannot separate them. A genuine ideal today is the real of tomorrow' (106). And it was often those who, because of the relative backwardness of the objective social conditions around them, were least wedded to the moment's 'finite categories of understanding', who were therefore most within reach of the leap, leap, leap to other ways of seeing and doing. Hence, for example, his repeated suggestion that the model for the emerging West Indian writers of V. S. Naipaul and George Lamming's generation should be nothing less than the great Russian novelists who sprung from Europe's politically and economically under-developed hinterland (for example, James 1964a). Hence, likewise, one of Melville's great achievements, in James' view, was to encapsulate in the 'savage' trinity of Queequeg, Tashtego and Daggoo, ways of understanding and acting which were the antithesis of Ahab's relentless search after 'abstract purpose' (2001 [1953]: 15). This is not, to be clear, that old back-handed compliment which credits the 'primitive' with 'authentic' experience or understanding; a kind of spiritual payback for the various forms of dispossession which are their lot. The three harpooners, James is explicit in noting, are integral to the social relationships and to the labour processes within that floating symbol of capitalist modernity which is the Pecquod. What James credits Melville with recognising, although he does not use this phrase, is the fact that modernity has developed unevenly, so that neither its structures nor our understanding of those structures are uniform. While we may recognise that attempted creativity is in some respects curtailed by where and when the attempt is made, it is not the case in the unevenness of capitalist modernity, if indeed it ever was, that creative or intellectual insight is given by some fiat of History to those from the most technologically advanced societies. 'The *Other* of the age', he wrote to Webb, 'finds its greatest freedom and power where [...] the already established is weak or backward' (1996b: 364). A typically Jamesian twist: the advanced is also the most entrenched; the 'backward' closest to newness.

So here, it seems to me, James seeks to decouple assumptions which have long ridden in train. On the one hand, it is clear that in his account creativity is clay-footed, that it is rooted in the complexity of social relationships and historical situations and the often imperfect awareness that we have of these things. In this emphasis on the ways in which the practices and objects of culture are shaped by the world from which they are wrested he is very much a part of the historical materialist tradition. Even when, at its best, creativity helps us reach out beyond 'what is', it does so only by working through what is, by turning it into something else. 'The other of the age', after all, is both 'other' and 'of the age'. James famously begins *The Black Jacobins* with a subtle paraphrase from Marx: 'men make history, but only such history as it is possible for them to make' (1980 [1938]: x). That history includes the making of books and films, paintings and great innings by men and women. But such things are themselves, therefore, contingent: they depend on their circumstances. Of them too it can be said, that they are such as it is possible to make and therefore, also, expressions of the strictures under which they are produced. On the other hand, James very clearly unhitches this materialism from that self-congratulating story in which the West was assumed to stand, not just in the vanguard of technological progress, but in the vanguard of any possible understanding of history. As Kenneth Surin (1996) convincingly argues, James rejects the language of 'centre' and 'periphery', and demonstrates instead the ways in which historical experience in those societies often deprecatingly described as 'peripheral' actually encapsulated, in microcosm, many of the dilemmas that were characteristic of modernity as such. And not the dilemmas alone, but also many of the most resourceful and creative responses to those dilemmas.

A striking final example, and one which demonstrates both James' argument regarding the historical contingency of creative acts, but also his 'law of historical compensation', is provided by one of the very last pieces of cricket writing that he produced before leaving for America in 1938. This was James' report, written in his capacity as a correspondent for *The Glasgow Herald*, of the fourth Test match of the Ashes series between England and Australia. As with much of his sports writing his account is both a piece of journalism and yet also much more, alert as it is to the wider historical and social resonances of the events he describes. England had lost this particular match, capitulating to Australia on a badly worn pitch, where the unpredictable bounce and deviation of the ball made batting increasingly difficult. In purely cricketing terms, James concludes, England failed because their batsmen refused 'to use their feet' (1938c: 17).

An explanation is probably unavoidable for those not familiar with the cricketing vernacular. There is, on a cricket pitch, a line marked behind which the batsman is, as it were, 'safe'; equivalent to having a foot touching a base in baseball. If, however, in attempting to facilitate a more aggressive shot the batsman goes beyond this 'crease', any member of the fielding side who can hit the stumps with the ball before the batsman returns can end their part in the game. In other words, to use your feet, to advance past the point of safety, is a calculated risk indicative of aggressive intent and a refusal to be intimidated. It is precisely in this respect, James says, that the English players failed:

> I saw every ball from 11.30 on Monday to 1.20 and not a single English batsman left his crease [...] They stood as if chained [...] One simply ached to see the batsman come out and play with the resolution that the situation demanded [instead, they] went down without one batsman playing for death or glory [...] all heads were bowed meekly to the slaughter.

Of course, for James, the cricketing judgement is tied to a historical one. Here he makes this explicit by introducing a framing device: his report is filtered through the eyes of 'three men who lived in a far country' and who had left their 'remote islands' with the intention of seeing the greatest spectacle that the heartlands of the game can offer. The 'far country' in question is presumably Trinidad, because after the match James reports a meeting with his three compatriots:

> He had heard of their long and hopeful journey and congratulated them on their good fortune at seeing so interesting a day's cricket.

> But to his surprise – which, however, was only immediate – they broke out in remonstrance, which came near to imprecation. They said they had hoped to see some great batting, some fine strokes and resource, such as they had never seen and did not hope to see in their restricted sphere; but that instead they had seen such scratching and poking as made them regret their great Odyssey [...] The expert had to uneasily shift his ground, as is the way of experts, and agree that there was much to be said on both sides. The above is a true tale.

Here, very obviously, are the defenders of 'what is' at play. Or, perhaps more accurately, at work. James had written earlier about what he called the 'ugliest shot in cricket', that 'long questing forward defence stroke' (1937b) in which the batsman stretches out to smother the bounce of the ball while cautiously keeping one toe anchored behind the line of safety. For him, this inability on the part of contemporary English batsmen to leave the crease, the refusal of creative daring and the consequent rise of a riskless and standardised form of batting was itself an expression of something fundamentally ugly about twentieth century Western society. Years later, looking back at this time, he would argue that the shift in cricketing technique during the 1930s 'was not an accident, it was not a temporary aberration. It was the violence and ferocity of our age expressing itself in cricket. The time was the early thirties, the period in which the contemporary rejection of tradition, the contemporary disregard of means, the contemporary callousness were taking shape' (1983 [1963]: 189). Although these words are written in description of the win-at-all-costs English tactics in the infamous 'bodyline' series of 1932–3, it is clear that for James more generally changing cricketing form provided its own expression of what he called 'the decline of the west'. This new and constraining rationality in the styles of cricket was an echo, however distant, of the instrumental rationality of a world which saw Stalinist totalitarianism established on one side of the Atlantic, and Fordist production processes perfected on the other.

Hence, of course, the importance of the way in which he frames his report. The desperate surrender to formal constraint which he describes is witnessed by astonished figures who know only too well the ways in which, in their own 'restricted spheres', the same cultural practice was coming to express the hopes of 'what might be'. In James' 'true tale' three colonial migrants, whose arduous journey he records in detail at the start of the article, are deliberately juxtaposed with a line-up of English batsmen unwilling to venture one inch beyond the point of safety. James thus allows voices from the 'periphery', not only to unsettle his own 'expert' judgement, but to 'read' the cricketing form back to its own implied audience, to make clear to his British readers what the 'scratching and poking' of supposedly great English players reveals in social terms. The historical irony is nailed by James' description of the English batsmen 'standing as if chained', a phrase drawn directly from the archives of slavery and slave revolt in which he was then so deeply immersed as he prepared to write *The Black Jacobins* and to which he returned on other occasions, as in his later description of a wider culture of defensiveness as a 'ball and chain' on the feet of English cricketers (1986: 188).

James' law of historical compensation applied no less to those whose 'restricted spheres' were defined by class. He ends the article by appealing to the same demotic Northern voices which had provided the chorus to his elegy on S. F. Barnes – the 'thousands of Yorkshiremen who thronged the ground' (1938c: 17) – confident that they too knew what they wanted to see in this situation: some positive intent, some 'swinging of the bat' (ibid.). In other words, a willingness to risk 'what is' for the sake of 'what might be', the longing for a leap, leap, leap. Thus the day's play bore its historical meaning on its face. In this case the meaning had to do with the way in which a means-end rationality which was taking hold of twentieth-century working life had come to take a hold, no less crushing, on what had once promised to offer a means of escaping the limits of working life. And this relationship between social context and cultural event was discernible not simply as a kind of formal equivalence that could be traced at an intellectual level, but as something which the crowd knew in its guts, in its 'tactile consciousness'. History recognisable in an aesthetic refusal, in disgust. History as something felt, no less than thought.

IV

Reading the report which I have just discussed, with its references to 'slaughter' and 'death or glory', it is hard not to be a little unnerved by James' willing acceptance of the bellicose language which is another part of cricket's inheritance from its imperial past. The game, after all, along with the other field sports adopted by the public schools, had long been seen as providing the best possible inculcation into the martial values of bravery, camaraderie and submission to the chain of command which would be required by those second and subsequent sons of the ruling classes who were abandoned by primogeniture to careers in the colonial forces. It is an ideological role that is celebrated most famously in the syrupy violence of Henry Newbolt's *Vitaï Lampada* in which the admonishment to 'play up, and play the game' is passed unhesitatingly from playing field to battle field, and from one elite generation to the next. One does not need to find excuses for James: there were clearly aspects of the wider culture of cricket which he began to view critically in the late 1930s, but from which he only fully detached himself during his period away from the game in America. But there is also a pointer towards an interesting conjunction here, one that can be traced between the kind of argument that James makes concerning sporting forms, and his little discussed writings on the forms of modern warfare (although see Buhle 1988: 81).

James was, as Stuart Hall has emphasised (in Farred 1996b: 42–4), a strikingly non-doctrinaire thinker. Even in that period of his life when he was working in the close confines of small political parties, he admitted the influence of various writers with whose politics he was in profound disagreement. While, for example, Trotsky's *History of the Russian Revolution* provided the unsurprising model for *The Black Jacobins*, *American Civilization* draws a large part of its inspiration from the somewhat less predictable source of de Tocqueville's *Democracy in America*. *Beyond a Boundary*, meanwhile, owes a significant debt, by James' own admission, to Oswald Spengler and, for that matter, to Hemingway's *Death in the Afternoon* (Dhondy 2001: 174). All this no doubt provides ammunition for those who point towards unresolved political or intellectual contradictions in James. It seems to me, however, that it is precisely because the idea of contradiction itself came to be so central to James' thinking, including his thinking about cultural forms, that he was open to the lessons to be learned from a variety of accounts of the contemporary world, even when he rejected the conclusions that some of those accounts led towards.

Among the more surprising influences on James, and certainly among the least discussed, is Clausewitz's *On War*. In one long article, published near the beginning of the Second World War (1940a) and filling an entire issue of *New International*, and then in a shorter article, published as the war in Europe was drawing to its conclusion (1944), James turns to Clausewitz in an attempt to explain the rapid successes of the German armies, as well as their subsequent defeat. What he takes from Clausewitz is precisely the possibility of understanding the 'forms of war' as themselves socially and historically conditioned. That is to say, as events whose outcomes are not simply decided by the shrewdness or stupidity of generals, nor by the bravery or otherwise of the troops, but by the wider historical contexts in which both are forced to make their choices. In this respect, he specifically describes the second of these articles as a lesson in what he calls 'the method of judgement [...] of historical materialism' (1944: 247), albeit a method that, he insists, must resist 'that schematism which is the besetting danger of Marxism' (1940a: 1).

What I want to emphasise in James' account of the war is his claim that the early successes of the German blitzkrieg could only be understood in relation to the social and ideological contradictions which hamstrung European democratic societies. James understood fascism, as indeed he and his colleagues increasingly came to understand Stalinism (1986 [1950]; James, Lee and Chaulieu 1974 [1958]), as a derivation of, rather than a break from, capitalism; as one possible extension of its economic and social logic. Fascism, he wrote, is 'capitalism [...] stripped to the waist and trained for war as its sole means of survival' (1940: 7). 'Survival' because, following Lenin (1993 [1916]) and Bukharin (1996 [1929]), James believed that capitalist systems of production and exchange were increasingly out of sync with the territorial limits of individual nation-states, even while those systems continued to require certain kinds of order and predictability of which the state remained the most efficient guarantor. Here, then, is a much darker version of his law of historical compensation. It was in Germany, James argued, economically crushed after the First World War, and where popular forces had been likewise crushed, that one possible resolution of the contradictions of capitalist society emerged, based in the forced alliance of private capital and authoritarian state. An alliance which ensured domestic political constraint even as it drove an aggressive policy of external expansion. And it was from this social context that the blitzkrieg emerged as theory and practice. Tactically, James noted, the blitzkrieg was modelled on the extraordinary offensive strategies of the French revolutionary armies which had so changed the face of modern warfare. But this was form stripped of its social 'content'. The German military effort relied on a concoction of blood and soil patriotism and, as necessary, the force of totalitarian discipline. This was the stuff from which it tried to manufacture what James took to have been a more rational and thus durable identification, among the levies of the revolutionary armies, with a popular cause. In this respect, James saw fascism – as indeed Alexis de Tocqueville might have done – as the culmination, in many respects, of the development of new forms of centralised political control in the Napoleonic era.

For their part, the professedly democratic governments of rival European powers found themselves outflanked by a fascism which represented one possible and particularly efficient version of a capitalist future. This outflanking merely heightened the social contradictions in whose knots these elites were already entangled, James argued, caught as they were between their own ruinous economic imperatives and the simmering resistance of both their local citizenry and the independence movements in the colonies. It was, after all, to this citizenry, and against this backdrop of colonial unrest, that they were now forced to issue a call to arms in 'defence of democracy'. Words, James writes, which 'turned to ashes in their mouths', given that they feared what victory under such a banner would bring just as much as they feared defeat. And hence the only military strategy of which the European bourgeoisie could conceive, the strategy which had gradually become an orthodoxy during the inter-war period, was that of the defensive: a defence aimed simultaneously outwards, against the claims of rival imperial powers and inwards, at the potential disorders of their domestic and colonial scenes:

> which country torn as the democracies were torn could even attempt to consider any other strategy than the defensive, in other words, the strategy of temporization, of hesitation, of waiting and seeing, of trying to compromise. (ibid.)

It is in this respect, in a striking moment, that James 'reads' the Maginot line as an exemplary product of early twentieth-century French and British societies. The line, in his view, gave tangible expression to the stalemate that existed between the destructive drive of European capitalist imperialism and the recalcitrance of popular forces being dragged towards a state of perpetual and unheroic conflict. Those miles of more or less useless casements and tunnels were the (literally) concrete form of a historical contradiction.

At this point it becomes clearer what it was that James thought he saw being expressed, even in the seemingly distant netherland of English cricket of the period: that same inability to consider any strategy other than the defensive, the same temporisation and hesitation. The same paranoid clinging, indeed, to the line of defence. It becomes clearer also how crucial was the idea of contradiction, both to James' view of history, and to his view of those human activities in and through which history is figured and, occasionally, figured out. In the end, of course, the democratic powers were gifted that victory which they feared as much as defeat. The blitzkrieg broke itself against the forces of a rival totalitarianism amid the terrible suffering of the Russian front. Even in 1940 James had argued that, as a tactic, the fascist total offence was hollow at its heart and would be able to perpetuate itself only by complete and immediate success in all directions. Dragged into a drawn-out war, as Clausewitz might have predicted, troop morale faltered and then collapsed. But the contradictions of capitalist society were not resolved by this victory, rather they were cinched up further and tighter. In America, where the European bourgeois 'theory of the defensive' appeared all too obviously stagnant, a new theory of the offensive found its apotheosis in the emergence of weapons that could ruin entire nations in moments. Weapons which would, indeed, make victory indistinguishable from defeat. With this, James writes, 'the theory of the offensive, which safeguarded the birth, is now herald of the death of contemporary society' (1944: 251). This society, as he wrote a few years later in 1947, is now terrified by the very idea of progress under whose banner it had once marched (see 1980: 70).

V

James had ended his earlier article by stepping back, and by imagining the events of the mid-twentieth century in another form:

> Great states crash, communities of millions are torn up by the roots; shocks, catastrophes, sudden reversals and annihilations, drawn-out agonies, events unpredicted and unpredictable follow and will follow each other with bewildering speed. As we look at the film of history it seems that the operator has gone mad. (1940a: 32)

His point here, and more generally, as I have argued, is not to challenge this madness by claiming for himself privileged foreknowledge of the way in which the film of history will finally spool out. Rather, his 'method of judgement' places an essentially Hegelian focus on contradiction. What one can discern in the here-and-now is the tension between all that the conditions of the present close down, and all that responds with a longing to turn that present inside-out, the longing to turn these negations into a new affirmation. One seeks to grasp the historical world, in other words, by latching onto and clarifying the strange, locked embrace of what-is-not and what-might-be. Reason, he writes in *Notes on Dialectics*, 'catches hold of the variety and seeks out the Opposition, the Contradiction, *and drives them together*, ties them together, makes one the Other of the other' (1980 [1948]: 91).

For James, of course, it was a necessary assumption of any rational engagement with the world that the contradictions of here-and-now must, in the end, lead onwards; onwards to a world that is humanly fuller and better. But in general, it seems to me, he is explicit in saying that this is a presupposition or postulate, as he called it. It is the something that critical activity requires to be going on with: better day coming.

Reason, he followed Marx in arguing, cannot substantiate itself. Such suppositions are truthful, or otherwise, only by virtue of what happens. Nor are the fundamental contradictions of capitalist societies to be understood as intellectual artefacts, they are what run deep and gratingly through the lives of those who live in such societies (see 1986 [1950]: chapter 11). It was only from the popular response to that condition, from the stubborn creativity and the refusal to acquiesce, that a future 'other' than this fractured and volatile present could emerge.

And something of that last point is displayed in James' revealing choice of metaphor here: history as a flea-pit. It is not, one suspects, an image that he would have chosen whilst he was in Trinidad or in Britain, although his early short story 'The Star that Would Not Shine' (in 1984: chapter 2) suggests that he was interested in cinema rather earlier than has sometimes been assumed. All the same, it was certainly in America that James was forced to clarify his response, not just to the movies, but to what gets called 'mass' culture more generally. For many of his immediate contemporaries, of course, the spectacle of the glitzy and often trivialised productions of the American entertainment industries sounded the death knell of a culture that could be said to belong to the people in any meaningful sense. For James this is certainly one half of the story, but only one half. Just as his response to the mad film of twentieth-century history was to emphasise contradiction as central to any 'method of judgement', what he found in the mainstream cultural production of that historical world was, above all, evidence of deepening and potentially explosive contradiction.

This means, of course, that James discovered, even in Hollywood films, something more than just the dead hand of capitalist production, he discovered also traces of the needs and demands of a popular audience. Like Theodor Adorno, James rejected a view in which mass culture was swallowed whole by its passive or stupefied recipients (on the relationship between the two see Alleyne 1999). The difference is that when Adorno emphasised the agency of the filmgoer or jazz fan, he did so largely in order to accuse them of complicity in their own dispossession. 'People are not only falling for the swindle', he wrote with a typical turn of phrase, 'if it guarantees them even the most fleeting gratification they desire a deception that is nonetheless transparent to them' (1991: 103). For James, by contrast, popular culture was essentially contested territory. Even where, as in post-war America, the production of such culture had been cornered by powerful cartels, James argued that the resulting products would be split by the very inconsistencies from which they appeared to provide distraction, or comforting resolution.

It is in *American Civilization* that he makes this argument most explicitly, although much of the case is also laid out in his study of Herman Melville: *Mariners, Renegades and Castaways*. In both contexts he follows de Tocqueville (1966 [1835/1840]) in claiming that modern America was defined, above all, by the ever-starker contradiction which existed between its founding historical promise of personal and political freedom, on the one hand, and the contemporary regimentation of both working and domestic lives, on the other:

> Upon a people bursting with energy, untroubled by feudal remains or a feudal past, soaked to the marrow in a tradition of individual freedom, individual security, free association, a tradition which is constantly held before then as the basis of their civilization, upon this people more than all others has been imposed a mechanized way of life at work, mechanized forms of living, a mechanized totality which from morning till night, week after week, day after day, crushed the very individuality which [that?] tradition nourishes. (1993: 116)

It is this fault-line, then, that James saw running through the archetypal products of American culture. In even the crassest studio movies, he argued, one could witness the hopes and resentments of a popular audience facing off against the strictures imposed on content by the studios and their financiers. In this sense, for example, the gangster movies of the thirties were themselves a kind of celluloid Maginot line. In them the hopes of a mass audience found thwarted expression in the doomed rebellions of bank-robbers and other renegades from state authority. The public, James noted, could not get enough of these brief and violent representations of lives which rejected order, constraint and submission. The films sold out even though, in the final reel, they sold out; even though, at the last, social order was restored. Adorno emphasised this final message of conformity in the thriller genre. Yet what struck James was the easily overlooked fact that such a message was bought only at the expense of all that went before. In his view the audience swallowed this tacked-on morality for the sake of being able to witness that vivid display of disordered, autonomous action, however perverse and misdirected were the adventures in which it expressed itself. In this, as in other respects, he comes close to the account offered by Antonio Gramsci, who emphasised the degree to which stories of adventurous revenge such as *The Count of Monte Cristo* gave expression to a subterranean popular longing for justice even if, in doing so, they tended to misdirect that longing towards belief in a transcendental agency capable of administering such justice

(Gramsci 1985: 328). Such, in any case, were the lines of engagement that were drawn in what James called American popular culture's state of 'armed neutrality' (1993: 123) or 'armed truce' (1992: 225).

Cultural forms for James, then, are not merely a 'mould into which something is poured' (1992: 232), whatever that political or ideological something might be. Whatever the more or less explicit political agenda of the masters of mass culture, they too go about their work in a social context which conditions what is plausible or manageable. The films or music that they create are subject to formative pressures over which their control is, at best, incomplete, and open to appropriations and reclamations by a popular audience over which their control is equally limited. In even the most trivial examples of that culture, therefore, James saw something more than the irresistible triumph of control. For Adorno and Horkheimer, 'Donald Duck in the cartoons [received] his thrashing so that the audience can learn to take their own punishment' (1997 [1944]: 138); a view which is wholly concerned with what mass culture does to its audience. For James, contrastingly, 'Donald Duck voiced a perpetual exasperation with the never-ending irritations of modern existence' (1993: 135); a view which is all about what the popular audience does with, or brings about in such culture as it has access to.

None of this should be taken to imply that James celebrated the products of mass culture in uncritical fashion. Crediting the average movie- or concertgoer with critical resources is not at all the same as an indiscriminate endorsement of these cultural products themselves, or of the wider systems of mass cultural production. In this respect, it seems to me that Neil Larsen (1996) and Stephen Howe (2003) are absolutely right to claim that James would have dissented from the shiny happy populism of contemporary cultural studies. Against such a view Larsen (see also Ross 1996; Porter 2006) helpfully reiterates James' view that the products of popular culture contain within themselves the contradictions of the society in which they are produced. Contradictions as yet unresolved. We can note, for instance, that James was particularly struck by the emergence of a new level of violence in American cinema and comic literature after the Great Depression, and equally by the rise of a star industry centred on Hollywood figures who were defined, *not* by their extraordinary personal qualities, but by the absence of any such qualities. In both developments he found, not the proof of a popular duping, but the proof of a popular demand: the on-screen and off-screen lives of the stars were latched onto, he claimed, because they provided some image of a 'revolt against the general conditions' (1993: 142). And the gangster film, as suggested, gave to millions a glimpse of something that they desperately sought: 'a sense of active living' (127), ninety minutes of unmechanical life. Yet if these developments, in some respects, responded to the longings and resentments of a popular audience, they offered no lasting or satisfying resolution to such longings. Moreover, both the cultish worship of celebrity and the frustrated, desperate and violent refusal of the world found obvious echoes in the structures of feeling that had been exploited by fascism and communism:

> The violence on the one hand, the absence of any creativity and the decline to accepting a few individuals as the raw material of the functions art must fulfil is a sign of a profound dislocation in society [...] Between them they are the psychological preparation on a vast social scale of the most striking social and political actuality of our times – the emergence of the totalitarian state. (148)

About this threatening possibility, at least, one can imagine James and Adorno agreeing in those meetings which Paul Buhle reports took place between them over coffee at the New School.

In short, James was not blind to the degree to which those forms of cultural expression which began among people as 'arts of their own' (James, Lee and Chaulieu 1974 [1958]: 85) – jazz, the comic strip, film – were quickly appropriated by 'official society'. Nor was he blind to the degree to which the mass produced, mass distributed products of the entertainment industry represented something stultifying and regressive. Yet if there were negations here, they were negations which themselves bear witness to that popular search for something better of which they were the 'other'. To see in all of this merely defeat meant, for James, surrender to an intellectual version of the theory of the defensive. But it also meant a flattening out, or an overlooking, of the contradictions of modern society and of the way in which those contradictions were expressed in its artistic and creative products. Such contradictions, notwithstanding the increasingly awful human cost that they exact, imply something still undecided about the film of history. Although James found a way of expressing this thanks to Hegel and Marx, this is not where he learned it. He learned it, as we will discuss in more detail in the next chapter, from his encounters with those who were neither elite nor intellectual but who recognised, even in the compromised, 'synthetic' forms of culture made for their consumption, lessons which 'official society' found unspeakable:

> [T]he American public has developed an extraordinary awareness and sensibility with regard to these, its popular arts. [...] What the

American audience does is to reject, often with good-humoured if not contemptuous cynicism, the synthetic conclusion. Beginning from the problems and the types of people placed before it, it works out for itself the answers which producers and directors have evaded. (60–1)

Conclusion

How are we to talk about, or to describe, the historical meaningfulness of cultural practices and artefacts, without making it appear that those practices and artefacts are nothing more than reflections of their historical circumstances? How to recognise the degree to which these practices are entailed in politics and in situations of social struggle without implying that this is, as it were, all that they mean or, indeed, all that they are good for? These are, it seems to me, the kinds of intricacy in which any attempt to think sociologically about culture quickly becomes entangled. What I have tried to suggest, in this chapter and that which preceded it, is something of James' response to such dilemmas, exemplified in the way in which he went about interpreting particular games, texts, films or broader cultural traditions.

James clearly emphasises culture as something which is made and made use of by human beings. Culture is historically meaningful not because it provides some blank wall on which the disembodied hand of History writes its grand story, but because men and women fight for possibilities, for ways of understanding and for forms of happiness, including such of these things as are denied them in the lives they lead, and because books, films, games and so forth are some of the places where they look for such things. James, to use a sociologist's word, emphasised the degree to which cultural practices and objects gave evidence of the agency of men and women. Not an unconfined agency, of course, but an enduring struggle with the here-and-now in all of its limits and compromises. In all of its contradictions, above all. And to do this, therefore, to talk about the active making and making use of culture is, of necessity, to talk about the historical meaningfulness of such activity, the way in which it is shaped by, as well as a part of the effort to shape, the social context from which it came. But it means that such questions can be asked without losing sight of what is specific to cultural practices in themselves, the symbolic spaces they offer, the creative possibilities which, at their best, they open up and which draw us to them in the first place.

3
Crowds

Introduction

In 1948 C. L. R. James delivered a report to the national conference of the Socialist Workers Party in America, entitled 'The Revolutionary Answer to the Negro Problem in the USA'. The report, which was published under a pseudonym in *Fourth International* later that year, is widely seen as the culmination of his decade-long grappling with the experience and history of racism in America, and with the question of the relationship between the politics of black resistance and those of class struggle (see James 1996a: introduction and Grimshaw in James 1992: 424). It was here that he most explicitly laid out the claim that black political struggles should be treated as ethically and politically significant in their own right. That the struggle against racism, in other words, could not be dissolved into the category of class and that black resistance to oppression pointed towards its own conclusions about what socialism might be. In his peroration James appealed, as he did often in his writings and speeches, to a kind of ethnographic evidence. The 'awakening passions' (James 1977a: 126) which simmer among the black population in America, he says, are there to be recognised by anyone who takes the time to get to know that population and its history 'intimately'. And for James, it becomes clear, such intimacy begins with the willingness to watch that population as its gathers, not only in public rallies or marches, but 'at their own theatres [...] at their dances [...] in their churches' (126–7).

Given what has been discussed in the preceding chapters, there is nothing particularly surprising here, even though we should perhaps remember that James' willingness to emphasise the political potential of these kinds of popular cultural activity may have raised a few eyebrows, if not hackles, amongst audiences such as the one that first heard this address. But there is a reminder of something else here as well, and it is this that I want to turn to in this chapter. It is easy to overlook the fact that James, for all the close critical attention that he pays to the action up on the screen, or to the texts in front of him, spends just as much time glancing sidelong at his fellow watchers and readers, at those up on the dance floor or sitting in the bleachers. Repeatedly in his writing about culture James steps back from the events or texts at hand in order to watch those who bring themselves and their longings to these objects and events. This is, of course, part of the reason why James' approach to art, literature or sport is so different from many of those approaches which treat such things as merely ideological or as instruments of discursive control. James simply did not accept that cultural objects and practices were the means by which people were bound ever tighter to their social fate even if this is, as it no doubt often is, the purpose which their purveyors intend them to serve. In this respect, his lifelong emphasis on popular agency is at the heart of whatever he has to say about audiences and about the interpretation of culture: his is almost always a consideration of what particular crowds, in particular historical circumstances, do with what they hear or read or see. This is precisely why he ends that conference report by urging his comrades to pay proper attention to the dancers in the dance halls and the congregations in the churches. Because here was evidence, not of passive consumption or of an audience force-fed that which served to distract it from its troubles, but rather, evidence of something being done, of an ongoing effort to make sense of, or to find some purchase on, the contradictions of the present. James points his immediate audience towards what other audiences do with culture, confident that the active 'doings' of that audience offer promise of even more consequential 'doings' in the future: 'the hatred of bourgeois society and the readiness to destroy it when the opportunity should present itself' (ibid.). A rapprochement between the struggles of workers and those of black men and women in America could not begin while it was assumed, as Frantz Fanon once accused Jean-Paul Sartre of assuming, that 'it is not I who make a meaning for myself, but it is the meaning that was already there, pre-existing, waiting for me' (1967b: 134). What James urged his comrades to recognise was precisely the degree to which black men and women, even amid the many curtailments and confinements of their lives, actively sought to make meanings for themselves. And it is precisely this emphasis that characterises his interest in the readers, crowds and audiences of cultural practices and objects generally.

I

In this, as in so many other things, James was a pioneer, pre-empting a now well-established interest in various branches of literary and cultural criticism with the role of the audience in interpreting, and making use of, different forms of culture. It seems to me that, for his part, James' awareness of such things was whetted in two particular ways. The first was his long experience of being part of the crowds that flocked to cricket matches, both in the Caribbean and beyond. Consistently in his writing about the sport, James makes clear the degree to which the crowd is a constitutive part of all that happens in it. Those who watched, applauded or jeered at the play in the middle were, in his view, not just a backdrop: their responses and demands made themselves felt as an integral part of the meaningfulness of that play. When famously, at the start of *Beyond a Boundary*, James remembers the shot making of the local 'ne'er-do-well' Matthew Bondman, it is a memory secured by the 'long, low "Ah!" [which] came from many a spectator' (1983 [1963]: 14) as those shots were played. Indeed, in a sense, it is the memory of that 'ah', that James records. Although Bondman is the one who makes his shots, it is the 'ah' of the crowd that makes something of them. And it is that response, therefore, which raises for James all of the subsequent questions regarding the true definition of art, and the relationship between popular culture and politics. 'My own little soul', he tells us, 'thrilled with recognition and delight' (ibid.). Recognition and delight in the shot, of course, but recognition also of the crowd and delight at his part in it (compare Murray 1996: 209).

That same thrill of recognition and delight was there when James watched the first Ashes Test of 1938, in which Australia batted for nearly two full days in order to save a game which they had looked certain to lose. James wrote a detailed report on the match, relishing the confrontations between key players and describing the pivotal moments. At the end of the article, however, he pointedly turns his attention to the role of what he calls 'the crowd militant' (1938d). And what he focuses on in this respect is what defines his wider approach to culture's many audiences. That is to say, the fact that 'the crowd refused to practise non-intervention', that they were themselves a part of what happened. He describes, in careful detail, how the events on the pitch and the response of the spectators were interwoven: wickets greeted with 'delirium', the all-or-nothing rearguard action of the Australians with cheerful admiration, and their later resort to delaying tactics with loud derision. Even though he engages in some rather prim tut-tutting about the heckling provoked by the Australians' time wasting, James was never really impressed by the idea that cricket should be watched with the kind of silent reverence accorded to objects of high culture: '[The crowd] barracked when Fingleton and Brown were playing slowly, and there is no valid reason why a crowd should not barrack when it wants to. You cannot treat 30,000 people at a match as if they were children in a kindergarten.'

In any case, James' real concern is with what happens next. Fingleton is dismissed late in the day. The light is disappearing, the home team are jubilant, their massed supporters equally so. The great talisman of Australian cricket, Don Bradman, is expected to bat next, but these are notoriously difficult circumstances in which to start an innings and there is a general assumption around the ground that he will send in a junior player and bat himself in the morning when conditions are less demanding. James recounts the moments that follow with deft narrative control.

> Would Bradman come? He means everything to the Australian side and I would wager that more than one of his men must have offered to go instead. 'He would be a fool to come' whispered a wise and experienced critic at my side. And then in the gathering darkness came the Australian captain, striding down the pavilion steps as jauntily as ever, and never so much the 'Don' as in this brave gesture. Practically the whole ground stood up and greeted him with roars and roars of applause that lasted almost all the way.

In this act is encapsulated much of what cricket meant to James. In particular, the way in which the game provided its own demonstrations of the human ability to respond creatively to, and to thereby challenge, a 'gathering darkness'. Such a demonstration, he insisted, speaks to something in all of us which lies beyond parochial loyalties. But if he recognised such things in cricket, he did so because they were made recognisable in and through the roars and roars of applause with which they were acclaimed by the crowd:

> It was the biggest moment of a game that had many, and if only a crowd could be as unintelligent as to barrack Fingleton and Brown when they were saving the game, what else but a crowd could so spontaneously and generously lift up all hearts and justify humanity?

There is nothing hedged or apologetic about James' language here, and he clearly intends to draw attention to something that he feels is important when he subtitles his article 'the crowd had an honour all its own'. Such, indeed, might be a subtitle to his whole intellectual project, given the central emphasis that he placed on the spontaneous and generous actions of popular crowds, and given how consistently he looked for a justification of humanity in such actions.

The history of modern crowds, of course, includes many moments that do nothing to justify humanity. One thinks of Durkheim's warning, in this respect, that 'a group of individuals, most of whom are perfectly inoffensive, may, when gathered in a crowd, be drawn into acts of atrocity' (1938 [1895]: 5). This is one reason why, it seems to me, it is important not to overlook the counter-emphasis in James' work on the irreducible and never fully predictable capacities of the individual, as will be discussed in the following chapter. But in general it is clear that he saw the popular crowd as a promising rather than a threatening phenomenon. He celebrated the fact that those drawn to sports and games demonstrated not a glassy-eyed conformity but energies and unities that came from shared longings, shared joys and even, as here, shared disappointments. Of course, as James admits in *Beyond a Boundary*, a sociological or historical response to sport – or any other cultural activity – is not necessary, nor is it the only kind of response that is possible to such things. But such a response *is* possible precisely because of the popular audience who, in all their own varied responses to such activity, make those activities socially and politically consequential. There is thus a deep complicity between those approaches which seek to strip cultural activity of historical or political meaning, on the one hand, and the dismissal of popular audiences as stupefied, on the other. Each claim provides the other with its alibi. By contrast, James' recognition of the significant, albeit constrained, role of readers, viewers and listeners in making and making sense of the games and texts of culture is what justifies, in large part, his sociological reading of such things.

II

James' approach to these matters is informed by something else as well: that is to say, by his work on the histories of slave resistance and anti-imperial rebellion. These histories, after all, are littered with examples of the way in which texts and idioms of all kinds, especially those of Christianity and European liberalism, were taken and turned to uses that their supposed 'owners' did not expect. It is noticeable that James is alert to the significance of such appropriations even in his earliest works such as

A History of Negro Revolt (1938e). Here, in a way that pre-empts by the better part of a century issues that are now fashionable in anthropology (for example: Comaroff and Comaroff 1993; West and Sanders 2003; compare Kelley 1996), he discusses the role of millenarian religious literature in articulating emerging working-class discontent and the first stirrings of African nationalism. As ever, James begins by subjecting the texts themselves to a considered close reading, examining in particular the eschatological pamphlets of the Watch Tower movement, with their world-upside-down attacks on established churches and governments and their prophecies of a coming justice. If Toussaint L'Ouverture wrote in the language of 1789, he says, 'the grotesqueries of Watch Tower primitively approximates to the dialectic of Marx and Lenin' (1938e: 85). While we may baulk at his choice of adverb here, we should not mistake the fundamentally dignifying claim that he is making. The millenarianism of the Watch Tower matters, not for itself, but for what is done with it. It matters because of the way in which the texts come to give expression to 'the ideas moving in the minds' of its readers already (83). Culture, in other words, is not just something 'received', in the way that a radio receives a signal. Acts of reading, listening or viewing are, for James, indeed acts. They include the possibility that texts of all kinds can be originally construed, or even deliberately misconstrued by their audiences. Moreover, such acts take place in, and in response to, particular social and political contexts: for James, the reading of culture is inextricable from the effort to read the world in which the reader finds themselves. And hence it is that reading, or listening, can become part of the articulation of what he called an 'immanent' political consciousness, a consciousness which, in this instance, was finding a corresponding expression in the wave of strikes and uprisings then sweeping the African continent.

Earlier in that same study James had examined the impact of Marcus Garvey's movement in exactly these terms, making his focus the question of what the rank and file membership of the movement found in it, or brought to it. He was clearly still thinking about this a year later, in America, when he castigated the 'two-cent' revolutionaries who could point out all the absurdities of Garvey's claims without once considering what expressions of present resentment or future hope might have been found in those absurdities by the thousands who flocked to join the movement (James 1996a: 115; see also 1939b). '[D]esperate men', as he puts it here, 'often hear, not the actual words of an orator but their own thoughts' (1938e: 69). The note is a typically Jamesian one, recognising that texts of all kinds belong not just to their creators or stewards, but also to their popular audience, and unafraid to credit that audience with the ability to wring greater significance from these texts than less desperate, more elite readers might recognise or even imagine.

This same emphasis can be found in *The Black Jacobins* as well as in the corresponding play which James first wrote – under the title *Toussaint Louverture* – and starred in alongside Paul Robeson in 1936. The original version of the play is not available to us but the text of the 1967 revival is included in *The C. L. R. James Reader*. While there has been some debate about the extent of James' involvement in this revision (see Cudjoe 1992b), the text that we have was clearly one that James was willing to see published under his own name. Moreover, and more significantly, it draws out the role of the wider slave community in the San Domingo revolution in a way that accords very clearly with James' own critical reconsideration of *The Black Jacobins* later in his life (James 1964b; see also N. King 2006). What can certainly be said is that much of the dramatic structure of this piece – and of the historical study to which it relates – hinges on the idea that the rebellion in San Domingo was an event which involved a critical re-reading of the public statements of the French revolution and the texts of the European Enlightenment more broadly, by a constituency which made their own meanings of those texts, and which took the promises they contained as their own (compare Blackburn 1995). In the version of the events presented in the play, this is made explicit through a series of carefully staged acts of reading or listening. Thus Toussaint's rise to leadership is presented as something catalysed by his reading of Abbé Raynal whose comment on the precariousness of slave-owning societies – 'a courageous chief only is wanted' – Toussaint takes as a prophetic word: 'I have read it a thousand times before', he tells his wife, 'but it is as if I had seen it for the first time' (1992: 71). In a similar way James sets up a neat piece of dramatic irony at the start of the play by introducing the wife of Toussaint's owner, Madame Bullet, singing Donna Anna's 'vendetta ti chieggo' aria from *Don Giovanni*, with its demand for a 'just anger' and for vengeance against the murderer of her father. As Madame Bullet sings the lights come up to reveal Marie-Jeanne, her mulatto house slave, at the piano beside her, joining in the song. This obvious act of appropriation is superimposed on another as the massed slaves in the distance take up a ragged version of *La Marseillaise*. And so, moments later, with the lines from the libretto 'I demand revenge of you' still ringing, the revolution announces itself with the entrance of Dessalines and his words: 'Revolution in France. Revolution in San Domingo. Freedom for slaves. Kill master. Burn down plantation' (72).

Later, it is Marie-Jeanne who entraps the French general Hédouville as he seeks to manoeuvre against Toussaint's authority. As she sits down to write the letter that will reveal this conspiracy, a letter which will lead in the end to the establishment of an independent Haiti, she hums to herself snatches of the same aria. In such moments it is made clear that resistance to slavery and colonialism often involved a critical translation of aspects of European culture, and a reclamation of the routinely broken promises of European modernity. Here, very obviously, is a lesson in the ability of readers and hearers to find in the texts they read and the words they hear all kinds of unexpected promptings and purposes: *La Marseillaise* used as a rallying cry against the French plantocracy; Mozart as the inspiring soundtrack of one of the great revolts against European imperialism.

What follows, of course, quickly descends into tragedy, foreshadowing the course of later revolutionary events in the modern world. And in this as well it is the role of the crowd that is crucial. The play's stage directions begin by specifying that throughout the production a large upstage area is to be left open. At the beginning, this area is filled with a number of working slaves in silhouette, singing a song in dialect whose meaning is revealed to be a pledge to destroy the rule of the masters. Subsequently, as the revolution fulfils that pledge the area is taken up by crowds representing the free slaves. James comments: 'Crowds say very little but their presence is felt powerfully at all critical moments. This is the key point of the play...' (1992: 68). Indeed it is, because Toussaint's great error is precisely that he loses sight of this audience, that a sense of their critical presence ceases to guide his decisions. James, who knew his Aristotle, has Toussaint point out the very danger to which he later succumbs. During a scene in which he negotiates with a Spanish general he says: 'Look at these people, General. Some of them understand only one French word – *Liberté*' (77). At this point Möise, the one figure throughout the play who most clearly understands Toussaint's dependence upon those he leads, gestures 'to the crowd of men, who are eagerly listening' (ibid.). 'They will join anything', Toussaint continues, 'or leave anything for *Liberté*. That is why I can lead them. But the day that they feel I am not for liberty, the day they feel I am not telling them everything, I am finished. They are all listening to us now' (ibid.).

This is, of course, exactly what happens. Toussaint makes his decisions increasingly alone, pursuing an accommodation with Napoleonic France, and failing to recognise how his policy jars with that single-minded desire for liberty which drives those who are 'eagerly listening' upstage. In the more historical account provided in *The Black Jacobins*

James presents these fateful decisions as forced on Toussaint by the counter-revolutionary threat of European armies on all sides, and by the impossibility of developing a new and effective system of production out of the wreckage of the plantation system. But these contingencies become fatal because of his growing detachment from those he leads, a point which is forcefully dramatised in the play. The second act ends with the announcement of an invasion by Napoleon's forces and thus with the disastrous unravelling of the accommodationist policy. It ends also, in a skilful piece of dramatic orchestration, with Toussaint signing the death warrant of Möise, his last link with those who were the 'key point of the play'. With this the way is paved for the betrayal of L'Ouverture and the ascent of the despotic Dessalines in act three. Yet even in the tragic finale the critical voice of the crowd continues to make itself heard. The play ends with Dessalines calling for music to celebrate his self-appointment as 'Emperor of Haiti', but this is interrupted from upstage by a song of mourning for Toussaint, whose death in exile has just been announced.

The story of Toussaint clearly fascinated James and in it are caught many of the intellectual and political issues with which he wrestled for much of his life: the ties between a leader and a social movement; the problems of political organisation in an economically underdeveloped society; the dangerously fissiparous relationship between anti-colonial struggles and the intellectual and cultural heritage of European modernity. The tragedy that James has to describe, of course, was a historical one. Yet Athenian drama was a reference point throughout his life and Kara Rabbitt (1995) is surely correct, in her excellent reading of the original study, to show how deliberately and how successfully James interleaves the conventions of classical tragedy with a scrupulous materialist analysis of the structural underpinnings of Toussaint's fall from grace. James' treatment of this history has been usefully criticised by Alex Dupuy (1995) for its failure to adequately recognise the emerging class divisions of the post-slavery society. But I am much less persuaded by Paul B. Miller's reading (2001), which represents James as fatefully wedded to an Enlightenment distinction between the heroic leader and the pliant masses. This seems to me to ignore the degree to which, in both the historical and dramatic telling of the story, James' presentation of the ex-slaves as a kind of chorus is deliberately intended to unsettle such a distinction. The play is interesting not least because it makes this scrupulously clear, allowing those who fill the upstage space to interrupt the dialogue of the central characters with bursts of collective song and movement, both of which are defining characteristics of *choros* in its original sense (Ley 1991; Griffith 2007; Zafiri 2007). The slaves and ex-slaves represent a critical presence within the play whose demands and outcries cut across the spoken dialogue of the central characters and whose responses are, as I have suggested, crucial to the course of events that the play relates. And this is, moreover, indicative of James' whole approach to popular crowds. Understanding, in his view, comes not as a consequence of detachment or contemplative distance, but as an entangled consequence of doing things. It is Toussaint's error, his *hamartia*, to forget this. It is an error much like that into which James believed many modern intellectuals had fallen, a refusal to heed or even believe in the possibility of popular critical insight. James, for his part, continued to find in the many audiences of contemporary games and texts some echo of that classical chorus: vocal, interrogative, not easily bidden. I find little evidence in either version of *The Black Jacobins*, nor in his wider writings on popular culture, that 'James must to a certain discursive degree share responsibility for [Toussaint's] flaw which consists of a distrust, alienation or severance from the "masses"' (Miller 2001: 1075).

The preceding discussion perhaps helps us understand a little more clearly what James meant when he said, in a much quoted phrase from *American Civilization*: 'To believe that the great masses of the people are merely passive recipients of what the purveyors of popular art give to them is in reality to see people as dumb slaves' (1993: 122). On the face of it, this seems like a rather weak riposte given that the kinds of argument that James has in mind here clearly did (and do) see mass culture as securing a dumb popular enslavement. In this respect, James appears to be rephrasing the position that he is opposed to rather than giving us grounds to contest it. It is only if one reads the comment in the light of what has just been considered that its critical edge begins to show. He, of all people, knew how little evidence there was of slaves being merely dumb. He recognised, on the one hand, how the political and ethical assertions which accompanied European colonialism had been critically refashioned by those to whom they were addressed. And he recognised, on the other hand, and as *The Black Jacobins* makes very clear, the degree to which any postcolonial social order worth fighting for would need to remain open to the demands and actions of that same critical popular audience. It is precisely because he knew these things, because he knew that neither slaves nor freed-slaves were simply dumb, that James did not overlook the degree to which the audiences and crowds of twentieth-century mass culture were capable of refusals and refashionings with regard to the cultural texts of their own times.

III

Having described his general position in this way, I want now to turn the tables somewhat on James and to move away from his discussion of how other readers or viewers respond to cultural texts and practices. Instead, I want to consider *his* response to a particular text. James' reading, it seems to me, provides its own clear demonstration of the degree to which audiences are able to turn even unpromising material to surprising political and sociological use. After all, and as was noted in the previous chapter, his work often involved a critical redeploying, or even the 'wilful misinterpretation' (Springfield 1990: 88), of writings whose social and political presuppositions he certainly repudiated (in the case that Springfield is referring to, for example, Edmund Burke's *Reflections on the Revolution in France*). And of all the books in his life, none seems to have mattered more to James than Thackeray's *Vanity Fair*. It is his relationship to this novel that I want to consider in what follows, treating it as an exemplary instance of his own practice as a reader. James talks famously in *Beyond a Boundary* about the impact upon him of this book, which he first read at the age of eight, which he was still re-reading regularly in his eighties, and much of which he learned by heart. What might he have found in *Vanity Fair* that led him to cherish it in this way, and to claim that it was Thackeray, even more than Marx, that bore responsibility for his development as a person and as a thinker (1983 [1963]: 47)? Or, to ask the question as James asks it of the readers of *Watch Tower*: what did this particular reader *do* with this particular piece of writing?

A number of James' biographers have sought to say something by way of explanation, if not expiation, regarding his obsession with *Vanity Fair*. Paul Buhle, for example, suggests that the novel's satire gave James his first glimpse of a British empire that was 'fallible within and vulnerable without' (1988: 16). This is certainly a persuasive comment, and one that I will seek to develop, in certain respects, in what follows. Moreover, it chimes with James' recollection in *Beyond a Boundary* of the unsettling shock he experienced when George Osborne is killed before *Vanity Fair* is two-thirds complete. It seems a reasonable assumption that this 'novel without a hero' would have done something to puncture the heroic air which many British imperial projects and interventions claimed for themselves. Kent Worcester, for his part, argues that the novel's simultaneous subversion of and preoccupation with manners and subtleties of convention would have found some resonance in the equally status-conscious and manner-bound world of the black middle class in Trinidad

(1996: 4; see also Anderson 1985 and Phillips 2001: 153). This too seems probable, and fits with James' memory of laughing 'without satiety at Thackeray's constant jokes and sneers and gibes at the aristocracy and at people in high places' (1983 [1963]: 47). Indeed, in one of his first publications, *The Life of Captain Cipriani,* James provides a vivid picture of members of this very class, drawing obviously from Thackeray's satirical repertoire as he describes them fawning on colonial government officials and awaiting 'the nod distant, the bow cordial, the shake-hand friendly, or the cut-direct' (1932b: 56). Apart from these suggestive comments, however, there seems to be something of a consensus of silence around James' love of *Vanity Fair.* Farrukh Dhondy perhaps comes closest to explaining why this should be, finding in James' obsession with Thackeray an example of his catholic taste when it came to reading matter, but also something so deeply rooted in James, so 'personal', that it remained 'unanalysable', even to James himself (2001: 8).

It is true that James did not leave us any extended interpretation of Thackeray, as he did for Melville or Whitman and, aside from the comments in *Beyond a Boundary,* he said little about what *Vanity Fair* meant to him or why. And in this respect, although it seems to me that we can venture some analysis of his reading of the novel, such analysis is necessarily a little speculative, and is consigned for the most part to work back to front, moving from what we know of James back to the novel itself. All the same, some suggestions can be made. One is struck, to begin with, by the fact that the first character that the reader encounters in *Vanity Fair* is a black footman who rings the bell which announces the start of the novel and who, in taking Amelia and Becky to the Sedley's Bloomsbury townhouse, sets in train all that follows. Sambo, as the footman is called, is precisely the kind of peripheral figure towards whom postcolonial studies have so effectively directed critical attention. Nothing in the book happens to him, as it were, in his own right. More importantly, his interior life appears largely hidden from the otherwise all-penetrating gaze of the narrator, a gaze which extends often enough to the private thoughts and motives of other servants and valets who appear in the narrative. The result is an ambivalence. While, on the one hand, Sambo's apparent unknowability insulates him from much of the cutting edge of Thackeray's satire, it also debars him from taking part in that satire on his own behalf. Although his silence gives him a certain dignity amid the empty chatter of the novel's other characters, it is also a sign of dispossession: he is never afforded the chance to join in with those 'jokes, sneers and gibes at people in high places' which is granted to many of the story's other subsidiary characters.

In this respect, on the few subsequent occasions when he appears, Sambo seems like a character who is discrepant or out-of-place in the fictional world that Thackeray creates. And it is precisely that out-of-place quality which sets him up to be the butt of the joke when the aristocratic Miss Crawley first deigns to descend to the grubbily commercial world of Bloomsbury in search of Amelia. 'Miss Crawley', the narrator tells us, 'was waiting in her carriage below, her people wondering at the locality in which they found themselves, and gazing upon honest Sambo, the black footman of Bloomsbury, as one of the queer natives of the place' (1933 [1848]: 121). In common with most jokes in the novel this has more than one target. Thackeray has a great deal of fun in what follows mocking the mutual snobbery of the contending classes here: the hypocritical aristocrats of Park Lane and the hopelessly pretentious middle classes of Bloomsbury. Yet there is no question, in the end, that the joke is on Sambo, of whom, the implication is, it could only ever be a mistake to imagine that he was native to this place. The term, of course, comes with its own spiteful double entendre, hinting at the possibility that Sambo is nothing other than a 'native' in the derogatory sense of that term popularised by Victorian anthropology and colonial travelogue. But more damaging still is in the word 'honest' which, appearing here without qualification, and in the absence of any later evidence by which it might be qualified, condemns Sambo to a peculiar kind of non-existence in the world of *Vanity Fair* where hypocrisy and ulterior motives are apparent among even the most sympathetic characters, and where moral messiness defines what it is to be human.

We have no easy way of knowing how James responded to Sambo in his many re-readings of *Vanity Fair*, nor whether he came to view him with a certain poignancy as he became increasingly involved in anti-imperial and anti-racist struggles. What we can say something about is how James approached the reading of fictional characters in general. As we have seen, in *Mariners, Renegades and Castaways* he fiercely refuses any attempt to reduce the crew of the *Pecquod* to a series of allegorical or symbolic portraits, emphasising instead their 'reality', their live historical meaningfulness. It was, he argued, one of the great failings of contemporary intellectuals to so hanker after 'literary self-consciousness' (2001 [1953]: 85) that they lost sight of what the crowds and audiences of popular culture well understood: when we applaud, or reject, or fight over the personalities and characters who appear in our cultural games and texts we do so because they are of our lives, and a part of how we come to make sense of our lives.

This explains why, for example, in the course of an article describing the development of a cricketing culture among the 'plebeian' masses of the Caribbean, James drops in a passing reference to another peripheral black character from a classic Victorian novel: Quanko Samba, the bowler who plays an important role in the game described in Dickens' *Pickwick Papers* (1963: 8). Unless one keeps in mind his emphasis on the immediacy of fictional creations such an aside seems puzzling. According to the protocols of both academic literary criticism (working from one direction) and those of a crude materialism (working from another) this apparent muddling of the worlds inside and outside of the text is the sign of an unforgivable naïvety. James, of course, was guilty of no such confusion, nor did he imagine there to be any such confusion on the part of the men and women who watched sport or films or who read novels. The naïvety, in his view, was to imagine that literary or other creative activity could somehow transcend the contradictions and contentions of the world from which it sprang; to imagine that the characters invoked by such activity were not riddled through and through with the traces of those contentions. In this respect, his passing reference to Quanko Samba reminds us of his famous preface to *Beyond a Boundary* which had been published earlier in the year and in which he predicts that in order 'to establish his own identity, Caliban [...] must himself pioneer into regions Caesar never knew' (1983 [1963]: xix). Those who turned their hands to that most beloved pastime of the English imperialist were unquestionably a part of the struggle to establish or own an identity that been historically over-written. Typically, of course, James' comment looks forward not backward. His naming of Quanko Samba in this context is not about rehearsing all that has been done to those who were presumed to fit that name, but is rather an assertion of triumph. It serves to emphasise what has been done to Quanko Samba as Wes Hall, Roy Gilchrist, Malcolm Marshall and the other heirs to that struggle pioneered into regions that Dickens never knew.

And in just this way, although we cannot say what exactly James made of Thackeray's Sambo, in the sense of knowing how he interpreted that character, we do know what he made of Sambo. That is to say, we know what he did with that characterisation. After all, no sooner had James disembarked at Plymouth in 1932 than he headed *not* for Lancashire, where he was due to meet Learie Constantine, but for Bloomsbury (much to the disgust of some subsequent commentators: Rohlehr in Agozino and Edwards 2007). And there, with no little audacity, he became a part of the literary and artistic scene, revelling in the chance to display his mastery of the Western canon as he engaged in artistic debates and accepted invitations to deliver public lectures. The articles that he wrote for the *Port of Spain Gazette* reporting on his first weeks in Britain read like dispatches from the front-line in some distant campaign, and there is a definite air of intellectual conquest when James concludes at the end of one of these reports: 'by instinct and training I belong to [Bloomsbury] and have fit into it as naturally as a pencil fits into a sharpener' (2003: 54). It is indeed as if he were keen to demonstrate how easily and unambiguously he could pass as a native of this place which was the symbolic heartland of British intellectualism but also came, one imagines, with a heavy personal symbolism for a compulsive reader of *Vanity Fair*.

Of course, 'nativity' continued to be defined in other ways as well and James quickly encountered British racism. As elsewhere in his biographical writings, he says little about this directly, aside from promising one day to 'strip the question raw of all the cant and hypocrisy with which it is covered' (87) and apart from his description of a few chance encounters in a lift or train where he was made to feel distinctly out of place. Even in his reticence it is clear that, despite the degree to which he felt culturally and intellectually at home in Bloomsbury, he was aware of those for whom he could only ever appear incongruous. If, on a personal level, James found all this hurtful, he does not say so. Rather he turns that recognition of hypocrisy to use, feeding it into a series of increasingly deflating revelations about British life for his Caribbean readers. Satire conventionally relies on a perspective that allows discrepancy to be revealed between promise and reality, pronouncement and action – a perspective, of course, that men and women living under British imperial rule had only too much opportunity to occupy. In this respect James' articles for *The Port of Spain Gazette* certainly owe something to a long tradition of subversive satire from the colonial world. But they are also, of course, in the tradition of Thackeray and there is more than a hint in these pieces of Thackeray's disdain for pretension and his skill with the barbed comment. So although, in one sense, James' letters from London record a partially thwarted quest to claim nativity – the English intellectual going to England, as he put it in *Beyond a Boundary* – his triumph is to make of that thwarting the means to a critical distance which allows him to stand above the world of Bloomsbury as a 'secondary thing' (54) and to record the gap between claim and achievement in British social life more generally. It is this voice, which makes itself heard most clearly in the later articles, that witheringly points out the statues of 'aristocratic nonentities' (113) dressed in Roman clothes in the London park that they once 'happened to own', or which describes the houses of the suburban middle classes where 'there is usually a piano, if even played badly [...] a good bookcase, if even it holds rubbishy books' (68). James' targeting of the pomposity of the aristocracy and the affectations of the middle class, as well as his turn of phrase, suggest very clearly something of what he, as a reader, drew from Thackeray. Yet, as befits someone who saw in our engagement with culture both evidence *and* site of struggle, his achievement in this respect rested on his doing something *to* Thackeray and to the characters created by Thackeray, involving as it did the recovery of the satirical voice, the right to sneer and gibe, of the queer native of Bloomsbury.

IV

This is, however, not the whole story, because James' relationship to Thackeray's novel reveals something about the way in which his discussion of the popular audience relates to his political perspective more generally. A justification of this claim might begin with an admission: Sambo is not, as I suggested previously, the first character that one encounters in entering *Vanity Fair*. Before the action of the novel begins, Thackeray presents us with another figure: the 'Manager of the Performance', sitting before the curtain and looking 'out into the Fair' (1933 [1848]: 9). At first glance, of course, it is not clear whether this is really a 'character' in the usual sense, because the manager appears to be a fairly transparent alter-ego of the author, casting his mind back over the success of the serialised novel and proud to think how his 'Puppets have given satisfaction to the very best company in this empire' (10). (An eight-year-old boy in a distant fragment of that empire is not, one imagines, quite the company he had in mind.) All the same, this scene has an ambiguity about it which unsettles the assumption that the manager of the performance and the author of the novel are one and the same. We are introduced to the former, after all, sitting with his back to the stage looking, not at his puppets, but out towards the audience themselves. Back, indeed, at us, so that when he concludes that 'Yes, this is VANITY FAIR; not a moral place, certainly; nor a merry one, though very noisy' (9), he clearly challenges us to recognise ourselves in his description and, 'with a reflective turn of mind', to consider where exactly we point when we say 'yes, *this* is vanity fair'.

And if this is a moment that implicates the reader in the performance, it implicates just as completely the storyteller himself. He too, it seems, is a part of the Fair, sitting not in some position of external authority but just slightly apart from his characters, and exuding not certainty but 'profound melancholy' (9). And it is this scepticism regarding the trustworthiness of the narrator that seems to me to be what resonates most clearly between *Vanity Fair* and James' developing political and intellectual view. As Peter Shillingsburg has argued recently (2001), *Vanity Fair* is precisely *not* a satire conducted from some point of Olympian self-assurance. If satire requires an omniscient storyteller who is able to counter-pose characters' claims to morality and probity with knowledge of their true intentions and actions, *Vanity Fair* is a very uncertain satire. Its narrator is too obviously contradictory and insincere for that, too obviously in cahoots with the interests of particular characters. Too obviously equivocating, for that matter, allowing the reader privileged access to private thoughts one moment and feigning ignorance of events the next. This disingenuousness is captured with particular clarity in the climactic scene in which Rawdon finally confronts Lord Steyne on suspicion of his having had an affair with Becky Sharp. 'What *had* happened? Was she guilty or not' (1933 [1848]: 482), the narrator asks, before sheltering behind the fallibility of his own creation: 'She said not: but who could tell what was truth which came from those lips; or if that corrupt heart was in this case pure' (ibid.)? Who can tell indeed? For if the narrator is unable or unwilling to answer such questions then the reader is pushed to ask themselves: whose lips are we to mistrust? As Shillingsburg quite rightly says, *Vanity Fair* above all cautions its reader to be wary of what we are told, to alert ourselves to the possibility that it is the heart of the narrator which may be corrupt. By making the manager a part of the performance he describes – not moral, nor merry, merely noisy – Thackeray denies the reader the consolation of access to a superior or definitive moral perspective. The effect, Shillingsburg says, is that the laughter provoked by the story is not bitter and mocking, but sad and sympathetic. It is a self-deprecating laughter inasmuch as the narrator's own claims to know, in the words of James' famous question, 'what it is that people live by', seem hollow or insufficient.

A revealing comparison might be offered here with James' own novel *Minty Alley*, which was written in the late 1920s, but first published on his arrival in Britain in the next decade. It too is a story narrated by a pompous and archaic Victorian voice, replete with obvious Thackerayisms. It, like *Vanity Fair*, is a book about the subtle codes and practices by which class is marked out. It is, also like *Vanity Fair*, focused particularly on the way in which economic calculations cast a doubtful light over the authenticity or spontaneity of human relationships, particularly romantic or sexual relationships. And it is a book, above all, where the reliability of the narrator is thrown into question. So when, to give one instance, the narrator says of the hired help, Philomen, 'she was a simple soul with a golden disposition' (1971 [1936]: 85), this judgement is undermined not only by its triteness, but also because it is so obviously complicit with the voice and values of Haynes, who is the central character of the novel, an intellectual who rents a room in a down-market boarding house where the action takes place. It is, indeed, this complicity between Haynes and the narrator which defines the book as a whole. As Kenneth Ramchand has pointed out (introduction to James 1971 [1936]; compare Nielsen 1997: chapter 1), James orchestrates the novel in such a way that the narrator's view is extraordinarily confined, limited to peering through the same chinks in doorways and the same chance revelations in the backyard that are available to Haynes. One result of this confinement is that the popular characters of *Minty Alley* are granted a private life. They are not, however, rendered mere blanks, as is 'honest Sambo', because a whole wider world of understandings and practices reveals itself in references to 'science' (i.e. the occult), in snatches of gossip, and in the unexpected turns of event which neither Haynes nor the narrator find wholly explicable. Just as, in *Vanity Fair*, the narrator is revealed at one point to be just someone who happened to have dinner with someone who happened to be an acquaintance of some of the central characters in the novel, so in *Minty Alley*, the narrator is implicitly revealed as a lodger in the house, only dimly aware of what passes in other rooms, and in a vibrant popular cultural life beside which their judgemental voice sounds staid and artificial. Miss Atwell, a fellow lodger with Haynes, says in the course of a fight with her landlady's philandering husband: 'when God take a turn in your skin, you goin' to know something' (81). Until such an event occurs, a God's-eye view seems like a pretension that only intellectuals like Haynes could ever contemplate. And a pretension, moreover, which leaves Haynes at the end of the novel much where Thackeray's manager of the performance sits as he packs away his puppets: sitting to the side of popular life and looking on, detached in a way that grants no compensating authority or certainty.

V

Whatever else James took from *Vanity Fair* in his lifelong relationship with the novel, this emphasis on the fallibility or doubtfulness of the supposedly authoritative voice seems to me to be crucial. What can certainly be said, in any case, is that it is this sceptical disposition which is at the heart of his own account of reading, of the audience or the crowd. Indeed, it is this disposition which is at the heart of his politics more generally, the keynote of which is precisely a refusal to grant to the conventional voices of authority the last interpretive word, the right to pass definitive judgements. It is absolutely characteristic of James' cultural writing that he resists any attempt to interpret cultural activities or works on the basis of political first principles. And he makes this argument as staunchly as he does precisely because he never lost sight of the margin of freedom which popular audiences had in interpreting, appropriating and re-tooling cultural stuff. James repeatedly searched for and found evidence of this process of active 'making use' which proceeded oblivious to, or at least largely unconcerned by, whatever assumptions about the meaning or worth of the texts in question reigned among the literati or among party ideologues. This is why, as was discussed in the previous chapter, he came to emphasise the contested nature of 'mass' culture, the degree to which it involved a series of highly strained compromises between the largely antagonistic demands of its elite makers and its popular audience. Hence also, the truly great artistic innovations of the twentieth century, in his view, those which managed to escape the three-fold trap of introspective modernism, the diktat of the party line and the stifling imperatives of the market, were innovations catalysed by the artist's awareness of a popular audience with its urgent demands and desires, its desperate grappling with the dilemmas of new social relations and possibilities. It was in this vein, for example, that he celebrated Eisenstein's achievement in the crowd scenes of *Battleship Potemkin* (1990 [1954]) or Picasso's *Guernica* (James 1992: chapter 29).

In developing this position James looks both forward and back. Back, in that he repeatedly cited both Elizabethan and Athenian drama as exemplary instances of the way in which art might become an integral part of the lives of popular audiences. And, conversely, of the way in which the social and political demands of those audiences might become an integral part of art. In his never-completed *Preface to Criticism*, James returned to Aristotle's *Poetics*, scornfully dismissing those who boiled that text down into a series of 'how-to' lessons in literary structure or organisation: 'If that is what Aristotle has to contribute [...] then he has no more to say than any instructor who undertakes to teach the writing of saleable fiction by post in ten easy lessons' (1992: 256). Against this hopelessly ahistorical formalism James insists, much as recent critical work on Greek tragedy has insisted (Hall 1997), on situating Aristotle's approach in relation to its specific social time and place. And in so doing he recentres Aristotle's work around the concept of audience: 'The principle which unifies Aristotle's ideas is the popular audience, whose modern counterpart crowds into the cinema in every modern city' (1992: 256). Aristotle's definition of the functions of drama and the structure of plot are made, he says, specifically in terms of that audience. Dramatic work is successful for Aristotle if, and in so far as, it poses questions and posits solutions which the audience lives as their own. Moreover, while modern criticism 'from Saint Beuve to T. S. Eliot' (257) dismisses popular culture as anodyne and treats true art as a kind of exclusive hill-top retreat, James insists that Aristotle saw things the other way around: 'literature for the popular audience, dealing with things that concern it vitally [is] not easier but more difficult than literature for cultivated persons' (ibid.). The popular audience, in short, is the making or breaking of any cultural product worth keeping; the forms or effects of that culture are not magically 'given' to us, but can be named only in terms of a relationship to their audience. Not catharsis as an abstract principle, for example, but catharsis *for* those who watch and find in the drama some aspect of their lives refracted. Not actors on a stage practising mere technique, but 'Actors, imitating actions, as though they were living it themselves *in the emotions of a popular audience facing a situation in which they feel themselves to be profoundly involved*' (256, my italics). As was argued in Chapter 1, James did insist that it was crucially important to take account of the specific intrinsic properties of particular cultural practices. But one could do this, in his view, only by thinking through what those forms meant to their audience, and what their audience did with them. Anything that we might say about cultural practices or forms is conditioned by the question of their significance, a question which ties their meaning to specific times and places, to the needs and struggles of the particular crowds or readers for whom, and by virtue of whom, they matter.

James thus insisted that the classical critical heritage to which current intellectuals retreated as a 'bomb-shelter' (James, Lee and Chaulieu 1974 [1958]: 85) was actually a hidden cache of 'explosives' (ibid.) by which existing intellectual approaches to culture and its audiences might be demolished. As his reference to those crowding into the city cinemas suggests, he firmly believed that modern technology offered the promise of a new kind of integration of cultural or artistic activity and daily life. This remained, as I noted in the previous chapter, a deeply ambivalent prospect. He recognised that such an integration was approaching one kind of completion in the fascist and Communist states with the public drama of the show-trial and the degraded public poetry of propaganda. But as yet, James insisted, the contradiction between the audience's desire for creative expression and the increasingly centralised control of cultural production was unresolved:

> Art, film, radio, television, offer arts of the mass, for the mass, offer the means whereby great artists in the infinite complexity of modern life, in the way great artists always have done, will simplify and dramatize and attack the emotions as well as the intellect with dramatizations of the great problems [...] A modern society *must* do this in the manner of the totalitarians or in the manner of the Greeks. (1993: 157)

James refused to concede defeat here not because he was blindly optimistic, but because he insisted on recognising what he might have called the dialectical truth of things, the affirmations that can be found in even the worst of contemporary negations. If Henry Ford, for example, required armed mercenaries to keep his workers tethered to their assembly lines, what clearer testament could there be of the depth and endurance of the demand for creative control among those workers (1993: chapter 6)? And it is precisely in this vein that he approached the audiences of modern culture. Even in those early *Letters from London* James is thinking along these lines. In his essay on 'the houses' of London, for example, he describes his own experience of living in a bedsit, amid terraces of identical, anonymous, rented rooms: 'whatever you do', he says, 'the loneliness of the room is dreadful', once the door is locked 'there is an end of you' (2003: 64–5). And it is 'when you appreciate what this means that you see why there is a cinema or a theatre or a show of some sort every fifty yards in a London street' (65), or why there should be young women sitting all afternoon in cafés reading the paper 'from cover to cover' (66). The audiences for popular culture, those who 'fill the cinemas, from twelve in the day to twelve at night' (70), even those who lap up sensational stories about 'the Rector of Stiffkey', demonstrate not compliance or defeatism, but the refusal of men and women to accept what capitalist modernity has given them: 'anything rather than work from nine till six and then go and lock [your]self away from the world in that prison of a room' (66).

This, it seems to me, is the first hint in James of the argument that he will develop more fully only in *American Civilization* and *Beyond a Boundary*: that the readers and viewers of popular culture are involved in an ongoing struggle, not just over the meanings and implications of the books they read and films they see but, in and through that, over the very conditions of their lives. A struggle that begins with the refusal to accept that working nine-to-six followed by a prison-house of a room is sufficient to be given the name freedom or happiness. 'They do what they feel to do – get at any price', James concludes, 'I know what I am talking about. I have seen it. And then, you see, I myself in one of those dreadful rooms have felt the same' (70). Unlike his creation Haynes, who is left to look backwards at the house of popular culture as something belonging safely to 'old times' (1971 [1936]: 244), James' own encounter with that culture was enduring and led him to emphasise the social and political longings articulated in its acts of reading and viewing. It was among those newspaper readers and film viewers that one could find clearest evidence of a widespread refusal to settle for the present, and the traces therefore, of a possible future forthcoming.

VI

The comments of James which I have just cited are intriguing not least because they suggest something of what might tentatively be called his method. After all, one response to his whole approach to culture, the kind of response which is always on the tip of the sociologist's tongue, is: 'says who?' On what basis are the claims that James makes about the historical meaningfulness of such things as bowling technique, or artistic style, established or demonstrated? His account of the meanings and uses of culture might well be accused of being just as subjective, and in its own way just as full of hubris, as those provided by the bourgeois intellectuals whom he scorned. It is his concern with the popular audience which, it seems to me, provides some basis for a counter to such accusations.

The first thing to say is that not all sociological claims about cultural objects or practices can be empirically tested in any obvious way. Max Weber's claim, for example, that 'the piano is by its very musical nature a bourgeois domestic instrument' (1978b: 382), rests upon an observation about the particular properties of the piano as an object, and how those properties accord with the equally particular properties of bourgeois life, including the nature of its household arrangements, its characteristic aesthetic sensibilities and its patterns of consumption. Our response to such a claim relies primarily upon the degree to which we are convinced or otherwise by the observations it rests upon with regard to both the object and the historical context in question. Much of James' interpretation of modern culture involves propositions of the same order. Such, for example, is the case when he describes the displacement of adventuresome batting by a containing, defensively minded technique as indicative of the 'welfare state of mind' (1983 [1963]: chapter 17); that is, of a whole social and political arrangement in which the state substitutes security and standard of living for autonomy or creativity. This interpretation is convincing, it seems to me, but not in any way that can be easily tested. It appeals, rather, to our sense of its truthfulness, to the extent to which it elicits from us something like that long, low 'ah' of recognition which Matthew Bondman's shots drew from his audience.

Yet such interpretations did not come from nowhere. In general, it is a defining feature of James' writing about culture that he consistently pays attention to what popular audiences and crowds had to say about the things which he was concerned to understand. There is, indeed, something like a method here. A method not unlike that adopted by an unconventional historian such as Studs Terkel, based in nothing more grandiose than small day-to-day acts of conversation. A method based, more particularly, in a willingness to listen. Many of those who knew James best, particularly during his time in America, have recalled how much time he spent talking to the working men and women he met, and asking them in detail about their lives and labours, desires and despairs (for example: Buhle 1986: 98; Rawick 1986: 233; Boggs 1995: 166). In the same way, much of his most insightful writing about cricket begins or builds from comments that he has overheard around him, or from questions asked to his fellow members of the crowd. I think here, for example, of an early article from 1934, published in the *Manchester Guardian*, which begins with James watching a soporific day's play at Dover, listening to the grumbles of those around him and casting his eye about the 'terrace after terrace dotted with people looking lazily on and talking of Woolley' (1986: 39–40). It is precisely in response to this crowd's own response to the game that he goes on to draw an imaginative parallel, for the first time that I am aware of in his writing, between modern sport and Greek drama of the fifth century BC:

> The ancient Athenians had terraced seats in the open air, and if they looked on Aeschylus and Sophocles, they had their Olympic games too. What would an Athenian have thought of the day's play? Probably that the white-flannelled actors moving so sedately from place to place were performing the funeral rites over the corpse of a hero buried between the wickets. (ibid.)

Later, in chapter 12 of *Beyond a Boundary*, James will develop this analogy with increasing seriousness, using it to substantiate his claim that organised sport is quite capable of bearing the name 'art' and that it offers to those who watch it a creative exhilaration which they long for more generally in their lives. Thus it is that he arrives at this view, and therefore some answer to the question 'what do people live by', not just by reading or by scholarly inquiry, but also because he begins by sitting and listening to the subdued frustration of a crowd who saw in the dull play in front of them the death of something that mattered. The analogy that he draws between Athenian drama and a modern Test match is meant to dignify cricket as an activity, no doubt, but it is also meant to dignify the modern crowd who brought to their own games a critical attentiveness and an undimmed desire for freedom which made them the historical heirs to those who sat and watched the plays of Aeschylus and Sophocles.

It should be added, perhaps, that there are plenty of anecdotes which suggest that James was quite capable of hectoring his own audiences. However, in the little material that we have in which James provides an insight into his own experiences, he does appear as someone who was engaged in what I am tempted to call a radical 'ethnography' of ordinary life. His early 'letters from London' provide one example, his later letters to Constance Webb provide many others. None are more striking, in this respect, than those first letters he wrote to Webb from Nevada, where he had gone in order to secure a divorce from his first marriage, and where he was forced to wait out a residency requirement, working and living on a ranch a few miles from Reno run by a one-time champion rodeo rider (1996b: part four; see also the helpful article by Dworkin 2007). His accounts to Webb certainly show James as someone unfamiliar with, and not altogether comfortable at the prospect of, manual labour. All the same, they also reveal James as a careful, quiet observer of those around him as he sits 'in the back among the baggage' on the weekly ride into town, or watches the course of romances and relationships playing out in the kitchen of the ranch. By his own account, James' willingness to listen has a kind of empowering effect on those to whom he listens: 'as soon as they see that their knowledge has significance far beyond what they dreamt, they *all* talk' (329). James was not, of course, a worker and his time adrift in the desert must have driven home to him how different his experiences and assumptions were from those who were less educated and less widely travelled. But he had enough humility to remain open to the experiences of working men and women, not only listening to their accounts of their lives, but watching as well. More than once he remarks on the resilience with which those around him responded to day-to-day crises in their places of work, and the remarkable resources of energy and improvisation which they are able to draw upon in such moments. He continued to read and to write, of course. He could hardly do otherwise. But he also did something else: paid close attention to the stories and to the savoir faire of working men and women, feeling in both the shifting of 'that volcano that is clamped down in every human being' (326).

It is worth remembering, in this respect, that James turned his back on the possibility of either an academic career or of a mainstream political role. Indeed, much of his most fruitful intellectual work was carried out while he was illegally resident in America. He deliberately chose to work in this way, and his choice cost him much of his health, many of his closest relationships and almost all semblance of economic security. He chose as he did because he believed in the importance of a political struggle rooted in and responsive to popular experience. This does not mean, as I have already made clear, that James was an uncritical populist. His public speaking is characterised by his urging audiences of all kinds to engage with the most challenging writers – Kant, say, or Karl Jaspers – or to engage with familiar texts such as the gospels in newly demanding ways. Yet he certainly does offer us some model of what it might mean, in practice, to refuse to give the last word to those he self-deprecatingly called 'writers and talkers like myself' (1973 [1960]: 61). A model of what it might mean to develop an account of modern culture, in other words, and of modern society more generally, which begins by listening to those without the privilege of much education or much wealth. In this he remains a profound challenge to anyone interested, not just in thinking through, but in doing, the politics of popular culture today.

Conclusion

In the end, then, it seems to me that James' approach to the crowds and readers of popular culture is underwritten by the faith he had in the ability of the oppressed to read accurately, and to respond appropriately, to 'the text of their own lives', as George Rawick puts it (1986: 233). His rejection of what he called a Stalinist, or simply a doctrinaire approach to culture, was of a piece with his slowly worked out rejection of the structures of political organisation that were conventional on the left, especially the idea of a vanguard party that would orchestrate and explain to those involved the true meanings of otherwise chaotic mass action. In a series of publications through the forties and fifties, James and his collaborators questioned the conception of a politics based in this notion of parties which would speak for the working class.

Their scepticism was honed on what they took to be the key lesson of the Soviet state, that 'By a remorseless logic [...] representation of the proletariat turns into its opposite, administration over the proletariat' (James 1986 [1950]: 116). Rather than the revolution posited as some forthcoming state of affairs which intellectuals, with their God's-eye view, could guide the masses towards, James' developed position was that socialism was already immanently there, in the ceaseless popular struggle for happiness and in the refusal of much that people were consigned to by their working and domestic lives. In a sense, therefore, this position was precisely about overturning an idea of socialism as something narrated to people by those better able to read the text of history, and replacing this with the idea of socialism as that which can only come from people's critical reading of the story of their own existence. Here, as in so much of his work, James' politics and his cultural analysis are part of the same thing. And perhaps it is not too much to suggest that there is a distant hint here of that caution in *Vanity Fair* about the act of 'speaking on behalf of', which may explain something of James' enduring devotion to the book.

All of this is also, of course, why James and his colleagues were finally so dismissive of a politics aimed at the accumulation of more stuff: 'quantitative, vulgar materialism', as he called it (1973 [1960]: 97), in both its Stalinist and welfare-statist guises. What is it that people live by, what are the desires and needs that animate popular life? In *Minty Alley*, as we have seen, James specifically qualifies and undermines the stature of the narrator and Haynes the intellectual by recognising that an answer to that question was not theirs to give. And that assumption moves increasingly to the heart of James' political position. The answer to the question 'what is it that people live by?' cannot be asserted from above, nor calculated in terms of an 'increased use of goods'. Rather it must be searched for inductively, in what people do with what they have, including what uses they make of the expressive stuff of culture. This is, above all, why James was so concerned with the audience. This is why he turns his attention not only to the text or game in front of him – neither of which ever slips from sight – but also to the crowd itself and its responses. To do so was not only to defend a political assumption (that the crowd has an autonomous critical sensibility and interpretive authority); it was also to watch for, to learn from, a politics in action.

4
Players

Introduction

C. L. R. James' first book was planned and researched in Trinidad but ultimately published, thanks to the support of Learie Constantine, by a local press in Lancashire in 1932. On the face of it, the book takes as its subject a populist union leader and thorn in the side of the island's colonial administration, hence the title: *The Life of Captain Cipriani.* Yet James clearly intended it to bring other targets in range, as is indicated by his subtitle: *An Account of British Government in the West Indies.* Although it has not been much discussed subsequently, *The Life of Captain Cipriani* is an intriguing piece of work. On the one hand, it is in many respects wholly untypical of James. It is, for example, stylistically unsteady, shifting gears gratingly between political invective, novelistic description and investigative journalism. It is also somewhat politically unsteady, mixing condemnation of the crown colony system with a rather diffident note, even in the demand it makes for West Indian self-determination. Although the book apparently played its part in subsequent political uprisings in the Caribbean (Hill 1981: 20), one can understand why the experienced trade-union and socialist organisers who had befriended James in Nelson, as well as critically minded reviewers at home, were nonplussed (ibid.; also Worcester 1996: 21–5).

On the other hand, it also contains much which, read in the light of James' subsequent work, seems richly suggestive. As I have noted already, the book features some wonderfully biting moments of satire, not least when James is describing the sudden and desperate adherence to ideas of national and racial superiority which characterised expatriate officials on their arrival in the Caribbean. No wonder he insisted that men and women dismissed as 'backward' were often well placed to recognise the contradictions and hypocrisies of the mighty: for the colonial regime that he describes such contradictions were not merely incidental but intrinsic to its very claims to authority. That authority, James notes coolly, justified itself on an assumption about the moral superiority of a British way of doing things, including a celebration of the supposedly British virtues of liberty and tolerance, virtues that were simultaneously and paradoxically treated as 'the greatest crime' conceivable in a colonial society (1932b: 7). The book, moreover, discusses a noteworthy incident of sporting politics, when James describes Cipriani's role in a small-scale revolt among black troops of the British West Indies Regiment. These troops, stationed in Taranto after the First World War, refused to take part in a series of recreational games because of the insistence of their South African commanding officer, General Carey Bernard, that these should take place on racially segregated lines. Subsequently, a member of the same regiment was called to court martial, accused of starting a rumour that the victory of the General in a number of swimming races had been suspiciously easy. James, clearly, was not the only one who recognised the importance of defending the autonomous criteria of success and failure that define sporting practices, nor the only one who recognised the possibilities for challenging forms of social authority, and authority's justifying ideologies, which those practices opened up. The black troops of the British West Indies Regiment obviously knew what was at stake in such events as, it would seem, did General Bernard, given that he considered rumours of his cheating sufficiently subversive to warrant the full weight of military discipline.

The most typically Jamesian aspect of this, the first of his major publications, however, is the fact that he chose to present his critical *Account of British Government in the West Indies* in the form of a biography of a leading figure in the resistance movement which that government was then provoking. The nature of the relationship between James' title and his subtitle, after all, is anything but self-evident and it is clear that he was aware of this. He begins, for this very reason, with an explanation: 'This book is a biography, but a political biography. It is not written for the purposes of describing the personal career and probing into the motives of Captain Cipriani. It is written as the best means of bringing before all who may be interested the political situation in the West Indies today' (1932b: 1). This statement raises as many questions as it answers. Why should something as specific as a biography, albeit one concerned with a significant figure in a given political situation, be 'the best means' of throwing light on that situation? Conversely, what kind of biography is so blithely uninterested in the very things which are most subjective about its supposed subject? 'A fairly unsuccessful one' is one possible answer to that last question and an answer that even some of James' most supportive readers have arrived at (for example, Buhle 1988: 36). Not without reason, because his account of Cipriani is definitely too piecemeal to be really compelling, nor does it effectively personalise or bring to life the book's wider political arguments. There is, indeed, something of a tacit admission of this failure in the fact that James would, in the following year, pare out sections of his original text so that they could be published in pamphlet form by Leonard and Virginia Woolf's Hogarth Press, under a new, more explicitly polemical title: *The Case for West Indian Self-Government* (1933). In the filleted version, Cipriani all but disappears, becoming little more than a name among other names in the dedication.

Yet, whatever its faults, James was grappling with something in *The Life of Captain Cipriani* which remained a central problem and provocation throughout all of his subsequent work. The individual on the one hand and the social context on the other: James' title and his subtitle. These two scales of experience and an attempt to work through the relationship between them becomes one of his most characteristic concerns. At one point in the book, describing the peculiarly warped workings of the colonial legislative council, he writes: 'We need not go one inch out of Captain Cipriani's life to see [that government] on every conceivable occasion doing its damnedest' (1932b: 70). In general, the surrounding text does not do all that much to sustain this claim, and tends to wander a long way from Cipriani's life in pursuit of its political targets. Yet it is clear that James was reaching for something significant here. Much of what he would produce over the course of the succeeding half-century was driven by that same reach, by an attempt to reconcile the personal and the political; an attempt to reconcile the biographer's concern for human being in all of its precious idiosyncrasy with an understanding of the shaping effects of political and social structures. An attempt, in other words, to develop a vision of these things as inextricable, to see one without having to 'go one inch' out of the other.

Having put things in this way, I am perhaps at risk of giving credit to James where it is only partly deserved. The reminder that the personal is political is, after all, one that we owe to feminism, and part of what that slogan draws our attention towards is the degree to which the relationships, labour and exploitations which characterise the 'domestic' sphere require an ethical and political response of their own, even while they are integral to the successful reproduction of capitalism as a social system generally. James does discuss such questions. There are moments in his letters to Constance Webb, and more particularly in *American Civilization* (1993: especially 211–25), where he addresses directly the specificity of women's struggles, while also seeking to understand those struggles as related to a wider demand for freedom and a rejection of what he called 'mechanized, routinized living' (219). Much of what he says in this context seems to me to be insightful, and he recognises importantly the degree to which the oppression of women, like racism, rests on assumptions 'that are strictly a priori' (214), but which become effective, in part, by being embodied. All the same, *The Life of Captain Cipriani* typifies something in James that is a weakness, as well as much that will become a strength. While it focuses on an individual and seeks to balance an account of that person, in all of their specificity, with a sense of their particular historical and social context, the individual in question is a publicly prominent one, a political leader, and a man. The same can be said of almost all the other figures that James found it worth writing about, at greater or lesser length, in future years: Stalin, an analysis of whom is at the heart of his early history of the Communist International (1973 [1937]); Trotsky (see the essay in McLemee and le Blanc 1994: 92–130); Toussaint; Nkrumah (1977b); Lincoln (1996a: 108–11; 1992: chapter 18); George Padmore (1984: chapter 19); George Jackson (1977a: chapter 20) and so on. The only obvious exception to this pattern that I can think of is the play about Harriet Tubman that James planned, drafted and pitched to a commissioning agent in 1944 but which was never completed.

One of James' best loved essays takes its title from Lenin: 'Every Cook Can Govern' (1977a: 160–74). In it, and drawing as elsewhere on the model of Athenian democracy, James builds a claim about the startling capacity of ordinary individuals as political leaders, freed from the assumption that their rightful position is that of the passive objects of leadership by others. But the claim that 'every cook can govern', radical as it may be in terms of conventional political structures, is an easy sell. A corresponding but less easy proposition might insist that every governor should take their turn doing the cooking. James' critique of 'the politics of the vanguard', and of apostolic claims to definitive political truth, is a staunch one. But perhaps it needed to leave greater space for another critique, a willingness to ask about the hidden distribution of labour on which all leadership relies. This question and the perspective from which it develops are sometimes notable by their absence in James' writing. Indeed, according to Farrukh Dhondy, his response to the 'wages for housework' campaign started by Selma James, his third wife, was one of 'amused disdain'. 'They argue about who does the cooking.

Those who will cook will cook, those who won't cook, won't cook' (2001: 205), Dhondy reports James saying, although we should do him the fairness of placing this comment alongside his much more thoughtful response to black feminist writings in the same period (1984: chapter 20). Ntozake Shange, one of those writers who James encountered late in his life, has made clear more recently that the generally feminised work of cooking deserves more than amused disdain, not least because the skills and knowledge associated with it have themselves been politically important in the historical context of the African diaspora, providing a day-to-day demonstration of the resilience of oppressed communities and of their ability to recreate and defend distinctive cultural practices (Shange 1998). More encouragingly, at one point in the same book, Shange recalls a meal prepared in the very same Brixton apartment where James had spent his last years. Looking back, she says: 'I'm sure even in his nineties C. L. R. James would have assisted us' (25). Perhaps so: Young has interviewed those who knew James in Britain during the 1930s, a number of whom particularly remark on his habit of cleaning and cooking for those who hosted him (1999: chapter 3). Although his political writings tend to focus on the public and the masculine at the expense of the hidden labours and hidden politics to which, historically, women have been limited, it seems that in his own life James was not unprepared to take his turn with such things.

I say all of this, then, because it offers a necessary qualification to James' interest in the great historical figure, and one which should be placed up-front in a discussion of this aspect of his work. In what follows, I want to look more particularly at the way in which this concern of James' which I have described, the concern to reconcile the specificity of individuals to a wider setting of historical events, plays out in his cultural writings more specifically. Those writings, as we have already seen in his discussions of Barnes, Whitman and others, are no less fascinated by what he called the 'vagaries of individual persons' (1973 [1937]: 32), and by the particular quality of 'character' which artists bring to what they do. This is in one respect unsurprising because the work of art is part of its social and historical context only by virtue of those who do the work that is designated art. A materialist account of such things, therefore, cannot afford to overlook the role of the artist any more than it can afford to overlook the role of the crowd in making that work meaningful. Indeed the artist and the audience are what, between them, make culture historically determinate in certain respects, and what means that a materialist approach to these things may be plausible and worth troubling about. On the other hand, as with his emphasis on cultural form,

C. L. R. James' focus on the great artist skates out onto what has often been viewed as dangerously thin intellectual ice.

Here he is, for example, writing at the start of the chapter in *Beyond a Boundary* on the West Indian batsman George Headley: 'I believe that every great batsman is a special organism; it must be so, for they are rare, as rare as great violinists' (1983 [1963]: 139). This is absolutely typical James: a comment capable, and no doubt designed as such, of unsettling political enemies and political bedfellows in equal measure. On the one hand, of course, the comparison of a mere sports player with a virtuoso of the classical music world is part of a wider argument in *Beyond a Boundary* which challenges the established assumption that certain kinds of activity are exclusively praiseworthy as 'art'. On the other hand, this is one of many such comments that can be found in his cricket writing, and indeed in his wider cultural criticism, which define the artist or player that he is describing in terms of a quality which is unthinkable apart from the person in question. A quality which implies that, as he has it in the blunt subtitle to that chapter, a batsman like Headley is 'nascitur non fit': born, rather than made.

And this is puzzling, of course, because in many respects the idea of the natural genius, like the related idea of artistic inspiration, seems to be at odds with any attempt to foreground the historical qualities of art. Sociological discussions of art and literature in general, and Marxist accounts in particular, have tended to be understandably wary of such language. Hence Raymond Williams begins *Culture and Society* (1982 [1958]: especially chapter 2; compare Abrams 1953) by describing the emergence of the modern idea of genius as one part of a whole complex of responses among writers and artists, from the mid-eighteenth century onwards, to the partly liberating, partly threatening shift from patronage relations to a reliance on the purchasing power of a middle-class reading public. This reconception of the idea and ideals of art, and of the status of the artist, allowed a dignifying claim to be made about the enduring worth of creative work in the face of the anonymity of the market, but also served to justify a kind of retreat. A retreat which could easily end, as it often did, in the assumption that true art keeps its hands clean of social grime, being otherworldly or apolitical by definition. It is precisely against these assumptions, and their tendency to romanticise, individualise and depoliticise artistic production that Marxist accounts of such matters have tended to take their stand, from Walter Benjamin's provocative call to reconsider the artist as a producer (Benjamin 1970 [1934]), to more historical summaries of the social production of art (for example, Wolff 1993). In this respect, James' suggestion that a great batsman, like a great musician, is born not made, might well appear to buy into a mystification, a smokescreen which presents the great artist as the recipient of an unfathomable, quasi-divine gift about which no more can be said or asked. Apart from anything else the use of the term 'genius' as a kind of accolade serves to conceal the fact, as Bourdieu's work reminds us, that not everyone has equal access to whatever social resources are necessary to sustain creative originality in a given practice: the time and equipment required to master techniques, the freedom from economic necessity which allows risk-taking, and so forth.

Why, then, would James, who was so concerned to understand cricketing and other artistic achievement in terms of its social and historical conditions, and who knew very well the degree to which assumptions about race or class had historically curtailed the possibilities for creative expression for black or working-class men and women in the modern world; why would the James who knew these things and what they suggest about the historically and socially conditional nature of artistic success or failure, still find it possible to work with the idea of talent as something which is peculiarly and even inexplicably subjective? This is the question that I want to tackle in what follows. No work of secondary literature on James appears to be complete unless it has fashioned some kind of oxymoron in an attempt to describe the unsettling combinations that typify his work, and here I risk adding another to the list: does he offer us a 'materialist account of artistic genius'? Is such a thing, indeed, conceivable? Whether or not we are convinced that he resolves all the issues raised by this troubling proposition, he certainly pushes us, as he pushes us in so many other areas, to think towards the possibility that we are not faced with quite the contradiction in terms that we appear to be. That there may be here, in other words, reasons for keeping together lines of thought which are usually treated as dangerously fissile.

I

The first thing to say is that James' use of this language needs to be related to the questions that were discussed in the first chapter of this study: that is, his recognition that cultural practices such as sport define their own criteria of success and failure which we need to work with, rather than work around. If James talks about genius, as he does, he clearly means genius as established by the categories of achievement specific to particular symbolic activities in which human beings engage. This is, in itself, a kind of sociological qualification to the idea of genius as usually understood. When, for example, he seeks to describe the 'greatness' of his old friend Learie Constantine, in a fond essay from 1969, he does so by describing in the most detailed terms what Constantine achieved in his playing career, and also the particular effect that his play had on those who watched him. James uses two long citations from William Hazlitt, describing his own experience of watching Mrs Siddons in the role of Lady Macbeth, to give some sense of how the ephemeral events of a game of cricket were capable of producing something lasting for its crowds: 'The point about Constantine's fielding', James says, 'is that you came to the ground expecting the moment of artistic truth and were rarely disappointed' (1986: 236). If, then, Constantine's close-catching could be seen as providing an instance of 'artistic truth', it could be so described only because the peculiar forms of action which take place on a cricket field have come to be recognised as particularly consequential in some respect, aesthetically or symbolically. And only by virtue of the further fact that those watching shared this understanding, and therefore felt themselves 'dazzled by the sunburst (especially in the bleak English weather) of a great cricketer at his best' (ibid.), just as Hazlitt felt himself dazzled by Mrs Siddons' performances in her own form of play. To this extent, greatness is a contingent, contextual and ascribed quality: it depends on the social construction of certain categories of value, and on the contemporary acclamation of a particular performance in terms of those categories.

Yet this is not all. It depends also, or it is unthinkable apart from, the existence of Learie Constantine. There was, in other words, a quality or character to Constantine's play which was uniquely his, just as Mrs Siddons' Lady Macbeth was both uniquely hers but, at the same time, one instance in a long history of the playing of a given role. There is here an important corollary to be recognised. James' use of the language of greatness or genius makes it clear that he accepted as self-evident the fact that some individuals carry out creative activities better than others, and that a sociological or historical account of such things cannot avoid participation in such judgements: he clearly saw evaluation as a necessary part of any materialist analysis of cultural activity. Whatever the historical and political meanings of what Constantine achieved, those meanings are accessible for James only through the recognition of his greatness as a cricketer. He would, no doubt, have been sympathetic in many respects to contemporary attempts to storm the ramparts of the old cultural canons, and to open their gates to the many stories and forms of creativity which they have systematically left beyond the walls. Indeed, James himself laid siege to those same targets on more than one occasion, both in the name of overlooked writers from the colonial world such as J. J. Thomas, and in his general willingness to treat seriously popular forms of creativity such as comic strips (an effort which the cultural critics of his day assumed was merely a piece of cuteness on his part: see James 1992: 220). Yet James would also have scorned, it seems to me, any attempt to dissolve the idea of literary or artistic value, as such, whether in the name of cultural relativism, or because such ideas might be seen as inevitably culminating in exclusions and hierarchies. This follows, firstly, from what was argued in the first chapter: unless the fields of creativity sustain judgements of success and failure, and unless those judgements remain compelling to those involved, they cease to offer a social space on which those who are dispossessed in other respects can demonstrate the ways in which they too have the capacity to dazzle. Moreover, artistic or literary evaluation has its own role to play in wider social critique. Put simply, if we are not willing to follow James in admitting the sheer trashiness of much contemporary culture (see, for example, 1993: 36) then we risk losing a critical grip on our times, we risk losing sight of the depredations of capitalism and how much of human creativity and imagination it squanders. Cultural practices cannot point us to better possibilities beyond their own symbolic arrangements, as James certainly believed that they could, unless they also include (and unless we admit the validity of) the judgements of better and worse which take place in terms of those arrangements.

Here, as in other respects, it seems to me that James recognised something important precisely because he was willing to begin by thinking seriously about the lessons of a popular form of culture. After all, success or failure is defined in the course of sporting practice itself in a way that the success or failure of a novel, for example, is not defined in the act of writing or publication. Although sport does include a more fluid question of aesthetic appreciation, of who achieves its particular ends most beautifully (see Todd 2007), those ends themselves are clearly given. Evaluation was self-evidently part of historical understanding for James not least because it is so unavoidably written into the meanings of sport itself: a historical analysis which began by asking 'why was Muhammad Ali a failure?' would be nonsense even before it went any further. It seems an odd turn of events, in this respect, that it should be the same postmodern literary and cultural criticism which often claims to speak on behalf of 'the popular', which also seems to be so chary of evaluation and for which, culturally speaking, anything goes. James, by contrast, continued to insist that among novelists as novelists, and among cricketers as cricketers, there was better and there was worse, and he recognised the necessity of such judgements precisely because he began from the lessons to be drawn from a popular form of creativity.

II

James, then, assumed that cultural activities defined the grounds on which certain kinds of achievement and failure could be recognised. Such judgements are, in his account, not antithetical to a historical understanding of culture, but precisely where such an understanding must begin. It is through recognition of cultural success or failure, defined in terms of the activity in question, that we can begin to ask about the wider social and historical conditions in which that success is, or is not, secured. As I have argued already, James was deeply suspicious of a brute sociology which treated artistic, literary or sporting outcomes as straightforwardly determined by relations of production or by a political context more generally. His insistence on talking about the great player or the great writer is clearly related to this suspicion of 'determinist' accounts of what human beings do. His language repeatedly and deliberately brings us face to face with individual writers or players, and he treats them not as so much glass through which historical truth shines unbroken, but as men and women whose writing or play is historically expressive precisely because it required them to contend, more or less consciously, with particular conditions of possibility and difficulty.

James, it should be admitted, does not always work out the detail of this kind of claim as fully as we might wish; he does not always explain exactly *how* history is, to use a more theoretical term, 'mediated' by the work of such individuals. Often his accounts offer something looser, settling for the negative or ground-clearing claim that the outcomes of cultural practices cannot be wholly explained by factors which are intrinsic to those practices. This is neatly captured, for example, in the title of a motion he proposed during a Cricket Society debate in 1957: 'Neither Toss, Weather nor Wicket were Decisive Elements in the Defeat of Australia Last Season' (1986: 81–6). James warns his audience cryptically at the start of his address: 'I will be speaking to you on two levels [...] I am not going to disguise that the ideas which I am putting forward are governed by a definite attitude to the first-class game' (81). For the most part, however, he confines himself in what he says to precisely the kind of technical minutiae that many of those present no doubt expected the debate to involve: tactics, decisions about field placements and bowling changes and so forth. The secondary 'level' of analysis which he had promised appears mostly in hints and asides.

He talks, for example, about a newly static approach to batting among the Australian team, and relates this to a general sea-change in the culture of the game: 'The wicket is not bad because of what a bowler can make the ball do but because of what is in the hearts of batsmen as individuals' (86). He talks also about a new level of media scrutiny and the degree to which this increasingly exacting attention tends to inhibit expressive freedom on the pitch. Only at the very end of his address does he make explicit what he is implying about the nature of the relationship between these 'two levels' of analysis. Cricketing technique, he concludes, has 'absorbed' something of its wider historical context, of 'a security minded age' (86). The effect in terms of the game is a notable refusal of adventuresome play. Although he does little to fill in the details, the general claim is clear: the 'age' makes itself felt in the game primarily through the changing attentions and demands of its audience and, beyond that, at the level of consciousness or belief, in a sense of what is and is not possible, lodged deep in the hearts and bodies of those who play the game.

We have to take such accounts for what they are, addressed as they often were to audiences who may well have been disconcerted even by James' rather reticent relation of sport to its historical and political context. There are many places, however, where he gives us more to work with. As I suggested in Chapter 2, James' writings are full of detailed analysis, not only of cultural success, but also of failure, of attempts to achieve something in cultural activity which fell short or over-reached. A key example is his brief, elegiac chapter on Wilton St. Hill (1983 [1963]: chapter 7), the great Trinidadian batsman who confounded all expectation by performing abysmally during the 1928 West Indian tour of England. Here again, it is important to recognise that James' account is written in a literary rather than a sociological register. All the same it is, at least to my mind, surprisingly reminiscent of Pierre Bourdieu's description of Léon Cladel (1993a: 69–70; 1996: 262–3), the aspiring bohemian novelist who arrives in Paris from the provinces and is never quite able to overcome the contradictions that arise from this trajectory. It is clear that for James, St. Hill's heartbreaking under-achievement as a batsman, like Cladel's under-achievement as a novelist, has to be understood in terms of his social origins and a resulting lack of self-assurance. For St. Hill, James recognises, the ante on cricketing success was the chance to transcend his place in the black lower-middle class and his life 'selling yards of cloth and ever more yards of cloth over a counter' (1983 [1963]: 96) in a department store. Moreover, as Neil Lazarus has pointed out (1999: 165–8), James presents St. Hill's failure as a historical one in a more profound sense, as a failure to carry the weight of expectation which he bore as the great popular hero of a community in which resistance to British colonialism was becoming increasingly concerted. James barely talks about what happened to St. Hill in England in 1928, but the awfulness of it, in his discreetly veiled account, is that the batsman's wonderful wristy batting started to misfire in such a way that he appeared to confirm the condescending judgement already being passed on him by the London press: that he was guilty of too much 'exotic fancy'. James responds: 'His apparently exotic fancies were exotic only when he mistimed them', before admitting: 'he did so often in 1928' (1983 [1963]: 96). It was, in other words, as if St. Hill were caught in the very historical trap from which he was seeking to escape; an escape which many others were longing him to perform, on his account and on their own.

By James' own comparison, Constantine, whose rise to fame began with his signal success in the same tour, came from a family of real cricketing pedigree and from a social position that gave him 'ancestry' (106): his father held a position as an overseer on an estate, a job which had once been reserved for whites. For reasons that were no doubt partly generational, but also to do with this particular background, Constantine knew 'in his heart' that black men and women were capable of achieving anything that Europeans were capable of achieving. It was, after all, a lesson that he taught to James in what he would later recognise as a pivotal conversation in his life: 'You have it all wrong. You believe all that you read in those books. They are no better than we' (116). And it was this self-certainty, a self-certainty that was both subjective (how could it not be?) but also, in significant ways, of its time, that helped make it possible for Constantine to do what he did in the 1928 tour and afterwards as a professional player in the northern English leagues. In this comparison, then, James provides a careful tracing out of the relationship between what is done in the fields of culture, and a wider political and historical context. He recognises, clearly, that creative daring, which Constantine continued to exhibit all of his playing life, but which failed St. Hill at the crucial moment, is not reducible to intrinsic individual ability. At the same time, his use of the language of genius, or of artistic greatness, indicates his refusal to treat the individuals under discussion as mere conduits for some kind of historical meaning. Instead, James arrives at an understanding of what a Constantine, in all of his sustained brilliance, meant; he arrives at an understanding of what a St. Hill and his desperate under-achievement meant, precisely by working through the complex passages of individual lives across a broader historical and political setting.

III

Constantine provides one example of the dual quality which James took to characterise the truly great performer, whether in sport, literature or the visual arts. This quality is summarised most clearly in the claim, as he makes it for Gary Sobers, that 'All geniuses are merely people who carry to an extreme definitive the characteristics of the unit of civilization to which they belong and the special act or function which they express or practice' (1986: 218). What is interesting about this statement, it seems to me, is its deliberate compounding of two ideas. Firstly, all great artists exhibited, for James, a mastery of what they did. This does not imply, of course, a slavish surrender to cricketing or literary precedent. Far from it, for James it was the peculiar quality of the great artist that their mastery was what sustained their ability to improvise, their ability to establish new and exemplary 'special acts'. Such a claim perhaps brings to mind the brand of cultural traditionalism represented by T. S. Eliot (most obviously 1950: 47–59), but it might equally be seen as an offshoot of that old Marxist insistence that our ability to act appropriately in the here-and-now depends on our awareness of the history that got us here in the first place. This was, certainly, a common enough assertion in James' political writings and even late in his life he would argue in the wake of Walter Rodney's assassination in Guyana that there was a need to return with renewed seriousness to the texts and lessons of a longer revolutionary history (1983). Marxism, of course, has been guilty of venerating its own sacred wood often enough, but in general when James says such things he is looking forward, not back. In his dialectical view the fixing or mastery of a category, including not least a category such as 'batting' or 'writing', is precisely the means of cracking it open and making it new. Tradition is a constant putting-to-use, not a consecration.

Secondly, he insists that a figure like Gary Sobers mattered for more than what he was in himself, even though that 'more' is unreachable apart from what he was in himself. Sobers, in other words, is important not just for what he achieved, but also because his achievement rested on and was acclaimed by a specific community or audience as belonging to them and demonstrating something about them. I do not want to get too waylaid at this point by the much-discussed question of James and nationalism. It is certainly true that his analysis of Frank Worrell, for example, or Charlie Chaplin for that matter, tends to assume the nation as the 'unit of civilisation' to which such figures most obviously belong. But he also considered writers and artists in relation to audiences that were both transnational (Western civilisation, for example, as in his discussion of Alexander Dumas or Alejo Carpentier, 1980: chapter 13) and less than national (such as an oppressed minority, as he argued with regard to Richard Wright). Clearly, for him, as for so many others in the Caribbean, the genius of the great West Indian cricketers or calypsonians from the middle part of the twentieth century was indistinguishable from the nationalist assertion implicit (sometimes explicit) in what they did. But it does not follow that this is the only scale on which his cultural analysis might work, or that what they did could be seen as being meaningful only in one way, or to one particular community.

His general claim, in any case, is that cultural achievement plays a crucial role in the processes by which various kinds of community come to imagine themselves as a community, serving as a kind of symbolic centre-of-gravity for all that far-flung stuff to which we gesture with the word 'identity'. It is in this sense that he famously describes the West Indian cricket crowds bringing with them 'the whole past history and future hopes of the islands' (1986 [1963]: 225) to each match and finding in the performances of a Sobers or a Walcott something that might constitute a 'national tradition', and which might also constitute, therefore, some part of a 'conception of themselves' (ibid.). James made this claim of the relationship between all great performers and their audiences, although he also recognised that historical displacement and long-standing political disenfranchisement meant that cultural achievements took on a particular significance for black men and women in the Caribbean, as he underlines in his essay on one exemplary innovator in an exemplary innovated form: the calypso singer Mighty Sparrow (1977a: 191–201).

It is important to recognise that the two claims that James makes here for greatness are interleaved. The specific claim (that what the genius does is in some sense 'definitive' in terms of a particular activity) and the wider, sociological claim (that what they do becomes part of a process of historical self-definition for those around them) are part of each other. Someone like Sobers was not treasured by the crowds that watched him on the basis of a merely arbitrary symbolism. He was treasured, rather, because what he did was already markedly 'West Indian' in some sense; it was knowable as such because it was shaped in itself by the place where he had learned the game and by the specific social, political and material contingencies of that place. He was, writes James, 'a West Indian cricketer, not merely a cricketer from the West Indies' (1986: 218).

It was on this basis, in a short article from 1967, that James angrily repudiated, not for the first time, the suggestion of an English cricket pundit that Sobers' brilliance was merely a matter of fortunate physique (1986: 215–17). Against this belittling reading of Sobers' significance James deepens and widens, insisting that Sobers' play was in important respects the fruition of an unmistakably West Indian tradition of batting. This tradition, James argues, had its roots in a longer history of popular cricketing practice in the region, and in the ways in which that practice was shaped by the place in which it developed. Most cricketers in the region had been required to learn the game, he says, not on grass pitches, which were few in number and for the few in number, but on strips of matting rolled out to serve as a wicket. Because this matting produced exaggerated bounce and spin, the best batsmen tended to be those who played late, whose weight rested on their back foot, but who became consequently very adept at coming forward to drive the overpitched ball straight or through the covers. The characteristic strengths of West Indian batting, in other words, strengths which made Sobers even as he remade them, were rooted in a particular history of cricketing tradition in the region and of techniques of play which were, to some extent at least, determined by the local conditions in which that play occurred. Conditions means here, before anything else, material conditions in the most earthy sense: any cricketer quickly learns to recognise and respect the particular qualities of pitches and climates, and how these shape what is likely or unlikely to be achievable on a given day. Perhaps, one might go as far as speculating, no thinking cricketer can afford to be totally oblivious to a materialist view of human action. 'Conditions' also means, of course, the exclusions of 'race' and class which led to so many Caribbean cricketers playing on matting wickets in the first place and which, beyond that, shaped the formation of clubs and playing styles on the islands, as James famously discusses in *Beyond a Boundary* (1986 [1963]: chapter 4). All of this, from the ground itself to the social relationships in which the game was embedded, to the attempt of ordinary players to transcend the limits of both in their play, are thus a part of what produced a peculiarly West Indian tradition of which Sobers was, in his time, a 'consummation'.

It is worth reiterating the dialectical sensibility that underlies James' point here. His claim about the representative role of the great artist or writer should not be read as implying something settled or neat, as if the presence of a such a person somehow puts a symbolic capstone on a search for identity, finishing it off or completing it, and sealing it against the historical elements. If such a performer becomes representative this is because the way in which they do what they do makes recognisable the shaping effect of particular social and historical circumstances. It is in this sense that they can be said to belong to a particular time and place, and to belong also to those who feel those historical shapings as their own. But they are not just shaped by history, they also shape it for themselves. Important and necessary political work often gets done through the formation of that finite category: 'us'. It was central to what James called genius that it played a part in the affirmation of such categories and the expression of a shared history around which they might cohere. But at the same time, the lesson of genius, a lesson already taught in the long collective labour on which the achievements of such individuals rested, was the possibility of turning historical limits inside-out, making of them something new and something more. And in this respect his use of the term 'genius' implies a warning against any desire to settle for a moribund traditionalism in any practice, or for a closed and defensive idea of 'us' as an identity. Both would have been, in his view, instances of the futile attempt to 'torture reality [in order] to keep it finite' (1980 [1948]: 47). The best of culture, according to James, does precisely the opposite of this: it makes of the curtailments of a particular context the grounds for something newly creative and expansive. Sobers would be one obvious Caribbean example of how such limits could be turned inside-out. The recycling of discarded oil drums as instruments and from this the development of an entirely new musical tradition called steel-pan, led by innovators such as Spree Simon and Ellie Mannette, would be another (see James 1984: 221; Stuempfle 1995).

IV

James' use of the language of genius, then, involves a judgement which is strictly historical. It reckons greatness in terms of the historical role that a particular figure played in relation to political and social movements more generally. And it understands such significance as itself being made possible because of the longer and wider social labour which sustains even the most seemingly individual act of creative innovation. Yet, having said these things, the terms in which James describes a Gary Sobers or a Jackson Pollock still provide something of a jolt. After all, he was a lifelong proponent of a political project which is usually assumed to be egalitarian in its aims and understandings. Moreover, James is associated particularly with the critique of conventional notions of political leadership, of the vanguard political party, and with a corresponding emphasis on the unbidden creative resistance of ordinary men and women to the strictures of their workaday and domestic lives, and of all that this suggests about the potentiality smothered in such lives: every cook can govern. The idea of innate inequality expressing itself through cultural activities such as sport or literature seems more than a little incongruous when placed side-by-side with the profession of a politics of this kind. Are we to take it that James, who could write of Herman Melville, for example, that he was 'a unique individual, the type of human being who appears but rarely in the history of civilization' (2001 [1953]: 115), believed that to some ineradicable degree, human beings came with different inherent individual capacities and capabilities? That we are, in a word, unequal?

The simple answer to this question, it seems to me, is 'yes'. James would have been quite happy, I think, to join his voice to Terry Eagleton's provocative comment: 'It is hard to see what is so wrong about human inequality' (1998: 48). After all, as I have already noted, his developing critique of Trotskyist political organisation ran alongside an increasingly humanist inflection to his politics: the idea that political struggle was *not* about securing some kind of flat material or developmental equality but rather that it aimed at, and that it involved, the possibility of human beings developing their own collective and individual capabilities to the fullest extent possible: 'Freedom is creative universality, not utility' (1973 [1960]: 115), is how he summarised his view during his lectures on *Modern Politics*, as well as on other occasions. He certainly recognised, in other words, that the danger of equality as an abstraction was that it would override 'the sensuous particularity of individual men and women' (Eagleton 1998: 49; see also Marx 1972 [1875]: 16–17).

His reading of Marx's early writings was an important part of how James came to think through all of this, but no less important, I suspect, was his time in America, face to face with the most advanced capitalist economy of the era and its social consequences:

> In city after city, street after street, [...] the two or three rooms, kitchen and bath, the same breakfast cereal, however disguised, the same ride to work, the work itself, the evening paper, the same radio commentator, the packaged foods, the neighbourhood movie. (1993: 116)

While he did not share Tocqueville's wistfulness for lost aristocratic glories, James did share his predecessor's sense that America was defined by the extraordinary contradiction between its historical promise of heroic individualism and the 'deadly uniformity and monotony' (ibid.) which characterised the lives of most American men and women. More than this, James recognised very astutely the degree to which those past historical promises provided the lure under which the uniformities of mass-production were packaged and sold. The very language which Whitman fashioned in his great celebration of romantic individualism, 'his "body beautiful" and "body electric" and "seminal wetness"', became 'the reservoir from which advertisers of foods, toothpastes, vitamins, deodorants, draw an unending source of inspiration by which to cheat [...] the American people' (60). James, in short, was wary of the claim of equality, not simply because he had read his Marx, but also because he looked around him and he saw what a world made in the image of exchange value might look like. Unlike Adorno, of course, of whom this last comment is so reminiscent, James saw this contradiction as one that ran unresolved and at high tension through all parts of modern social life. His insistence on the fact that great individual acts of creative expression remained possible was part of his rejection of the idea that human beings, in all of their 'sensuous particularity' had been crushed flat by capitalism.

There were other reasons for James to be suspicious of claims about equality. Here, as elsewhere, his reflections on the experiences of those who were designated 'black' in the modern world were clearly an important part of his thinking. A striking example, in this respect, is a short article he wrote in 1946 for *Labor Action*, one of the very few pieces of dedicated sports writing he produced in America, on the occasion of Joe Louis' successful defence of his heavyweight title in a rematch against Billy Conn, who had come close to beating him five years earlier. Here James points out something very significant. On the one hand, in a way that pre-empts much of his later cricket writing, he recognises that Louis' success had become symbolically representative for African-Americans, representative of an emerging political identity, but also straightforwardly representative of what black men and women could achieve given a reasonable opportunity. 'A tense political or social situation', he writes, 'can take the simplest or most commonplace event and make it a symbol of political struggle' (1996a: 60). On the other hand, James points out that Louis' representative significance in this respect is shadowed by a second claim about his representativeness. That is to say, the degree to which the mainstream media in America treated him as a figure of the black population as a whole, so that all of his public behaviour was scrutinised as evidence of what 'negroes' were like. This is what Albert Memmi called, in relation to the perception of colonised populations: 'the mark of the plural' (1965: 85), the synecdoche upon which the concept of 'race' itself relies, whereby whatever Joe Louis achieved, he could achieve it only as someone who bore the levelling horizon of his blackness. This marking, as Memmi recognised, left the colonised, as it left African-Americans, emptied of human particularity. The common description of Louis as a 'model Negro' wasted a word, because to be designated a Negro was to be defined already in terms of a model, it was to be treated as an instance of a type, and to have all achievement or failure read as merely the exemplification of what such a type might be capable or incapable of.

It is at least partly in response to this experience, then, that James was driven to insist on a Marxism refocused around the idea of creative development as both a goal and method of struggle. And this is also, it seems to me, part of the reason why he refused to ditch the language of genius in his description of figures like Joe Louis or George Headley. In an important sense, the idea of genius works against the 'mark of the plural'. To describe such figures as 'born, not made' is to recover something about their humanness, their uniqueness or specificity, out from under the 'made-up-ness' of their racialised identity. Thus, part of what James loved about cricket was precisely the fact that its long, recursive patterns had the effect of stripping away the 'conventional aspects' of its players and allowing 'human personality', as he called it, to become recognisable (1983 [1963]: 195). The 'measured ritualism' of the game, in other words, allied to its symbolic 'apartness', is like those other rituals famously described by Victor Turner (1977), in which ascribed social identity is stripped away, and a space created in which social structure is, if not suspended, then at least rendered 'see-through'. Only momentarily, of course, but nevertheless, as Turner noted (128), a quality which makes ritual a close cousin to art. And cricket, in James' account, unquestionably belonged under that name.

Of course, in an important sense, the figures so revealed are still like us, indeed like us all the more for being so revealed. But they are like us in their inequality: that is to say that they show to us something of what Marx called our 'species being', our shared capacity for self-determination, even within and against the social and historical limits of our lives. The genius is a figure of human possibility in all of its riot of variety and unpredictability, on which we all have a claim.

Such an argument, of course, cuts both ways. In using the language of genius James was reasserting the uniqueness of particular individuals against the flattening assumptions of racists. But that same language marks a kind of limit, or a caution, against the danger of a black audience celebrating the successes of a Joe Louis or George Headley as a solely black achievement. Of course James knew why such celebrations took place, and he himself cheered without equivocation those figures who, through their efforts, allowed dispossessed communities to recognise and revel in the fact that 'they are no better than we are'. All the same he clearly also saw that the idea of 'race' could become a trap, even for those who wielded it defensively, or because it had been forced on them in the first place. One of James' most famous statements, a statement which became part of the epitaph on his grave in Tunapuna, reads: 'it is not the quality of goods or utility which matter, but movement: not where you are or what you have, but where you have come from, where you are going, and the rate at which you are getting there' (1986 [1963]: 116–17). The roots of this statement, it seems to me, lie a long way back in a series of articles James wrote for *Socialist Appeal* shortly after his arrival in America, in which he specifically sought to make clear that the concept of 'race' is a social construction, not a biological given. His way of doing this was to historicise the idea: in studying the question of 'race', he argued, we must, as with any social question, 'see it from all sides and particularly [...] see in what direction it is moving, what is likely to happen tomorrow'. The 'very opposite' of this dialectical method, he continued, is the treatment of 'race' as a cause in itself: the assumption, for example, that because a white worker gets selected over a black worker, the 'Negro problem is a race problem' (1939c: 3). He reiterated this point with some urgency in the next column in the series: 'History is moving very fast. That is why it is necessary to know where we come from, where we are, and infinitely more important, in what direction we are moving' (1939d: 3). It is precisely an access to this sense of movement, of change and possibility, which is implicit in James' use of the language of genius. In this it challenges the racist's idea of race as something which stabilises and fixes human difference, packing it away into eternally tidy boxes. But, by the same token, it acts as a warning to those forced by historical circumstance into a form of anti-racist racism, not to forget that such ideas are useful only as a means to movement or change. In the end, for James, the great achievements of truly creative individuals point us not towards static answers to the questions of who we are, or what we have, but towards the historical and always forward-looking question of where we have come from and where we may yet reach.

V

James, then, recognises that the judgement about greatness in sport, literature or any other human activity is, of necessity, a historical judgement. This is the case because such judgements are made in terms of the categories of value specific to particular kinds of human activity which have been historically construed, and which, moreover, occur in particular places and times, with audiences for whom cultural achievement or success is always likely to come to matter for more than its own intrinsic and largely arbitrary reasons. To say all of this, however, is a very different thing from saying that the existence of genius is historically predictable. Or, indeed, that it is somehow historically called forth. Here, then, there is a last question around the concept of greatness as James uses it. If, as he argues, the play of a Rohan Kanhai filled a historical need for those who watched him take guard in the Caribbean, did that need somehow bring a Kanhai into being? Is the genius the person who happens to be, in the way that they happen to be, because in some historical sense it is necessary that they should be? Here, as might be expected, James' use of the term marks a further limit; a limit against theories which explain human beings and their actions in terms of history, instead of understanding history in terms of the human beings and human actions which constitute it.

He broaches many of these issues, of course, in *Beyond a Boundary*, but he returned to them more concertedly in the essays that he wrote on a number of the great West Indian cricketers in the later part of the 1960s. And most particularly when he returned to reconsider George Headley, the sportsman 'born, not made', in a piece for a book edited by John Arlott in 1967. James begins that essay by explicitly foregrounding the question of the relationship between individual talent and social context. He starts off with a bare-bones summary of Headley's achievements in the game and then says, startlingly: 'That historical account is, for historical purposes, quite adequate. However, it leaves unanswered the question of questions.' And that question of questions is, of course: 'how comes it that a little West Indian boy untaught [...] would have made himself into a cricketer who would have been welcome in any eleven that has existed in England or Australia between 1886 and the present day?' Having framed the question in this way, James continues: 'when all allowances are made for qualitative individuality, for historical idiosyncrasy, we still remain face to face with a miracle. And with a miracle one either faces up to it or evades the issue behind a barrage of words of [sic] mystification of phrases' (1986: 191).

James goes on, then, to 'face up to the miracle of George Headley' (ibid.) on three grounds. First of all, he describes his 'qualitative individuality', those particular personal and bodily qualities without which he would not have been George Headley, and which James, with his sharp eye for playing style, describes in detail. Secondly and thirdly, he describes two related issues: what Headley learned of the game of cricket and how he managed to learn it. Here, drawing on his own conversations with Headley, he summarises in a now familiar way the historical positioning of the sport in the development of West Indian society. This includes, of course, the central place which cricket had come to hold in popular culture, which gave Headley both context and reason to learn the game, which allowed him to watch and learn also the lessons of the great players who visited the region, and which ultimately gave to his play something of the 'glamour of [cricket's] best days', James says, 'just at the time when the game was about to sink into its present defensive spell' (201). Yet James' point in separating out these different factors in this way is not to turn any one into a simple explanation of the others, but rather to insist on their mutual causality. His point, one might say, is to treasure the miracle rather than dispel it. Headley could not have been what he was historically apart from what he was personally, apart from his qualitative individuality. But nor could those individual qualities in themselves have transcended his social and historical context. They found a way to some kind of fruition because of, and in response to, the popular political energies which were themselves being canalised in the game at that time. It is the close entanglement of these things which is what matters to James: the fact that they are 'tightly intertwined, closer to being strands of a unity, than they appear at first sight' (191–2). The miracle is not simply Headley happening to be. Rather it is the inextricability of his happening to be and the context in which he came to be.

Towards the end of the essay James makes this clearer as he takes stock: 'Now after all this analysis, the opening of historical avenues of investigation, and so on, the entity which makes all the information and perspective alive, that entity is George Headley, the unique individual who has brought all these material facts into an existential vividness, the entity without whom they would be mere statistics and observations on a sheet of paper' (201). He goes on to insist that there is no way of conclusively marking the line at which the individual ends and the social or historical begins. The miracle, rather, is that we might learn to see something of our social and historical circumstances – 'these material facts' – more clearly because they are given 'existential vividness' in one supremely talented person and that, conversely, the other side of the same claim, this person could become what they become only because those circumstances are a part of their becoming. That these things are 'tightly intertwined', twist over dialectical twist, into something close to a unity.

I read James' description of Headley as a genius, then, and his use of the language of genius generally, as a way of leaving space for the human messiness of history and the unpredictability of individual creativity. As a way of leaving space for everything that Derek Walcott calls the 'sheer *is*', and which he inexplicably accuses James of overlooking (1995: 42–3). Yet it is also a recognition of the fact that Headley's genius was not just an achievement of his own, but one reliant on a whole popular social and political context which was entangled in formative, material ways, as well as in emotional and political ways, with what he achieved. Here, as in all of the best of his writing on sport or art James strives to develop a historical explanation of something which does not explain out of existence the very thing that is its concern. This was, as he puts it in his discussion of Melville, the 'fatal' mistake that threatens any attempt to relate the products of human creativity to 'the social movement': the danger that such explanatory effort forces the very thing that it is explaining to 'fade into the background [and to] become a mere expression of social and political ideas' (2001 [1953]: 115). This is the great balancing act which defines James' whole approach to understanding culture. Indeed, it was the great balancing act of his politics in general, characterised as this came to be by a willingness to accept, rather than by a desire to resolve, that open and productive tension in Marxism between, on the one hand, a recognition of the degree to which we are products of our historical circumstances and, on the other, an emphasis on the never wholly predictable human ability to change those circumstances.

Years before, in that period of his life in which he was most vigorously rethinking all of these things, James had written to Constance Webb describing the experience of discovering 'the world around you, its infinite diversity' and 'accidentalness', and yet, miraculously, the fundamental logic of society, the 'necessity' of development. As Hegel says: 'all chance is the expression of necessity. And all necessity expresses itself by chance' (1996b: 79). Although he might not, in later years, have accepted all of this language without qualification, one can recognise that here he was grappling with a question in regard to cultural practices which was no less central to his politics. Bringing the two claims together we can perhaps summarise his point as follows: we cannot fully explain, in a way that is sociologically adequate, or in a way that is adequate to historical materialism, the 'chance' of a George Headley. Nor should we want to do so, because such predictability would come at the cost of imposing on processes of social and historical change a kind of rigor mortis. Not for nothing did James point out that the first West Indian Test match victory against England depended on the skill of two, young unheralded spin-bowlers, thus teaching a lesson to those 'critics of a sociological turn of mind [who] had proved that we are a nation which naturally produced fast bowlers' (1983 [1963]: 148). And the lesson, of course, was that 'we are moving too fast for any label to stick' (ibid.). What we *can* do, however, is explain how and why a George Headley became something more than a mere 'chance', we can recognise what popular political energies found their chance in him, found their vividness in him, learned to see how fast they were moving in him. And, by the same token, what sense of himself he found in them.

To put it another way: one cannot reduce the arbitrariness, the 'accidentalness', of the great player in James' account because that arbitrariness is indistinguishable from their concrete specificity, and from the vividness of what they achieve. But this is not, as it might be for a certain kind of romanticism, all that there is to say, because the accidental and vivid expression of the life that is in one particularly talented individual is, for James, the specific example of what he saw as a general necessity. Not necessity as a grand historical logic flattening out the peculiarities, the subjective qualities of human experience in the name of a pre-given purpose, but precisely the opposite: the necessity, common to all, to struggle to live the life that is in us even as that brings us into conflict with what passes for life for so many under capitalism. He did believe that the great players and artists were gifted in specific ways, and that what they achieved was partly made possible by an urgent subjective need to give expression to those gifts. as he wrote on Frank Woolley, in an article I have already discussed: 'he played the game that was in him to play' (1938a). And yet, unique as Woolley's gifts may have been in some respects, James took that desire for self-expression or for creative flourishing to be inseparable from what it was to be a human being. Indeed, a few years later, writing to Constance Webb, he would say in words that closely echo his comment on Woolley: 'It isn't that one does this or that "for socialism". No. One does this or that because in society as it is today, a substantial number of people are created who to express themselves and live the life that is in them, refuse to be bound by old traditions and ideas' (1996b: 150).

Conclusion

James, to put it colloquially, had a thing about satellites. In the public lectures which are collected and published as *Modern Politics*, for example, he takes the satellite as the characteristic product of a world dominated by the politics of the planner and the technician. A world in which, in other words, men and women were driven to 'constantly produce more means of production, and constantly improve means of production [... even when ...] they have become means of destruction pure and simple' (1973 [1960]: 102). A little earlier, in *Facing Reality*, he and his collaborators had used 'Hydrogen bombs and Sputnik' (James, Lee and Chaulieu 1970 [1958]: 45) similarly, summoning them up as evidence of the destructive wastefulness of what they called an 'official society' in which all vestiges of human 'ends' had been devoured by what were once the mere means towards such ends. Sputnik, they argued, was the objective correlate of a 'vertigo' (47) gripping the ruling class and of the fact that the perfection of political control had become the single compelling rationale of that class; a rationale in pursuit of which everything, including social life itself, was expendable. Here, as elsewhere, James treated Stalin and Hitler not as aberrations but as exemplifications of what might yet lie in store for modern capitalist societies.

If such an account questions, as it obviously does, a bourgeois view of progress, it questions also a Marxism which places uncritical faith in technological development as a cause of social change in its own right, somehow apart from the issue of the social relationships entailed in the production or deployment of that technology. There is, in other words, an explicit scepticism in James' later writing with regard to Marxism's alliance with what he calls 'dead rationalism', a rationalism in which the intellectual adventure of scientific discovery had been appropriated to the quest for mastery over both human and natural resources. It was in this respect that he and his collaborators insisted on the importance of a Marxism willing to think through its own tendency to emphasise means over ends, and willing therefore to displace the question of the ownership of technology in favour of a restatement of the proper aims of political struggle: space for collective creative potential, social relationships free from systematic exploitation and 'the free development of the individual personality, the right of the meanest intelligence to wander through the strangest seas of thought' (70).

Even, indeed, in one of those short stories which James wrote for his young son Nobbie in the 1950s, separated as they then were by the Atlantic Ocean and the hostility of the American immigration agencies, the main characters find themselves stranded at one point on a satellite which has spun loose from its orbit, and which is heading out into the cold of deep space. As elsewhere in these stories Boongko and Boo-boo-loo are rescued by the timely intervention of the superheroic Mighty Mouse, who tells them to return home with the advice for their friends to 'work as hard as you can studying satellites and missiles guided by the stars [...] There are some people on earth who are playing with these two things and preparing for war and they don't know what they are doing' (2006: 118). In the end, Mighty Mouse helps them push the satellite 'back into the shed' of 'Nicolas the worker'. James' simple but serious lesson for his son was, clearly, about the importance of judging technology by its usefulness to people, rather than understanding people as merely the makers or subjects of technology.

I mention all of this because the same lesson is there, bringing us full circle, in James' most famous description of that conspicuous genius of twentieth-century cricket, Gary Sobers. As I have argued already, James' various discussions of Sobers often begin with a deliberate repudiation of those accounts of him which naturalised his talent in such a way as to make it appear unconscious and instinctual, animal rather than human. Against such a view he insists on Sobers' careful and conscious mastery of technique and, as I have already described, the specificity of the context in which he learned to play, and by which his play was shaped. But more than this, and as with Headley, James points out how Sobers, in all of his sensuous particularity, responds to and redeems a world of which the satellite was an exemplary product. In a wonderful passage he asks the reader to imagine that world as the start of the third day of the 1966 Oval Test approaches, with the West Indies behind in the game and heading for probable defeat. James then presents his reader with a journey made from precisely a satellite's eye view, skimming over 'the crowded towns and hamlets of the United Kingdom', the 'scattered villages of the Caribbean', 'the green hills and veldt of Africa', 'the remote sheep farms of Australia', the plains and mountains of India and past 'planes making geometrical figures in the air above the terrestrial globe' (224). All these places are unified, in his visualisation, by the question being asked at some point in each: whether Sobers could make 200 and lead his team to a dumbfounding victory. The imagery here is quite deliberate, because later in the piece James specifically describes Sobers as a figure capable of responding to 'the age of Telstar' and the world dominated by 'engineers'.

His point, it seems to me, and the ultimate point in his use of the language of genius generally, is to show how the question of what one human being might achieve puts us within reach of a perspective on 'the human' as such. Against the vertigo of the powerful, against a world in which means dominated ends, the great acts of creative endeavour raise us to somewhere where we can start to recognise afresh what it might mean to talk about human potentiality. What Sobers in his individual brilliance made possible, for James, was the question of what is possible for us all. An open question, and one which turns the idea of genius inside-out. Instead of treating that concept as one which clinches a fatalistic assumption about inequality, it turns it into a provocation, a proposition or an invitation to imagine again what any one of us might be. What we might be in all of our wondrous individual diversity but also, equally and interrelatedly, in and through our inescapable need of each other's society.

5
Uses

Introduction

Any study, such as this one, which focuses particularly on C. L. R. James' cultural writing should expect to face, at some stage, a challenge. Such a challenge might come from one of two directions, both of them leading ultimately towards the blunt question: why? On the one hand, it could well be asked: what justification is there, given James' wider political and historical concerns, for singling out for consideration his interest in, and his analyses of, art and literature, sport, film and other kinds of creative or symbolic activity? As Selwyn Cudjoe pointed out following the publication of the *C. L. R. James Reader* (1992), there is a danger of James becoming a staple reference in the discussions of cultural and literary theorists – much as has Frantz Fanon, for example (Robinson 1993) – in such a way that his lifelong struggle for revolutionary social change gets shuffled discreetly off-stage in accounts of his work or in the way in which that work gets used contemporarily. Or worse, that James is used to lend a radical glamour to increasingly inward-looking academic discussions and expositions. Indeed, it has been alleged that James himself turned towards questions of culture in the period of his life following his departure from America as a response to his growing sense of detachment (geographical but also intellectual) from the work of those political groups of which he had been both member and mentor, or even that this apparent shift in his concerns was a means of organising a retreat from Marxism more generally (Paul Buhle, for example, goes some way towards suggesting this in his biography of James, 1988: chapter 4). It follows from such claims, or at least so it could be argued, that a specific focus on James' cultural writing risks celebrating something which was, in certain respects, a defeat.

On the other hand, from a more strictly sociological perspective, a different question might be asked, but with similar effect: if what is interesting about James' approach to culture is that it seeks to reveal important things about the wider social and historical conditions in which cultural stuff is made or used, if this is what matters about his approach to such things, why not skip the culture? In other words, why not simply study the history, the politics or the social movement directly? Both questions, in their different ways, suggest that there is something potentially disingenuous or wasteful about the effort to focus on James' cultural thought. Or that, at the least, carts are being put before horses.

One way of responding to such questions is to insist on the deep-seated unity of James' approach. We are, of course, now expected to be suspicious of such claims, and unity or totality have become dirty words so far as some kinds of intellectual discussion are concerned. They were not so for James, although this does not mean that his thinking was perfectly coherent. As I have argued already, precisely because so much of what he wrote was framed in the context of day-to-day political activism, James' arguments contain a certain amount of circumstantial position-taking. Yet, as Neil Lazarus rightly insists (1999: chapter 3), if there is one characteristic that can be appropriately labelled Jamesian, it is the struggle to treat seemingly disparate experiences and phenomena together, to seek out the relationships between the politics of class and 'race', for example, between the overlapping histories of the Atlantic world, between British Puritanism and Caribbean street traditions or Western classicism and the radio soap opera.

No doubt James might be accused, on this score, of that forlorn longing for a lost totality which Robert Young claimed was the nostalgic heart of Marxist visions of the world and of history (1990: chapter 2). Such an accusation has bite, of course, only if we assume that capitalist modernity has not, in real and traceable ways, led to damaging forms of social fragmentation. Or, perhaps, if we accept a counsel of despair which says that such fragmentation is irresistible. James, needless to say, would have scorned both suggestions. And the fact that the synoptic reach of his thinking so often brings us up sharp, that it is such a challenging, provocative or even inspiring part of reading his work is, it seems to me, itself sufficient evidence of the reality of these social and historical fractures, just as it is evidence of the possibility of contesting them.

In this respect, then, one might argue there is simply no conclusive line to be drawn between James' cultural writings and his politics, or between his historical analyses and those he provides of novels, films or sport. This seems to me to be broadly true, which is why I have sought, at various points in this study, to demonstrate how his conclusions regarding political questions affected those which he arrived at regarding cultural questions, and vice versa. Moreover, as his letters to Constance Webb make all too clear, James never stopped thinking about art and literature, form and audience, even when these concerns did not break the surface of his public writings. Anna Grimshaw is surely right to argue that questions of literary and artistic creativity were never far from his politics, and that it is important not to participate in a posthumous dismembering of James' legacy in this regard (Grimshaw 1992).

Having said this, however, we need to tread carefully. James' first response to the kind of challenges which I have imagined here, it seems to me, would not have been to defend his interest in culture on grounds of its political expediency. He would rather, I suspect, have insisted that culture matters in its own right. As I have argued from the outset, James consistently rejected the claim that the many activities which can be grouped under the name 'culture' required some sort of political justification, just as he rejected the idea that success in those activities could be judged on the basis of an author's politics. What I want to look at, in what follows, is precisely the question of the 'uses' of culture in James' account, of what culture might help us see, socially speaking, and what it might help us to do, politically speaking. Yet it is crucial to begin with the reiteration that whatever those uses might be they belong to cultural objects and practices in and of themselves. We are not justified, in this respect, in wanting to wish away the peculiar demands of cultural practices in order to arrive more quickly at a political destination. Rather, as I will argue in due course, James turns that old demand about, insisting that our politics needs to admit, rather than exclude, the desires and longings which express themselves in those practices.

I

A way of beginning to justify, or to flesh out, this claim is to make explicit James' essentially hopeful (and hope-providing) assumption that cultural practices produce a space in which, or by virtue of which, it can become possible to achieve a critical reflection on social conditions more generally, and that this is the case precisely because those practices are defined as being 'apart', in some respects, from the wider social world. I have outlined this argument briefly already in the first chapter of this study, but it is worth elaborating on some of the implications here. The distinctiveness of cultural practices is a matter of symbolic or formal definition, of course, but such definitions have their history, and these histories make them socially consequential. For James it is this symbolic distinctiveness which means that cultural fields can become the places where we can learn to see truths about our social existence in often startling or disquieting ways. We can get a clearer sense of the distinctiveness of his position by comparing it with the view of cultural politics which featured in and was popularised by the work of the late Edward Said, for example, notwithstanding the latter's own interest in James (for example, 1990). Said's argument in *Orientalism* (2003 [1978]) famously emphasises the degree to which imperial power rested (and still rests) on the construction and perpetuation of images of self and other through the control of knowledge formation in various kinds of literary, scientific, historiographical and popular cultural discourses. Epoch-making as this argument has proved to be, it leads into problems which are almost as famous as its original claims. Not the least of these is the fact that Said's representation of cultural and intellectual production as the necessary accomplice of power appears to leave very little space for the possibility of critical thought. As a number of critics have pointed out, the presuppositions of Said's account suggest, paradoxically, that his own critical project should be impossible (see, for example, Ahmad 1992: chapter 5; Moore-Gilbert 1997: chapter 2).

James, in common with Said, continually emphasises the ways in which cultural practices provide us with 'ways of seeing the world' (Hamilton 1992). For him, however, such ways of seeing the world were very often at odds with the vision of things that ruling groups might wish to promote. There are various reasons why James insisted on this claim. Not the least of these is his recognition that dispossessed communities have often sustained critical and at least partially autonomous creative traditions amongst themselves. James, like du Bois before him, realised the degree to which enslaved and ex-slave communities, for example, had cultivated what might be called (without any belittling undertone) a folk sociology, a reflective consideration of collective experience and of suffering which frequently found its expression in vernacular story-telling practices, in syncretic or millenarian religious beliefs, or in particular forms of music, dance and festival (compare Burke 1978). Like du Bois, James learned this partly as a result of time spent among impoverished rural black communities in America. This included his involvement, as agitator and organiser, in the sharecropper's strike in south-east Missouri in 1942. James facilitated, in that context, the writing of a pamphlet in which the strikers' demands were publicly justified and which is vibrant with their shrewd reading of their own social experiences, and of the causes and consequences of their treatment at the hands of employers and state agencies (1977a: chapter 6; see also 1996a: 22–34). It was precisely this sense of the fierce critical resources to be found in long-defended popular cultural traditions which led du Bois to preface each chapter of *The Souls of Black Folk* with snatches of musical notation drawn from the sorrow songs (see also 1978 [1900]; 1986 [1926]), just as it led James to produce a wonderful pamphlet version of Roosevelt's 'fireside chats', in which the president's tone of patriarchal authority is 'dubbed over' by the vernacular scepticism of 'native son' (see 1996a: 17–22). It led, more generally, to James' consistent refusal to ignore the possibilities of distancing and questioning that were contained in those cultural practices of which ordinary men and women were the innovators and defenders.

James departs more markedly still from Said in his insistence that even in those cultural forms whose production or distribution is controlled by elites, and in which we might therefore expect to find the clearest evidence of an effort to justify domination, there are vulnerabilities to be recognised and subversive forms of meaning-making to be taken into account. Cricket was one obvious context where this was true: few of the crowd who watched Learie Constantine fire the ball past the head of the Honourable F. S. G. Calthorpe, captain of the MCC touring side in 1926, could have failed to understand the implicit meaning of that aggression, or what was revealed by Calthorpe's inability to cope with it (1983 [1963]: 111). But this was not only true of cricket. As we have seen, James insisted that even mass-produced cultural forms could become the context in which potentially explosive social contradictions made themselves felt anew, and by virtue of which an audience might recognise with particular clarity the nature of their experience and the power of a possible collective response. As proof of this James pointed, apart from anything else, to the telling fact that the producers of mass culture were themselves clearly on their guard against such dangers. He noted more than once that the magnates of the popular press or of movie-making repeatedly refused to sanction material which might give symbolic expression to particular social antagonisms (a comic strip dealing 'realistically with the life of a Negro family' would, he argued, lead to 'riots in a dozen cities' (1993: 158)). Conversely, James noted, those same elites were careful not to use their various products as the mouthpiece of overt propaganda precisely because they recognised that popular audiences refused to be preached to in this way. The caution exercised by those who controlled the most commercialised forms of cultural production was, for James, a compelled admission that the

American public retained a strong sense that the resulting products were at some level 'theirs'. That they retained, if nothing else, a kind of negative sanction in this respect: the right to turn their backs on productions which appeared to refuse their role as the 'arbiter' (36) of their possible meanings.

In short, culture for James, by virtue of its particular and objectifying forms, is a highly uncertain context for the attempted reproduction of unequal social relationships. This is the case not least because, as this last point makes clear, the attempt to turn specific symbolic practices or cultural forms to political purposes often requires power, as it were, to break cover, to reveal itself in the extent to which it tramples on the formal autonomy of the cultural practices which it intends to make its instruments (as in the case of General Carey Bernard's segregation of races at Taranto). And this in turn implies the point just made: that the popular audiences for cultural practices play their own role in deciding on the meaning of those practices, and are often more than willing to cheer the anti-hero they are supposed to denounce or to pick out those verses which promise liberation for the oppressed from texts which they have been encouraged to read for lessons of humility and submission.

James' insistent defence of the liberating possibilities of cultural practice contrasts not just with *Orientalism*'s air-tight theory of discourse, but also with the approach of other writers as well. Take Pierre Bourdieu, for instance. Bridget Fowler has argued convincingly, in my opinion, that Bourdieu's account of the social world leaves more space than his detractors allow for the possibility of action informed by a sceptical self-awareness, and for the possibility of change generally (2006; 2007: 65–7). This is certainly clear in his discussion of sport where he is careful to insist, for example, that 'sporting practice, in its technical "intrinsic" definition, always presents a great elasticity, thus offering a greater availability for usages that are altogether different and even opposed' (Bourdieu 1990: 163; compare Baucom 1999: chapter 4). Bourdieu, in other words, emphasises what he calls the 'objective polysemia' (ibid.) of sports, the degree to which the same activity can be appropriated in different ways and can become the site of various and contesting symbolic meanings. James obviously anticipates such a claim in many respects and in this, as in his account of the refraction of social and historical tensions through sport, he shares significant theoretical ground with Bourdieu (see Smith 2006b). Nevertheless, there are recognisable differences of emphasis as well. Bourdieu ends the essay I have just referred to by suggesting that the bodily disciplines of sport will often serve to reproduce social conformity. There is, he argues, an important link between the learning of such disciplines, which take a more extreme form in the drill-halls and parade-grounds of the military, and the enforcement of a kind of pre-conscious acceptance of social authority: 'obedience is belief', writes Bourdieu, 'and belief is what the body grants even when the mind says no' (Bourdieu 1990: 167). Hence he ends his essay with what is a more or less characteristic underscoring of the general tendency of a particular kind of cultural practice to solidify, rather than unsettle, social order. Sport is, he suggests, among those practices which 'by symbolizing the social, contribute to somatizing it' (ibid.). That is to say, sport is one of the many ways in which social authority gets under our skin.

For James, by complete contrast, it is precisely the bodily quality of sport which puts it beyond easy reach of the forces of social authority. Famously, in *Beyond a Boundary*, he argues that cricket reproduces many of the central postures of dramatic art: attack, defence, defiance, cooperation etc. Moreover and more importantly, though, he goes on to argue that it entails also the repeated performance of physical movements or actions from which, in the end, a merely circumstantial significance falls away, and which speak to something which is elemental in human beings and lies at the heart of our response to all great works of visual art. Some commentators have found this claim inadequately defined, or merely mystical (see the useful discussion by McKenzie 1995), yet it is worth noting that James explicitly pre-empts this charge. For him, it is clear, there is a strictly material and historical question here. We respond to these bodily actions, he says, because they are part of who we have historically become: 'The use of the hand, the extension of its powers by the tool, the propulsion of a missile at some objective and the accompanying refinements of judgement, these marked us off from the animals' (1983 [1963]: 203). These movements and our responses to them, in other words, are the 'common possession' (204) of human beings, given to us not by a once-and-for-all human nature but by virtue of our historically shaped bodies. This does not mean that such things are somehow unchangeable and James talks in the same place about the rise of a new 'angular jerk' (199) in batting which he sees as akin to, and born of the same social context as, Cubism. It is, however, very obviously true that James had no qualms about talking of shared human qualities, possibilities and longings, any more than did Marx. Any more, indeed, than can any proponent of a politics which argues that some social arrangements are better for us than others and which therefore assumes that there are terms in which such judgements can be made.

The important point so far as the present discussion is concerned, in any case, is that it is precisely because he saw sport entailing particular bodily qualities that James rejected the idea that it could be regarded primarily as part of an ideological apparatus, a means of 'appeasing or distracting the urban masses on their way to democracy' (206). The physicality of sport is what helps it, in crucial respects, elude the control of the powerful. The playing of a given shot or a moment of brilliant reflex action in the field is, after all, instantaneous. Such moments and the response they elicit from those who see them are, in that respect, inalienable: they cannot be bought or owned, they cannot be hung in a private art collection or left to adorn the lobby of a company which manages hedge funds. They are inalienable, therefore, in that they offer a form of tactile pleasure and recognition to anyone who sees them. This is where he departs from the great cricket writer Neville Cardus, of course, whose defence of the sport's aesthetic qualities stumbles, according to James, precisely because he refused to believe that the mass of ordinary spectators were capable of a response of this sort. James' rebuttal, in a nutshell, is that they are capable of such a response precisely because they have bodies. Moreover, he says, simply listen: 'The spontaneous outburst of thousands at a fierce hook or a dazzling slip-catch, the ripple of recognition at a long-awaited leg glance, are as genuine and deeply felt expressions of artistic emotion as any I know' (203).

Here James departs not just from Cardus, but moves further away also from Bourdieu (see Bourdieu 1993b: chapter 15). The latter saw in the growing division between sports' glamorised professionals and its paying fans a loss of autonomy, the ever clearer encroachment into a distinctive sporting practice of the imperatives of the market. The same development also explained, in Bourdieu's view, a new shallowness in the critical and aesthetic response of such fans, for whom sport increasingly became a scene of mere excitement, an excuse for blinkered partisanship, or a source of relentlessly accounted statistical data (1993b: 124). James would not have denied the creeping intrusion of the market with regard to sport or other cultural practices, but he would have denied the idea of its triumph. The crowds still flocked to cricket, he argued, because it speaks to a need which they continued to recognise for themselves and in themselves: a grasp 'at a more complete human existence' (1983 [1963]: 206). For all of the Norman Tebbits who seek to reduce the game to a test of national loyalty, for all of the marketeers who seek to make it simply the occasion for further advertisements, the game could still provide its viewers a renewed sense of human possibility. And that sense might appear in a flash during some scruffy backyard game, on an overcrowded maidan, or in any of the other places where the game was played and organised by ordinary people for its own sake. Such possibilities could be eliminated only through the destruction of the game itself, or by the destruction of humanity of those who watched it.

The general point from the foregoing discussion, then, is that for James culture makes possible new and sometimes liberating visions of the world and of ourselves. In *Notes on Dialectics* he describes, in the disarming conversational tone which characterises that book, the relationship between understanding and reality: 'Reality says: "Thought. Here are some new bits of me. They make a whole but I don't know what I am and you don't know. But take these scraps that I give you, organize your lenses, and you can tell me what I am, for without you I shall never know"' (1980 [1948]: 42). Cultural practices are, we might say, some of those lenses by which thought may come to organise the accessible scraps of reality into something whole and purposeful. Certainly this is the vision which James believed was made possible by a whole range of cultural practices in the Caribbean from calypso to carnival to cricket, and which allowed those who lived on the region's scattered 'scraps' of land, as he repeatedly called them, to see themselves as part of something newly whole, something nameable, something with a story to be told, even though that vision was itself only a beginning, and needed to be substantiated in ways that were not merely cultural.

II

So far, so hopeful. James' emphasis on the critical opportunities which cultural practices can afford their audiences is clear enough, as is his insistence on the stubbornly independent forms of meaning-making in which those audiences could engage in response to such practices. To a large extent, I have argued, James did not lose sight of this because he, in common with other writers from the colonised world, was familiar with a historical situation in which the spaces of symbolic and creative expression were often all that remained open to disenfranchised populations and the only context wherein a critical reflection on social experience, however dim or refracted, was able to carry on. However, we might well ask, does James' wilful optimism in this regard drown out what should be a more honest and more pessimistic intellectual conclusion as regards the political effects of cultural practices? Is he guilty, in other words, of overlooking or underestimating what many of his fellow Marxists would call the hegemonic role of culture: the degree to which both high and popular forms of creativity can serve to reproduce ways of seeing the world, and ways of seeing others, which sustain rather than subvert systematic forms of oppression?

The tension between James' often optimistic reading of cultural forms and their often regressive political content is neatly expressed in an anecdote given towards the end of Farrukh Dhondy's biography. Dhondy recalls the elderly James responding to a young questioner who had asked him about the racism in D. W. Griffith's film *Birth of a Nation*, which was then being shown retrospectively in London. James, according to Dhondy, reflected for a moment before suggesting: 'I would recommend you go and see it in the morning and picket in the afternoon' (2001: 136). This was not, it should be noted, merely an off-the-cuff or smart alec answer on James' part. Two decades earlier, he had admitted, talking to an audience in the Caribbean, that this was exactly the course of action on which he had himself decided, faced with a showing of the same film in America (1973 [1960]: 134–5). There is, it seems to me, something quite telling here, and something which provides us with a significant pointer with regard to James' whole approach to the question of culture and ideology.

On the one hand, as his call for a picketing makes clear, James was certainly not unaware of the degree to which cultural products such as Hollywood films helped shape and define contemporary racism. Nor was he unaware of the degree to which they fostered a historical amnesia with regard to both the systematic violence attendant on slave production and the continual resistance of the enslaved themselves. Indeed, James discussed these issues directly on a number of occasions (for example 1996a: 46–8), and campaigned actively in this regard. As instigator of the National Negro department of the Socialist Workers Party in America he would have been central to the Party's campaign denouncing *Gone With the Wind* in 1939. In an issue of *Socialist Appeal* from the end of that year the department (for which we can read, in all probability, 'James') condemns the film as 'false from beginning to end', and 'as likely to stimulate old prejudices and hatreds which were the natural outcome of chattel slavery and which must continue on the basis of the sharecropping system today' (1939e). He is more explicit still in a later statement where, writing under his pseudonym J. R. Johnson, he describes the film, with its rosy reimagining of life for African-Americans on the plantations, as 'dangerous' and deserving of a boycott (1940b).

Yet, on the other hand, James insisted no less that popular products of this kind contained more than just an untrammelled ideological message. Hence, in his writing about a film such as *Birth of a Nation*, with its equally revisionist account of the history of post civil-war reconstruction in America, and its celebration of the Ku Klux Klan, he is remarkably and disconcertingly commendatory, describing the film in one statement as a masterly epic (1992: 223). He was, of course, not blind to the film's racism and, indeed, he refers to this quite openly (1990 [1954]: 3). What he insists upon, however, is that this overt, reactionary content did not exhaust the film's potential meaningfulness. Evidence of something else could be found, James argued, in Griffith's formal innovations and, in particular, in the dual development of wide-sweep panoramic shots, on the one hand, and facial close-ups, on the other. James read these technical achievements much in the same way that he read the achievements of someone like George Headley. That is to say, as innovations made possible by the director's awareness of a changing historical mood and by his responsiveness, more particularly, to the challenge of finding a mode of representation adequate to a new sense of both 'mass' society, and to a new awareness, post-Freud, of the deep reaches of the individual personality. It was Griffith's achievement, in James' view, to make artistic choices which went some way towards encapsulating this partly threatening, partly liberating sense of interior and exterior expansion. '[T]he film techniques which Griffith created are', he writes 'the result of the extended interests, awareness, needs and sensibilities of modern men' (ibid.). However useless it was to read the film as history, in short, it was more than useful to read it historically.

James is thus completely serious when he suggests to his audiences that our response to the stuff of mass culture should be both an attentiveness and a protest. Indeed, in a sense this inherently ironic stance is forced on us by any attempt to negotiate mass culture's zone of 'armed truce'. We may not always be convinced by the particular ways in which James relates the formal properties of particular cultural products to their time and place of production. I agree, certainly, with Bill Schwarz that his interpretations can sometimes seem rather too neat or rather too convenient (2006: 139–45). His insistence, moreover, on a strictly formal reading of *Birth of a Nation* seems not a little scholastic placed next to W. E. B. du Bois' recollection of the way in which the film led directly to an increase in violence against African-American communities (du Bois 1986 [1940]: chapter 8). Nevertheless, there is something like a statement of practice here on James' part. Reading cultural products with an eye on their historical formation becomes a means of reading them against themselves, as it were, a way of reading them against their explicit ideological content. James is thus able to point towards the way in which a film like *Birth of a Nation* says both *more* than it ideologically intends (how, for example, the representation of the massed clan members seems like a fearfully prescient glimpse of totalitarianism for the mid-twentieth-century viewer: 1990 [1954]: 4), as well as *less* (how its apparently triumphant revision of American history is interrupted and shaken by the sense of a present crisis making itself known in the film: it is a film, he argues, with 'all the ferocity, the cruelty, the destructiveness of a real civil war' (1992: 225)). In this respect, for James, a response to mass culture which attends both the picket and the ticket office is not so much a contradiction as a way of making something out of the contradiction. On the one hand, we are required to protest in the face of various kinds of ideological assertion and to contest these openly. On the other hand, even the most reactionary kinds of contemporary culture say things other than they intend to say. And this last point, of course, should be read alongside James' recognition of the existence of unexpected against-the-grain popular responses to cultural products of all kinds. It is incumbent on any serious, critically minded account of cultural forms, he implies, to act in solidarity with this insurgent meaning-making, sneaking in at the back along with it and happy to unsettle the stuff of ideology, as it were, from within.

III

Having said these things, and having laid out James' general position with regard to the politics of culture in this way, it seems important to me to complicate matters in some respects. I say this because posing the question, as I have posed it here, of the possible 'uses' of culture quickly becomes misleading so far as James is concerned. I have hinted at this already in the introduction to this chapter, but some further elaboration may be useful. Our attempts to describe social or political action tend to return, time and again, to a debate about the relative weight of established historical conditions in shaping choices and possibilities, on the one hand, and the ability of individuals and groups to act to change those conditions, on the other. This familiar opposition is given various names in the literature of the social sciences: structure versus agency, most famously, determinism versus instrumentalism and so forth (see, for a useful discussion, Derluguian 2005). Yet this question can quickly become a trap and it seems to me that James' emphasis on culture often relates to an attempt, on his part, to rescue a viable politics from the jaws of that trap. James, in other words, often refuses to settle for a consideration of the role that culture may play in either constraining or enabling political action, or in challenging or maintaining particular kinds of social relationships. Instead, he frequently turns to cultural practices as a way of raising a question that is aimed at cutting through that old Gordian knot tied out of structure and agency, the question which is at the heart of *Beyond a Boundary*: what is it that people live by? James turns to culture, that is to say, as a way of asking not 'how', but 'why': what is it that we need from our lives, what do people feel is lacking in their lives as they are, and where might we look for possible answers to such questions? It is in this sense, particularly, that it can be insisted that his interest in culture does not mark a retreat from politics. Culture matters to James not least because it reasserts this question of ethical or political or merely personal desire as the issue around which politics takes shape. Too many political or sociological accounts, even those which are specifically interested in emphasising 'agency', simply step over this issue, leading to a vision of social action apparently emptied of its intended meanings or motivating longings. For James, such an approach, and the related tendency to treat culture only in terms of its ideological role, risks a kind of rigor mortis. It ignores the fact that cultural practice raises the issue not only of the means of political action, but of its possible or hoped-for ends.

We can expect such ends to be various, of course, and to some extent contextual. Nevertheless, I think that it is possible to draw out some general lessons from James here. One would be that he often emphasises the degree to which culture becomes the context for the recognition and celebration of a sense of togetherness. Arguments about the role that cultural products may play in the formation of shared identities are now fairly familiar traffic in the social sciences, and have been at least since Benedict Anderson famously emphasised the way in which various literary and artistic forms and settings (newspapers, maps, museums, novels and so on) helped make conceivable the idea of a national community (1991; see also Hobsbawm and Ranger 1992). Something like this argument is there in James as well, and not just in his later work, but from early on. Take, for example, his long elegiac essay on Trotsky, published shortly after the death of the latter in 1940. In some respects, this piece is representative of James in his most orthodox Marxist period, yet even here there is a kind of iconoclasm about his argument which is made clear, particularly, in his insistence on drawing out the specific qualities of Trotsky's writing, read as a literary as well as political endeavour. And it is in the course of doing this that James digresses at some length to consider the way in which history, more generally, has been written. His overarching argument is that the most enduring works of history have been those which gave expression to 'some powerful progressive idea' (James in McLemee and le Blanc 1994: 120), a claim which he seeks to substantiate in a typically grand rhetorical sweep beginning with Thucydides as a defender of Athenian democracy, passing through Livy and Tacitus and ending with Michelet's emphasis on the popular forces at the heart of the French Revolution (on James' debt to Michelet, see Foot 1995). Yet James clearly intends to make this argument in a way that refuses, rather than accedes to, a view of history as an external idea or logic speaking through the medium of the historian. Instead, he insists on a much more entangled or dialectical relationship. On the one hand, the writing of the most enduring history, like all creativity in James' account, is in some respects enabled by the way in which popular political actions open up new understandings or new horizons in the conceivable or the imaginable. On the other hand, however, he portrays the writing of history as a creative act which is itself a part of what furnishes a wider community with some sense of themselves, of their world and its possible futures. He is quite explicit about this: 'What [these historians] do is to hold *not a mirror but a banner* up to society. They give society or more often a class an image of itself, not as it was but as it thought it was, or as it would have liked be. In them is written the history of an age, but not in the sense that they thought they were writing' (James in McLemee and le Blanc 1994: 120, my italics).

Not a mirror, but a banner. This is an altogether characteristic Jamesian passage, one which suggests both the degree to which the work of literary creativity is in certain respects shaped by its context (it contains more than just the history of the age that the historian may have assumed that they were writing), but which also recognises the way in which such products become a part of the construction of a sense of being in history, a sense of historical subjectivity, such that they give back to social groups a sense of themselves and their own possible historical role. Hence when he comes to evaluate *The History of the Russian Revolution*, although he offers the expected encomiums to the rigour of Trotsky's method of analysis, he insists also on the way in which the book became 'a summons to action [...] a roll of drums' (123). In other words, the degree to which, for many of its contemporary readers, dispossessed and lacking 'confidence in their own powers' (ibid.), the *History* becomes a work whose subject is not the past, but the present and the possible future, serving as the basis for something like that 'unisonance', that community in anonymity, which Anderson describes.

The writing of a historical account, clearly, may have political mobilisation as an explicit part of its intended purpose as, no doubt, Trotsky's history did. Yet this example is indicative of a wider fascination on James' part with the way in which cultural practices and products generally can help create a collective sense of presence and purposefulness. We have seen already, in various places, his emphasis on those moments when crowds become aware of themselves as crowds in response to the shifting patterns of whatever film or game they happen to be watching. It is noticeable in this respect that James is often less interested in the collective responses to grand questions raised by a given cultural event and more interested in the ways in which the seemingly inconsequential fragments of such events can serve a similar unifying effect. One such instance comes in the course of an essay James wrote for a cricket journal in 1964, reflecting on a series between England and Australia which was widely seen at the time as marking a nadir in cricketing standards and as representing the triumph of a grimly attritional approach to the game. James begins his essay with Hegel's much-quoted aphorism about the owl of Minerva flying only at dusk. He provides his own idiosyncratic and upbeat interpretation: 'the bright light which will illuminate, clear away the darkness, appears only when the darkness is pretty dark' (1964c: 195). James thus sets the generally gloomy scene for his article, but also defines his challenge: to justify this interpretation of Hegel's comment, to find evidence of what he later calls 'the new sprouts' amid 'the desiccated remains of an arid time' (199).

It goes without saying, of course, that James does not have only cricketing time in mind when he says such things. And it goes without saying also that James, following his own repeated admonition to 'watch what the people are doing', turns first of all to the crowds who queued around the block in the London rain in order to buy tickets for one of the games in the series, even though they were faced only with the prospect of further gathering darkness, literally or symbolically: further rain or, worse, further tedious, grinding cricket. Why should this be, he asks, what is it that keeps the 'audience there waiting, in the damp and drizzle' (195)? His answer is that they come in search of 'the dazzling personality, the startling event [...] still the main attraction of a game so ritualistic as cricket' (196). They come, in other words, undertaking precisely the same search as James himself, the search for that moment in which something glimmers which makes clear that change is still possible.

And yet when James comes to choose his example of a 'startling event', he chooses something deliberately tiny, even underwhelming. There is, he says, 'never so deeply felt a response from the crowd as when the home side gains an overthrow – something for nothing' (ibid.). He is referring here to the fact that occasionally, in a cricket match, the batting side are able to claim an extra run because a fielder has been overly vigorous in their returning of the ball. This is a moment which, in almost every instance, means little in terms of the result of the game in question. But James, of course, is less interested in the result of the game than in its other outcomes and in the particular fact that out of this 'nothing' event, something emerges. That is to say, not simply another run to the score, but rather a moment of spontaneous recognition from the crowd that matters far more than the event which was its occasion. It is this social something from a cultural nothing, this coming together of the crowd in response to the more or less arbitrary symbolic goings-on taking place on the pitch, which provides James with an instance of the wider point he is making in the article and more generally: culture demands of us the question 'what is it that people live by?' Part of what we live by, clearly, and what draws us to culture, is the way in which culture can, as it were, unveil the social to us even in its most inconsequential moments. This is one of the ways, as he put it in another context, that a people might find a sense of themselves (1986: 127). Thus it is that even in the darkest sporting days, James says, we find revealed the fact that 'everyone has a vision, not only of what he would like to see, but of what ought to be seen' (1964c: 195). And so he ends the article by citing a second of his great influences: the crowds who still flock to sporting matches do so, he suggests, in their own quest for answers to Kant's invitation to consider 'the aims of mankind [...] "What do I know? What must I do? What may I hope?"' (198).

IV

This sense of togetherness, then, was clearly one part of what James thought people sought and found in and through cultural performances or practices. Togetherness, of course, is not an unqualified good and, as I have pointed out already, James recognised the degree to which mass cultural practices could become the occasion for both new exclusions and new conformities. It is in this respect that he describes, for example, a stultifying unity created among the audiences for various forms of mass culture: among those hammered by the 'perpetual gagging' (1993: 135) of Bob Hope or Jack Benny, for example, whose humour he took as the degraded after-image of Chaplin's attempt to provoke a laughter that might transcend the awfulness of modern times. He describes in similar terms the effects of the growing commercialisation of jazz. This form began, in James' account, as a thoroughly popular one, defined precisely by the back-and-forth creativity of performers and dancers: 'in a big hall [...] a sensitive leader caught the rhythm for the evening from the dancers' (137). It is arguable that James' account is, in this respect, rather more nuanced than that of Adorno (for example, 1941), although like the latter he believed that jazz was increasingly subdued by the very rhythms of mechanised labour of which it had once promised a kind of subversive mimicry.

For James, however, the threat of culture becoming the context for a new kind of conformity or for a crushing integration into more of the same, is challenged by a number of possibilities. The first is that cultural practices, however routine or mechanical they may become, never entirely lose the possibility of that 'startling moment' which brings the crowds out to queue even in the damp and drizzle. The possibility, in other words, of an act of spontaneous and disruptive creativity. This idea, and the idea of spontaneity more generally in James' work, has been the subject of a certain amount of criticism, even from those who are broadly sympathetic to him (for example, Callinicos 1990; Renton 2007). It is argued in this respect that, particularly in his later political writings, the idea of spontaneous popular political action provided a fig leaf for James' growing lack of concern for the hard practicalities of political organisation and the day-to-day work of grassroots activism. There is, it seems to me, some validity in such criticisms, but only some. It is important to be clear, to begin with, that James' idea of spontaneity is not millenarian, it is not a belief in a last trumpet upturning of things. He uses the term, rather, to insist on the fact that ordinary men and women are able to learn the lessons of their own historical experiences and to underscore the possibility that their actions, in response to such experiences, can come to shape a context for political leadership, rather than vice versa. Certainly when James wrote to his comrades in America reporting on a meeting with Martin Luther King Jr. in 1957, at which they had discussed the Montgomery bus boycott, this is precisely the lesson that he draws (see 1992: 271–6; see also Buhle 1986: 154–8). It was, he points out, the more or less spontaneous action of one black woman, in refusing to give up her seat to a white passenger, that opened the space for a wider movement of which King became the public voice. James' idea of spontaneity thus places centre-stage the often unheralded effects of small-scale demotic resistance in shaping and driving larger, more formally led, political movements. Apart from anything, he opens a path here to a consideration of those hard-to-pin-down, person-to-person modes of popular insurgency (rumour, mutiny, skiving, and so forth) which have been increasingly recognised as significant in recent work on colonial and postcolonial history (for example, Rediker 2007; White 2008).

In this respect, James' idea of spontaneity, much like his account of artistic genius, emphasises the way in which the seemingly accidental, arbitrary or merely subjective event expresses and illuminates a wider historical context of struggle. That it reveals, even, a historical necessity, although by this James did not mean an outcome imposed on events by a logic intrinsic to historical processes in the abstract, but simply the fact that human beings in the modern world are heirs to a promise of freedom which they continually seek to substantiate, in the face of and against all kinds of existing unfreedom. In the end, such grand ideas are thwarted or realised in and through small, specific, limited decisions. The seemingly limited freedom, for example, to choose a seat on a bus, such as Rosa Parks insisted upon. It is notable that, a long time before his current critics, it was Constance Webb who accused James of displaying an unaccustomed spontaneity in some of the love letters which he had written to her. His response, strikingly, was to insist that the spontaneity in his writing was actually the expression of a necessity, an impelled response to the startling discovery of 'something I have been looking for all my life' (1996b: 128). And this is, indeed, precisely the pattern which James saw playing out in all apparently spontaneous popular political activity, from the sudden eruption of resistance in Hungary (James, Lee and Chaulieu 1974 [1958]) to the groups of white and black kids who met during the riots in Moss Side, 'with nothing in the manner of their meeting which in any way reflected a prearranged plan' (1982: 100), and headed off in the direction of the police station.

James' emphasis on spontaneity, in short, can be read as a deliberate counter-point to the emphasis on totality or togetherness which I have already discussed. Although one assumes that he would have found Hannah Arendt's portrayal of black Africans infuriating, James' view accords to some extent with that expressed in the famous final chapter of *The Origins of Totalitarianism* (a text which made it onto at least one of his lists of 'books to read' (1973 [1960]: 157; see also R. King 2006)). In that passage Arendt argues that the great danger of totalitarian regimes, a threat which, like James, she saw overhanging modern society in general, is the fact that they 'are never interested in the miracle of being' (Arendt 1973: 469), but only in a continual relentless becoming, only in the degree to which things process towards an end determined from without, unchallengeable and pre-given. Against this 'tyranny of logicality', she writes, 'nothing stands but the great capacity of men to start something new' (473). And the operating condition for this kind of regime, Arendt concludes, is that of 'loneliness', a world in which we have no longer any sense of ourselves precisely because we have lost the sense of others, of our mutual interdependence, and of 'the world as the human artifice' (475). For human beings isolated in this way, debates about premises (why should this be so?) or of purposes (to what end is this done?) become impossible, and we are left only with that 'logical reasoning whose premise is self-evident' (477) and for which truth shrinks to the literally 'end-less' chains of deduction uncoiling from what is already given: 'You can't say A without saying B and C and so on, down to the end of the murderous alphabet' (472).

I say all of this because, in many ways, it seems to me to come close to James' own view. For him, as for Arendt, a response to the fact that the preconditions for this kind of experience have 'become an everyday experience of the evergrowing masses of our century' (478), is to be found, ultimately, in the paradox of human creativity, the possibility of an unheralded beginning. James' emphasis on spontaneity is precisely an emphasis on this possibility, not as a magical event, but as a historical something which men and women cherish: that possibility of freedom which we look for all of our lives. At the same time, this possibility is also what brings us together, it makes us aware, in Arendt's words, of the fact that for the confirmation of who I am, and what I might be capable of, 'I depend entirely on other people' (476).

All of this, then, is at the absolute heart of James' approach to culture, and why, for him, the question of culture may help rescue us from the tyrannous logicality of a politics that has lost sight of possible human ends. The audience that comes together around a great moment of creative spontaneity is brought together around a demonstration of the human ability to start something new. For James, as I noted in the previous chapter, this was always in some respects a profoundly individual achievement. But it is a demonstration which reminds us of the shared prospect of newness. A reminder also that the specificity of each one of us, our mental, bodily and experiential uniqueness, does not have to be a precondition for loneliness, but rather for a renewed sense of what we owe to each other and what we make possible for each other.

This is also why James was at such pains to emphasise the question of cultural form. At the heart of the best cultural performances, in his view, was precisely what these words suggest: the ability to take formal constraint and turn it into the necessary condition for freedom. He makes this clear in many places, but nowhere more effectively than in his famous essay on Rohan Kanhai. James watched Kanhai play in a series of matches arranged at the end of the 1964 season between a West Indies side and an England eleven. Earlier in the year he had reported on an England versus Australia series in the company of his old friend Learie

Constantine, and it was a comment of Constantine's about Kanhai which started James thinking: '"You know at times he goes crazy" [...] Going crazy. That could be Greek Dionysius, the satyric passion for the expression of the natural man, bursting through the acquired restraints of disciplined necessity. I played with that idea for a while. Tentatively' (1986: 168–9). And then, in the last match of the series, Kanhai scored a scintillating 170 which James watched, and watching him changed his mind. This was no Dionysian breaking loose, says James, 'Kanhai did not go crazy. Exactly the opposite. He discovered, he created a new dimension in batting' (169). There is no need to reiterate James' technical analysis of Kanhai's achievement, how he controlled what the bowler was doing in such a way as to set up the delivery which he would then crash out of the ground. What matters is James' conclusion. Other West Indian cricketers before Kanhai, he notes, had already proved that 'anything you can do, I can do better' (170–1). But this, James says, was something different, something for which the only fitting word was 'new': 'At that moment, Edgbaston in 1964, the West Indian could strike from his feet the dust of centuries [...] He was free as few West Indians have been free' (171). Kanhai, in company with all of the greatest artists, showed to James not craziness, not spontaneity as some unpredictable inward passion erupting outwards, but rather the ability to consciously create something original out of the very stuff that was seeking to prevent that happening. The ability, in other words, to take the rigidities of a particular form of doing something, culture's essentially arbitrary and symbolic set of constraints, and to make of them the conditions for the expression of a new freedom. It is this that keeps the popular crowds queuing in the rain, buying the books, watching the films. They too come to see that expression of freedom and those other horizons which such achievement opens up for our imagination, our sense of what may be possible. For James, watching Kanhai, what was opened up was a transfiguring glimpse of his home islands as the cradle of values which he thought were still worth preserving: 'Distinction. Gaiety. Grace. Virtues of the ancient Eastern Mediterranean city-states, islands, the sea, the sun. Long before Edgbaston I had been thinking that way. Maybe I only saw what I was looking for. Maybe' (171).

This, in the end, is the answer to the question that James posed with regard to cricket and, in different ways, with regard to other cultural practices. What brings people to sports and films, books and art, is the demonstration which they provide of what he called, in another context, 'concrete freedom' (1977a: 187). Freedom not as a flight of idealism, nor as airy abstraction, nor as some future destination which promises us an ability to transcend the historically given world of which we are part or the socially given contexts of our lives. Somewhere in the distance down that road lies the loneliness which Arendt describes. But rather, concrete freedom is what may be made out of all of the complicated, entangled webs of symbolic significance and practice which make up our social lives. A freedom which speaks of our reliance on each other, even as it reveals in a single sparkling act of individual creativity that all is not yet done, that new beginnings can still be made.

Conclusion

James' first report on arrival in Britain was produced for the *Port of Spain Gazette* and describes his experiences wandering round the London museums. As with some of the other articles which he wrote from the context of that first encounter with British life, there is a somewhat patrician note in his descriptions, yet this comes side by side with and is consciously undermined by James' drily humorous asides and by his appeals to local Caribbean knowledge. His 'letter', in any case, focuses in particular on two objects which he had come across that day. The first of these, which James met on an unplanned detour through the Science Museum, was a plane which had previously beaten the air-speed record, and which astonishes him not as a technical object (he does not quite manage to silence his question: '200 miles an hour, 300 miles an hour, 400 miles an hour – who cares?' (2003: 4)), but rather as an aesthetic one. 'What has been built solely for utility', he notes, 'turns out to be so beautiful' (ibid.). And then, secondly, at the end of a long day trawling through the art collection of the Victoria and Albert Museum, he stumbles across Rodin's statue of John the Baptist. James insists: 'it is no more John the Baptist that I am John the Baptist. It is a statue of a naked man walking, that's all, neither more nor less' (12). He goes on, with a now familiar superimposition, to imagine two other visitors encountering the work for the first time. On the one hand, an ancient Greek who would look at Rodin's statue, he notes, with 'much the same eyes' as his own. And on the other, 'three thousand years from now, some wanderer from the West Indies' (14), fresh from seeing the 'latest thought-plane' in the Science Museum, and for whom the record-breaking aircraft that James had earlier encountered would exist only as 'one of a crowd of obsolete designs' (ibid.). But in the Art Museum, James continues, he will come across something whose significance has not faded: 'he will see the statue of a man walking. It will be to him as it is to me' (ibid.).

That was 1932. Nearly half a century later, in another letter, this time written from Trinidad towards the end of his life, James includes a short critical comparison of the work of Picasso and Jackson Pollock. *Guernica* was certainly one of James' favourite pieces of art, and there are various stories of him carrying a postcard image of the painting in his jacket pocket during Test matches so that he could ponder it in the moments between deliveries. Nevertheless it was a work which presented its viewer, in his account, with a desperate and desperately unresolved attempt to represent 'the human' amidst all of the violence of the twentieth century. The final version of the painting, James argues, certainly contains images of defiance, particularly in the figure of the bull, and of possible regeneration: symbols of birth, for example, and of the lamp, which James reads as the flickering of those same, not-yet-exhausted classical virtues he thought he saw in, or by virtue of, Kanhai's batting. And yet the painting remains in some respects undone or without unity. These different, defiant elements exist in isolation: 'In opposition to the decay of society [Picasso] places sexuality [...] militancy and high civilization; but he cannot join them' (1992: 408). *Guernica* is an image of longing but also of irresolution, of an idea whose centre no longer holds.

It is at this point, faced with this broken mid-century scene, that James turns to Pollock. And what he finds in Pollock's paintings is not a completion exactly nor even a resolution of the quandary which Picasso faced, but nevertheless, something hopeful: the ability to turn that quandary into a new beginning and the possibility of a representation which might contain both diversity and order. The clinching image of this new start, James insists, is that in Pollock's paintings, especially in *One* and *Autumn Rhythm*, there is both a tremendous 'intricacy of design', but emerging 'unmistakably' out of this, 'the sense of feet walking along' (409). Faced with the contradictory, fragmented historical world of Picasso's painting, Pollock can imagine some new beginning, and he finds that beginning, says James, 'in [the idea] that men, or rather human beings, walked' (ibid.).

Any expositions of this sort are, of course, contestable. It might well be argued that James saw in Pollock's paintings, as he admitted might be the case with his mind's-eye image of a second Athens summoned up by Kanhai's batting, only what he wanted to see. What he wanted to see, and what he certainly insisted it was always possible to find in the greatest works of human creativity, was precisely that image of the human being moving, and moving forward. It is important to say that for James, this implies not just the idea of an endless contingency, a piling up of accidental starts and breaks. Rather, this is movement *from* particular historical conditions and their strictures, and movement in which is inherent (how could it not be?) the idea of *to*: from the contradictions of Picasso to Pollock, from the history of colonial repression to Kanhai. Movement vivid with some sense of purpose, in other words, not as a goal imposed from without, not as an end which is wholly sure of itself in advance, but as something implicit in the movement itself: human beings driven by the necessity to develop, to overcome barriers, to make some kind of freedom out of those conditions which seek to prevent freedom. Whoever chose as James' epitaph that famous quote from chapter 8 of *Beyond a Boundary*, chose well: 'it is not quality of goods or utility which matter, but movement: not where you are or what you have, but where you come from, where you are going, and the rate at which you are getting there' (1983 [1963]: 116–17).

Clearly such assumptions about the possibilities of human being, about this necessary reach for freedom, cannot be substantiated or falsified except in the course of what happens. They are 'postulates' for which, as James admitted in a letter to an American critic, 'the proof [or disproof] is in the future' (1992: 230). Yet this is not quite all, because for James there is a necessary rider to such a statement: 'the future is not born all at once. It exists in the present. The thing is to know where to look' (ibid.). Or, as he put it in writing to Webb: 'You know history does move. The thing is to see it' (147). Certainly one place that James insisted on looking for this future was in the working experiences of ordinary men and women, and the forms of innovation, cooperation and expression with which they repeatedly responded to the confinements of those experiences. But cultural and artistic practices, he insisted to Webb (1996b: 155), are also forms of production, in them too both individuals and social relationships are made and remade and reflected upon. In them also, therefore, it may be possible to see the glimmering of the 'future in the present'. Not as a merely symbolic gesture, nor as the promise of a sudden transcendence of what is, but in the demonstration provided by the best of human creativity that constraint can be turned into possibility, that form can become the basis of performance, that contradiction can be made into movement and fragmentation into the image of a human being walking forward.

Conclusion

I do not have a lengthy conclusion to offer here, but there is one comment which may be worth making, regarding the particular timeliness of a recovery of James at this juncture, and one image of him on which it seems appropriate to finish.

The comment is this. A few years ago a collection was published called *Theory's Empire* (Patai and Corral 2005). At nearly seven hundred pages, this self-proclaimed 'anthology of dissent' brought together writings from a wide variety of authors ranging from Noam Chomsky and Kwame Anthony Appiah to M. H. Abrams and Wayne C. Booth. This diversity notwithstanding, the tone of most of the contributions, as well as the editorial prefaces, make clear that the volume as a whole was intended as a kind of circling of the wagons around established principles of literary and cultural criticism: close textual exposition; a belief in truth and the distinctiveness of aesthetic sensibility; the wider ethical values of liberal humanism. Beyond this corral, as the story goes, the field is overrun by the barbarians and their beliefs: a politically correct relativism which judges work on the grounds of authorial identity rather than literary quality; a scepticism regarding objective critical judgement; a crude and reductive materialism or historicism; a thoroughgoing suspicion of rationality. Amongst themselves these particular barbarians jabber away in their own language, called something like 'theorrhea' (234) or 'theoryese' (105). Worst of all, they have hostages, having long since taken captive Jane Austen, Charlotte Brontë and many others.

This is a facetious summary, of course, but in a sense *Theory's Empire* invites facetiousness, not least because its 'dissent' often reduces to a straightforward defence of elitism. Frank Kermode, for example, ends up calling for a Coleridge-esque clerisy, a congregation of the gifted few who simply 'know', and instinctively defend, good writing when they encounter it (605–20). Ironic humour is also invited by the fact that the same critics who are defending a set of apparently settled and enduring aesthetic values do so by furiously representing their opponents as faddish or as the products of various unwelcome demographic or institutional changes in the arts and humanities. A kind of historicism, in other words, is summoned up as the very means of combating the alleged excesses of critical historicism.

Theory's Empire is, in any case, symptomatic of the kinds of struggle taking place within much literary and cultural criticism today. I mention it at the end of this study because it seems to me that James has a great deal to offer in this context, just as he did in relation to that battle in his own day between a crass political criticism, and those who responded by seeking shelter in 'the thing of value in itself' (that is, in close study of the cultural text or form as a kind of hermetically sealed symbolic world). James would also have sought to defend, we can assume, many of the cultural values in whose name this act of 'dissent' was organised, and he shared an underlying belief in the criteria of truthfulness. But he would, of course, have defended such propositions not as part of a 'call to order', an attempt to re-establish the exclusivity of these intellectual possessions, but as precisely the opposite: as a means of challenging such exclusivity. Those values can only be redeemed, he would have insisted, they are only worth what they claim to be worth, insofar as they cease to be elitist.

Facing in the other direction, however, James also offers a warning to a socially or historically minded criticism which, whatever its admirable intentions, too often seems willing to treat culture as simply the stuff with which politics gets done. Politics, of course, does 'get done' in culture, but not only that. James' point is that in its best moments, culture puts us within imaginative sight of something like an 'end' of politics, but that it only does this in its own terms. Lose those terms and we lose the possibility of that glimpse. This leaves us either lost in a maze of pure contingency in which all judgements evaporate, or it turns cultural creativity into an instrument for other purposes, at which point it must cease to be meaningful in itself and becomes useless for anything.

James' account of cultural practices is, of course, a historical one. He had, as I hope is clear by now, no time for static formalism; his interest lay in describing the way in which changing practices, expectations and ambitions in various forms of cultural production were 'of their time'. All the same, he also clearly believed that creativity at its most extraordinary should lead us to think about the possibility, or the possible shape, of a category called 'the human', and that it does this because it places before us some sense of common capacities and common longings. The capacity, that is, to turn a particular set of constraints into a means of expression. Culture, for James, does this within its many forms: no less when Ajantha Mendis turns the rigid mechanics of bowling into an astonishing array of loop and spin than when Alexander Pope makes the no-less rigid heroic couplet sing. But it expresses this also in the very histories of its formation, in the stubbornly resilient insurgent creativity which continually turns limits into the grounds of a provisional freedom: one thinks of the emergence of skateboarding, for example, or of agitprop graffiti. To talk about something 'shared' in this respect is not 'ahistorical' for James, because the point is always to ask about what it is that people do with the historical and social resources they have to hand. Whatever is common to us in all this is common to us not by virtue of some external, pre-given 'human nature', but rather in the innovative and restless creativity that is always making something new from the historical possibilities that lie at hand.

This brings me to my concluding image. This comes from one of James' letters to Constance Webb, where he tells her, in a confessional moment, that he has two favourite parts of a concerto: firstly, the momentary pause between the end of the orchestral introduction to the first movement and the entrance of the soloist: 'The end of the orchestra, *the pause*, and the entry of the piano form for me a combination from which I receive a thrill beyond description', he writes (1996b: 145). And then, secondly, he describes the moment which is usually found at the end of a final, quick movement when, beneath the trill which closes a cadenza, the orchestra comes creeping back in. As with so many of James' passing remarks and asides, this is packed with all kinds of resonance to his wider work. His sense of the 'organic social relation' (ibid.) within which both the performance of the soloist and that of the orchestra become meaningful suggests something strikingly similar, of course, to his account of the relationship between the great creative artists and their audiences or, for that matter, the great historical leaders and the movements which made them (an analogy which has occurred to others, in other contexts: see Waterman 1997).

Yet the idea of James listening to the momentary silences of a classical composition is provocative in another sense as well. One thinks of the protagonist of Ralph Ellison's *Invisible Man*, describing his love of Louis Armstrong's music: 'Instead of the swift and imperceptible flowing of time, you are aware of its nodes, those points where time stands still or from which it leaps ahead. And you slip into the breaks and look around' (1965 [1947]: 11). Here, then, is another way of grasping James' peculiar angle of vision: the figure who loved Western classicism dearly, but who also recognised its gaps, who sought out the breaks within that tradition. Who understood, moreover, how to slip into those breaks in order to look around. This gives us an image of James as someone positioned attentively on the cusp, on the cusp between a historical sense of all that has gone before, not as mere past-ness, not as something over and done with, but as something live and vibrating in the moment. And, the other face of that same thing: James listening out in that moment for the beginning of something new about to emerge, something which makes newly meaningful its past even as it is itself meaningfully shaped by that past. The sense, moreover, that all of this depends, that it is not in some way natural, 'a swift and imperceptible flowing' from one thing to the next. Rather, that it is possible only because of the work of those who are listening, attentively, at the cusp, insistent that whatever ending or silence we are faced with can be turned into a 'leap ahead', turned into the start of something new. A fitting place to end. Or, this being the whole point, a fitting place to begin.

References

Abrams, M. H. (1953) *Romantic Theory and the Critical Tradition*, New York: Oxford University Press.
Adorno, T. (1941) 'On Popular Music', *Studies in Philosophy and Social Science*, 9: 17–48.
Adorno, T. (1991) *The Culture Industry: Selected Essays on Mass Culture*, London: Routledge.
Adorno, T. and M. Horkheimer (1997 [1944]) *Dialectic of Enlightenment*, London: Verso.
Agozino, B. and Z. Edwards (2007) 'C. L. R. James: the Black Jacobins' Sociology: Interview with Professor Gordon Rohlehr of the University of the West Indies', *The Black Scholar*, 37 (3): 42–9.
Ahmad, A. (1992) *In Theory: Classes, Nations, Literature*, London: Verso.
Alleyne, B. (1999) 'Cultural Politics and Globalized Infomedia: C. L. R. James, Theodor Adorno and Mass Culture Criticism', *Interventions*, 1 (3): 361–72.
Anderson, B. (1991) *Imagined Communities: Reflections on the Origin and Spread of Nationalism*, London: Verso.
Anderson, J. (1985) 'Cricket and Beyond: the Career of C. L. R. James', *American Scholar*, 3: 345–59.
Arendt, H. (1969) *On Violence*, New York: Harcourt Brace and Company.
Arendt, H. (1973) *The Origins of Totalitarianism*, New York: Harcourt Brace and Company.
Aristotle (1996) *Poetics*, London: Penguin.
Bateman, A. (2003) '"More Mighty Than the Bat, the Pen ..." Culture, Hegemony and the Literaturisation of Cricket', *Sport in History*, 23 (1): 27–44.
Bateman, A. (2009) '"From Far It Look Like Politics": C. L. R. James and the Canon of English Cricket Literature', *Sport in Society*, 12 (4/5): 496–508.
Baucom, I. (1999) *Out of Place: Englishness, Empire and the Locations of Identity*, Princeton: Princeton University Press.
Benjamin, W. (1968) *Illuminations*, London: Collins/Fontana.
Benjamin, W. (1970 [1934]) 'The Artist as Producer', *New Left Review*, 1 (62): 83–96.
Birley, D. (1999) *A Social History of English Cricket*, London: Aurum Press.
Blackburn, R. (1995) '*The Black Jacobins* and New World Slavery', in *C. L. R. James: His Intellectual Legacies*, ed. S. Cudjoe and W. Cain, Amherst: University of Massachusetts Press.
Boggs, G. L. (1993) 'Thinking and Acting Dialectically: C. L. R. James, the American Years', *Monthly Review*, 45 (5): 38–47.
Boggs, G. L. (1995) 'C. L. R. James: Organizing in the USA, 1938–1953', in *C. L. R. James: His Intellectual Legacies*, ed. S. Cudjoe and W. Cain, Amherst: University of Massachusetts Press.
Bogues, A. (1997) *Caliban's Freedom: the Early Political Thought of C. L. R. James*, London: Pluto Press.

Bourdieu, P. (1990) *In Other Words: Essays Towards a Reflexive Sociology*, Cambridge: Polity Press.
Bourdieu, P. (1993a) *The Field of Cultural Production: Essays on Art and Literature*, Cambridge: Polity Press.
Bourdieu, P. (1993b) *Sociology in Question*, London: Sage.
Bourdieu, P. (1996) *The Rules of Art: Genesis and Structure of the Literary Field*, London: Polity Press.
Buhle, P. (ed.) (1986) *C. L. R. James: His Life and Work*, London: Allison and Busby.
Buhle, P. (1988) *C. L. R. James: the Artist as Revolutionary*, London: Verso.
Bukharin, N. I. (1996 [1929]) *Imperialism and World Economy*, New York: Howard Fertig.
Burke, P. (1978) *Popular Culture in Early Modern Europe*, London: Temple Smith.
Cain, P. J. and A. G. Hopkins (1993a) *British Imperialism: Innovation and Expansion, 1688–1914*, London: Longman.
Cain, P. J. and A. G. Hopkins (1993b) *British Imperialism: Crisis and Deconstruction, 1914*–1990, London: Longman.
Callinicos, A. (1990) *Trotskyism*, Milton Keynes: Open University Press.
Chinweizu et al. (1975) 'Toward the Decolonization of African Literature', *Transition*, 49: 29–37, 54, 56–7.
Colás, S. (1999) 'Silence and Dialectics: Speculations on C. L. R. James and Latin America', in *C. L. R. James' Caribbean*, ed. P. Henry and P. Buhle, Durham: Duke University Press.
Comaroff, Jean and John Comaroff (eds) (1993) *Modernity and its Malcontents: Ritual and Power in Postcolonial Africa*, Chicago: University of Chicago Press.
Cudjoe, S. (1992a) 'The Audacity of It All: C. L. R. James' Trinidadian Background', in *C. L. R. James' Caribbean*, ed. P. Henry and P. Buhle, Durham: Duke University Press.
Cudjoe, S. (1992b) 'C. L. R. James Misbound', *Transition*, 58: 124–36.
Cudjoe, S. (1997) 'C. L. R. James and the Trinidad and Tobago Intellectual Tradition, Or, Not Learning Shakespeare Under a Mango Tree', *New Left Review*, 1 (223): 114–25.
Derluguian, G. M. (2005) *Bourdieu's Secret Admirer in the Caucuses: a World System Biography*, Chicago: University of Chicago Press.
Dhondy, F. (2001) *C. L. R. James: a Life*, New York: Pantheon Books.
Dirlik, A. (1990) 'Culturalism as Hegemonic Ideology and Liberating Practice', in *The Nature and Context of Minority Discourse*, ed. A. Jan Mohamed and D. Lloyd, New York: Oxford University Press.
Douglass, F. (1969 [1855]) *My Bondage and My Freedom*, New York: Dover Publications Inc.
Du Bois, W. E. B. (1978 [1900]) 'The Religion of the American Negro', in *On Sociology and the Black Community*, ed. D. Green and E. Driver, Chicago: University of Chicago Press.
Du Bois, W. E. B. (1986 [1926]) 'Criteria of Negro Art', in *W. E. B. du Bois: Writings*, New York: Literary Classics of the United States.
Du Bois, W. E. B. (1986 [1940]) 'Dusk of Dawn: an Essay Toward an Autobiography of a Race Concept', in *W. E. B. du Bois: Writings*, New York: Literary Classics of the United States.
Du Bois, W. E. B. (1995 [1903]) *The Souls of Black Folk*, New York: Signet Classics.

Dupuy, A. (1995) 'Toussaint-Louverture and the Haitian Revolution: a Reassessment of C. L. R. James's Interpretation', in *C. L. R. James: His Intellectual Legacies*, ed. S. Cudjoe and W. Cain, Amherst: University of Massachusetts Press.

Durkheim, E. (1938 [1895]) *The Rules of Sociological Method*, London: The Free Press of Glencoe.

Dworkin, D. (2007) 'C. L. R. James in Nevada', *History Workshop Journal*, 63: 90–112.

Eagleton, T. (1998) 'Five Types of Identity and Difference', in *Multicultural States: Rethinking Difference and Identity*, ed. D. Bennett, London: Routledge.

Eliot, T. S. (1950) *The Sacred Wood: Essays on Poetry and Criticism*, London: Methuen.

Ellison, R. (1965 [1947]) *Invisible Man*, London: Penguin.

Fanon, F. (1967a) *The Wretched of the Earth*, Harmondsworth: Penguin.

Fanon, F. (1967b) *Black Skin, White Masks*, London: Pluto Press.

Farred, G. (1996a) 'The Maple Man: How Cricket Made a Postcolonial Intellectual', in *Rethinking C. L. R. James*, ed. G. Farred, Oxford: Blackwell.

Farred, G. (ed.) (1996b) *Rethinking C. L. R. James*, Oxford: Blackwell.

Foot, M. (1995) 'C. L. R. James', in *C. L. R. James: His Intellectual Legacies*, ed. S. Cudjoe and W. Cain, Amherst: University of Massachusetts Press.

Fowler, B. (2006) 'Autonomy, Reciprocity and Science in the Thought of Pierre Bourdieu', *Theory, Culture and Society*, 23 (6): 99–117.

Fowler, B. (2007) *The Obituary as Collective Memory*, London: Routledge.

Gair, C. (2002) 'Beyond Boundaries: Cricket, Herman Melville and C. L. R. James's Cold War', *Symbiosis*, 6 (2): 159–77.

Gair, C. (ed.) (2006) *Beyond Boundaries: C. L. R. James and Postnational Studies*, London: Pluto Press.

Gemmell, J. (2004) *The Politics of South African Cricket*, London: Routledge.

Gilroy, P. (1993) *The Black Atlantic: Modernity and Double Consciousness*, London: Verso.

Graeber, D. (2001) *Toward an Anthropology of the Present: the False Coin of Our Own Dreams*, New York: Palgrave Macmillan.

Gramsci, A. (1985) *Selections from Cultural Writings*, London: Lawrence and Wishart.

Gregg, R. (2000) *Inside Out, Outside In: Essays in Contemporary History*, Basingstoke: Palgrave Macmillan.

Griffith, M. (2007) '"Telling the Tale": a Performance Tradition From Homer to Pantomime', in *The Cambridge Companion to Greek and Roman Theatre*, ed. M. McDonald and J. M. Walton, Cambridge: Cambridge University Press.

Grimshaw, A. (1991) *Popular Democracy and the Creative Imagination: the Writings of C. L. R. James, 1950–1963*, New York: C. L. R. James Institute.

Grimshaw, A. (1992) 'Introduction. C. L. R. James: a Revolutionary Vision for the Twentieth Century', in *The C. L. R. James Reader*, ed. A. Grimshaw and K. Hart, Oxford: Blackwell.

Guha, R. (2002) *A Corner of a Foreign Field: the Indian History of a British Sport*, London: Picador.

Guttmann, A. (1994) *Games and Empires: Modern Sports and Cultural Imperialism*, New York: Columbia University Press.

Hall, E. (1997) 'The Sociology of Athenian Tragedy', in *The Cambridge Companion to Greek Tragedy*, ed. P. E. Easterling, Cambridge: Cambridge University Press.

Hamilton, C. (1992) 'A Way of Seeing: Culture as Political Expression in the Works of C. L. R. James', *Journal of Black Studies*, 22 (3): 429–43.
Hansen, J. (1940) 'Trotsky's Last Battle Against the Revisionists', *Fourth International* (November): 165–72.
Hartmann, D. (2003) 'What Can We Learn From Sport if We Take Sport Seriously as a Racial Force? Lessons from C. L. R. James' *Beyond a Boundary*', *Ethnic and Racial Studies*, 26 (3): 451–83.
Harvey, D. (2000) *Spaces of Hope*, Edinburgh: Edinburgh University Press.
Henry, P. (1992) 'C. L. R. James and the Antiguan Left', in *C. L. R. James' Caribbean*, ed. P. Henry and P. Buhle, Durham: Duke University Press.
Hill, J. (1994) 'Cricket and Imperial Connection: Overseas Players in Lancashire in the Interwar Years', in *The Global Sports Arena: Athletic Talent Migration in an Interdependent World*, ed. J. Bale and J. Maguire, London: Frank Cass.
Hill, P. (2001) *Eadweard Muybridge*, London: Phaidon.
Hill, R. (1981) 'In England, 1932–1938', *Urgent Tasks*, 12: 19–27.
Hobsbawm, E. and T. Ranger (eds) (1992) *The Invention of Tradition*, Cambridge: Cambridge University Press.
Høgsbjerg, C. (2006) 'C. L. R. James: the Revolutionary as Artist', *International Socialism*, 112: 163–82.
Howe, S. (2003) 'C. L. R. James: Visions of History, Visions of Britain', in *West Indian Intellectuals in Britain*, ed. B. Schwarz, Manchester: Manchester University Press.
Ismail, Q. (1999) 'Batting Against the Break: On Cricket, Nationalism and the Swashbuckling Sri Lankans', in *SportCult*, ed. R. Martin and T. Miller, Minneapolis: University of Minnesota Press.
James, C. L. R. (1932a) 'A Correspondent Writes [Tribute to Lord Harris]', *The Times (London)*, 29 March.
James, C. L. R. (1932b) *The Life of Captain Cipriani: an Account of British Government in the West Indies*, Nelson: Coulton and Company.
James, C. L. R. (1933) *The Case for West-Indian Self Government*, London: Leonard and Virginia Woolf at the Hogarth Press.
James, C. L. R. (1937a) 'The Pendulum Has Swung Back: Reflections Upon Watching an Older Generation at the Crease', *The Glasgow Herald*, 8 September.
James, C. L. R. (1937b) 'Hail and Farewell: Hendren Says Good-Bye With Ripe and Polished Century', *The Glasgow Herald*, 1 September.
James, C. L. R. (1938a) 'Cricket is Losing a Supreme Artist', *The Glasgow Herald*, 17 August.
James, C. L. R. (1938b) '"Tiger" O'Reilly's Farewell to England?', *The Glasgow Herald*, 31 August.
James, C. L. R. (1938c) 'Flat-Footed England Were at the Mercy of Spin', *The Glasgow Herald*, 28 July.
James, C. L. R. (1938d) 'One of the Greatest Matches in Game's History', *The Glasgow Herald*, 16 June.
James, C. L. R. (1938e) *A History of Negro Revolt*, London: FACT Monographs.
James, C. L. R. (1939a) 'Negroes and the War', *Socialist Appeal* (serialised in ten parts between 6 September and 3 October).
James, C. L. R. (1939b) 'The Negro Question', *Socialist Appeal*, 25 August: 3.
James, C. L. R. (1939c) 'The Negro Question', *Socialist Appeal*, 7 November: 3.
James, C. L. R. (1939d) 'The Negro Question', *Socialist Appeal*, 10 November: 3.

James, C. L. R. (1939e) 'Hollywood Epic Film *Gone With the Wind* Glorifies Old Slave Holding South', *Socialist Appeal*, 30 December: 3.
James, C. L. R. (1940a) 'Capitalist Society and the War', *New International*, 6 (6): 114–28 (cited version from www.marxists.org/archive/james-clr/index.htm; accessed 15 May 2009).
James, C. L. R. (1940b) 'The Negro Question', *Socialist Appeal*, 13 January: 3.
James, C. L. R. (1944) 'The Course of the War: the Bourgeois Theory of the Offensive', *Fourth International*, 10 (8): 247–51.
James, C. L. R. (1949a) 'Stalinism and Negro History', *Fourth International*, 10 (10): 309–14.
James, C. L. R. (1949b) 'Herbert Aptheker's Distortions', *Fourth International*, 10 (11): 337–41.
James, C. L. R. (1963) 'Cricket in West Indian Culture', *New Society*, 36 (June): 8–9.
James, C. L. R. (1964a) 'Rastafari at Home and Abroad', *New Left Review*, 25: 74–6.
James, C. L. R. (1964b) 'Black Sansculottes', *The Institute of Race Relations News Letter*, October: 26–9.
James, C. L. R. (1964c) 'Reflections on the Late Series', *The Cricket Quarterly*, 2 (4): 195–9.
James, C. L. R. (1968) 'Not Cricket', *Transition*, 37: 37–8.
James, C. L. R. (1970) 'C. L. R. James [Anthology]', *Radical America*, 4 (4).
James, C. L. R. (1971 [1936]) *Minty Alley*, Port of Spain: New Beacon Books.
James, C. L. R. (1973 [1937]) *World Revolution, 1917–1936: the Rise and Fall of the Communist International*, Westport, CT: Hyperion Press, Inc.
James, C. L. R. (1973 [1960]) *Modern Politics*, Detroit: Bewick Editions.
James, C. L. R. (1977a) *The Future in the Present: Selected Writings*, London: Allison and Busby.
James, C. L. R. (1977b) *Nkrumah and the Ghana Revolution*, London: Allison and Busby.
James, C. L. R. (1980 [1938]) *The Black Jacobins: Toussaint L'Ouverture and the San Domingo Revolution*, London: Allison and Busby.
James, C. L. R. (1980 [1948]) *Notes on Dialectics: Hegel, Marx, Lenin*, London: Allison and Busby.
James, C. L. R. (1980) *Spheres of Existence: Selected Writings*, London: Allison and Busby.
James, C. L. R. (1982) 'The Nine Year Old Leader', *Race Today* (May/June): 100.
James, C. L. R. (1983 [1963]) *Beyond a Boundary*, New York: Pantheon Books.
James, C. L. R. (1983) *Walter Rodney and the Question of Power*, London: Race Today Publications.
James, C. L. R. (1984) *At the Rendezvous of Victory: Selected Writings*, London: Allison and Busby.
James, C. L. R. (1986 [1950]) *State Capitalism and World Revolution*, Chicago: Charles H. Kerr Publishing Company.
James, C. L. R. (1986) *Cricket*, London: Allison and Busby.
James, C. L. R. (1990 [1954]) 'Popular Art and the Cultural Tradition', *Third Text*, 10: 3–10.
James, C. L. R. (1992) *The C. L. R. James Reader*, ed. A. Grimshaw and K. Hart, Oxford: Blackwell.
James, C. L. R. (1993) *American Civilization*, Oxford: Blackwell.

James, C. L. R. (1996a) *C. L. R. James on the 'Negro Question'*, ed. S. McLemee, Jackson: University of Mississippi Press.
James, C. L. R. (1996b) *Special Delivery: the Letters of C. L. R. James to Constance Webb, 1938–1948*, ed. A. Grimshaw, Oxford: Blackwell.
James, C. L. R. (2001 [1953]) *Mariners, Renegades and Castaways: the Story of Herman Melville and the World We Live In*, Hanover: Dartmouth College and the University Press of New England.
James, C. L. R. (2003) *Letters From London*, ed. K. Laughlin, Port of Spain: Prospect Press.
James, C. L. R. (2006) *The Nobbie Stories for Children and Adults*, Lincoln: University of Nebraska Press.
James, C. L. R., Grace C. Lee and Pierre Chaulieu (1974 [1958]) *Facing Reality*, Detroit: Bewick.
Kauppi, N. (2005) 'The French Intellectual Habitus and Literary Culture', in *Theory's Empire: an Anthology of Dissent*, ed. D. Patai and W. H. Corral, New York: Columbia University Press.
Kelley, R. D. G. (1996) 'The World the Diaspora Made: C. L. R. James and the Politics of History', in *Rethinking C. L. R. James*, ed. G. Farred, Oxford: Blackwell.
King, N. (2006) 'C. L. R. James, Genre and Cultural Politics', in *Beyond Boundaries: C. L. R. James and Postnational Studies*, ed. C. Gair, London: Pluto Press.
King, R. (2006) 'The Odd Couple: C. L. R. James, Hannah Arendt and the Return of Politics in the Cold War', in *Beyond Boundaries: C. L. R. James and Postnational Studies*, ed. C. Gair, London: Pluto Press.
Lai, L. W. (1992) 'C. L. R. James and Trinidadian Nationalism', in *C. L. R. James' Caribbean*, ed. P. Henry and P. Buhle, Durham: Duke University Press.
Lara, B. (with Brian Scovell) (1995) *Beating the Field: My Own Story*, London: Partridge Press.
Larsen, N. (1996) 'Negativities of the Popular: C. L. R. James and the Limits of "Cultural Studies"', in *Rethinking C. L. R. James*, ed. G. Farred, Oxford: Blackwell.
Lazarus, N. (1999) *Nationalism and Cultural Practice in the Postcolonial World*, Cambridge: Cambridge University Press.
Lemert, C. (2003) 'W. E. B. du Bois', in *The Blackwell Companion to Major Classical Social Theorists*, ed. G. Ritzer, Oxford: Blackwell.
Lemert, C. (ed.) (2004) *Social Theory: the Multicultural and Classic Readings*, Boulder: Westview Press.
Lenin, V. I. (1993 [1916]) *Imperialism: the Highest Stage of Capitalism*, New York: International Publishers.
Ley, G. (1991) *A Short Introduction to Ancient Greek Theater*, Chicago: University of Chicago Press.
Linebaugh, P. and M. Rediker (2000) *The Many-Headed Hydra: Sailors, Slaves, Commoners and the Hidden History of the Revolutionary Atlantic*, Boston: Beacon Press.
Macherey, P. (1978) *A Theory of Literary Production*, London: Routledge & Kegan Paul.
Mangan, J. A. (1998) *The Games Ethic and Imperialism: Aspects of the Diffusion of an Ideal*, London: Frank Cass.
Marqusee, M. (1994) *Anyone But England: Cricket and the National Malaise*, London: Verso.

Marx, K. (1972 [1875]) *Critique of the Gotha Programme*, Peking: Foreign Languages Press.

Marx, K. (1975) *Early Writings*, London: Penguin.

McKenzie, E. (1995) 'C. L. R. James on Cricket as Art', *Caribbean Quarterly*, 41 (3/4): 92–8.

McLemee, S. and P. le Blanc (eds) (1994) *C. L. R. James and Revolutionary Marxism: Selected Writings of C. L. R. James, 1939–1949*, New York: Humanity Books.

Memmi, A. (1965) *The Colonizer and the Colonized*, London: Souvenir Press.

Miller, P. B. (2001) 'Enlightened Hesitations: Black Masses and Tragic Heroes in C. L. R. James', *The Black Jacobins*', *M.L.N.*, 116: 1069–90.

Moore-Gilbert, B. (1997) *Postcolonial Theory: Contexts, Practices, Politics*, London: Verso.

Murray, J. (1996) 'The Boy at the Window', in *Rethinking C. L. R. James*, ed. G. Farred, Oxford: Blackwell.

Muybridge, E. (1901) *The Human Figure in Motion: an Electro-Photographic Investigation of Consecutive Phases of Muscular Actions Commenced 1872, Completed 1885*, London: Chapman and Hall.

Nandy, A. (1989) *The Tao of Cricket: On Games of Destiny and the Destiny of Games*, New Delhi: Viking Books.

Nielsen, A. L. (1997) *C. L. R. James: a Critical Introduction*, Jackson: University of Mississippi Press.

Oborne, P. (2004) *Basil D'Oliveira. Cricket and Conspiracy: the Untold Story*, London: Little, Brown.

Okara, G. (1963) 'African Speech ... English Words', *Transition*, 10: 15–16.

Patai, D. and W. H. Corral (eds) (2005) *Theory's Empire: an Anthology of Dissent*, New York: Columbia University Press.

Phillips, C. (2001) *A New World Order*, New York: Vintage International.

Pinsky, R. (1996) *The Figured Wheel: Collected Poems*, Manchester: Carcanet Press.

Porter, E. (2006) '"Summer of Hummer": C. L. R. James, *American Civilization* and the (Necro)political Crisis', in *Beyond Boundaries: C. L. R. James and Postnational Studies*, ed. C. Gair, London: Pluto Press.

Rabbitt, K. (1995) 'C. L. R. James' Figuring of Toussaint-Louverture: *The Black Jacobins* and the Literary Hero', in *C. L. R. James: His Intellectual Legacies*, ed. S. Cudjoe and W. Cain, Amherst: University of Massachusetts Press.

Ramchand, K. (1970) *The West Indian Novel and its Background*, London: Faber.

Rawick, G. (1986) 'Personal Notes', in *C. L. R. James: His Life and Work*, ed. P. Buhle, London: Allison and Busby.

Rediker, M. (2007) *The Slave Ship: a Human History*, London: John Murray Publishers.

Renton, D. (2007) *C. L. R. James: Cricket's Philosopher King*, London: Haus Publishing.

Roach, J. (1996) *Cities of the Dead: Circum-Atlantic Performance*, New York: Columbia University Press.

Robinson, C. (1993) 'The Appropriation of Frantz Fanon', *Race and Class*, 35 (1): 79–91.

Robinson, C. (1995) 'C. L. R. James and the World System', in *C. L. R. James: His Intellectual Legacies*, ed. S. Cudjoe and W. Cain, Amherst: University of Massachusetts Press.

Rosengarten, F. (2007) *Urbane Revolutionary: C. L. R. James and the Struggle for a New Society*, Jackson: University of Mississippi Press.

Ross, A. (1996) 'Civilization in One Country? The American James', in *Rethinking C. L. R. James*, ed. G. Farred, Oxford: Blackwell.
Said, E. (1990) 'Third World Intellectuals and Metropolitan Culture', *Raritan*, 9 (3): 27–50.
Said, E. (1993) *Culture and Imperialism*, London: Vintage.
Said, E. (2003 [1978]) *Orientalism*, London: Penguin.
St. Louis, B. (1999) 'The Perilous "Pleasures of Exile": C. L. R. James, Bad Faith and the Diasporic Life', *Interventions*, 1 (3): 345–60.
St. Louis, B. (2007) *Rethinking Race, Politics and Poetics: C. L. R. James' Critique of Modernity*, Oxford: Routledge.
Sandiford, K. (1994) *Cricket and the Victorians*, Aldershot: Scholar Press.
Sandiford, K. and B. Stoddart (1995) 'The Elite Schools and Cricket in Barbados: a Study in Cultural Continuity', in *Liberation Cricket: West Indies Cricket Culture*, ed. H. M. Beckles and B. Stoddart, Manchester: Manchester University Press.
Schwarz, B. (2006) 'C. L. R. James' *American Civilization*', in *Beyond Boundaries: C. L. R. James and Postnational Studies*, ed. C. Gair, London: Pluto Press.
Scovell, B. (2007) *Brian Lara: Cricket's Troubled Genius*, Stroud: Stadia.
Searle, A. (1997) *S. F. Barnes: His Life and Times*, Manchester: Empire Publications.
Searle, C. (1995) 'Lara's Innings: a Caribbean Moment', *Race and Class*, 36 (4): 31–42.
Searle, C. (2001) 'Murali's Match: Communalism and the Oval', *Race and Class*, 42 (4): 80–6.
Shange, N. (1998) *If I Can Cook/You Know God Can*, Boston: Beacon Press.
Shillingsburg, P. (2001) *William Makepeace Thackeray: a Literary Life*, Basingstoke: Palgrave Macmillan.
Singham, A.W. (1990) 'James and the Creation of a Caribbean Intellectual Tradition', *Social and Economic Studies*, 39 (3): 180–9.
Smith, A. (2006a) '"A Conception of the Beautiful": C. L. R. James' *Glasgow Herald* Cricket Articles', *The International Journal of the History of Sport*, 23 (1): 46–66.
Smith, A. (2006b) '*Beyond a Boundary* (of a *Field of Cultural Production*): Reading C. L. R. James with Bourdieu', *Theory, Culture and Society*, 23 (4): 95–112.
Smith, A. (forthcoming. 2010) 'Concrete Freedom: C. L. R. James on Culture and Black Politics', *Cultural Sociology*.
Souvarine, B. (1939) *Stalin: a Critical Survey of Bolshevism*, London: Secker and Warburg.
Soyinka, W. (1975) 'Neo-Tarzanism: the Poetics of Pseudo-Tradition', *Transition*, 49: 38–44.
Springfield, C. L. (1990) 'Through the People's Eyes: C. L. R. James' Rhetoric of History', *Caribbean Quarterly*, 36 (1/2): 85–97.
Stoddart, B. (1995) 'Cricket, Social Formation and Cultural Continuity in Barbados: a Preliminary Ethnohistory', in *Liberation Cricket: West Indies Cricket Culture*, ed. H. M. Beckles and B. Stoddart, Manchester: Manchester University Press.
Stoddart, B. (1998) 'West Indies', in *The Imperial Game: Cricket, Culture and Society*, ed. B. Stoddart and K. Sandiford, Manchester: Manchester University Press.
Stuempfle, S. (1995) *The Steelband Movement: the Forging of a National Art in Trinidad and Tobago*, Philadelphia: University of Pennsylvania Press.
Surin, K. (1996) '"The Future Anterior": C. L. R. James and Going *Beyond a Boundary*', in *Rethinking C. L. R. James*, ed. G. Farred, Oxford: Blackwell.

Taylor, L. S. (1999) 'The Purpose of Playing and the Purpose of History: C. L. R. James' Shakespeare', *Interventions*, 1 (3): 373–87.

Thackeray, W. M. (1933 [1848]) *Vanity Fair: a Novel Without a Hero*, London: Daily Express Publications.

Tiffin, H. (1995 [1981]) 'Cricket, Literature and the Politics of Decolonisation: the Case of C. L. R. James', in *Liberation Cricket: West Indies Cricket Culture*, ed. H. M. Beckles and B. Stoddart, Manchester: Manchester University Press.

Tocqueville, A. de (1966 [1835/1840]) *Democracy in America*, New York: Harper Perennial.

Todd, C. (2007) 'Cover Driving Gracefully: On the Aesthetic Appreciation of Cricket', *Sport in Society*, 10 (5): 856–77.

Trotsky, L. (1991 [1925]) *Literature and Revolution*, London: Red Words.

Turner, V. (1977) *The Ritual Process: Structure and Anti-Structure*, New York: Cornell University Press.

Walcott, D. (1995) 'A Tribute to C. L. R. James', in *C. L. R. James: His Intellectual Legacies*, ed. S. Cudjoe and W. Cain, Amherst: University of Massachusetts Press.

Wali, O. (1963) 'The Dead End of African Literature', *Transition*, 10: 13–15.

Waterman, C. (1997) '"Our Tradition is a Very Modern Tradition": Popular Music and the Construction of Pan-Yoruba Identity', in *African Popular Culture*, ed. K. Barber, Oxford: James Currey.

Weber, M. (1978a) 'Politics as a Vocation', in *Max Weber: Selections in Translation*, ed. W. G. Runciman, Cambridge: Cambridge University Press.

Weber, M. (1978b) 'The History of the Piano', in *Max Weber: Selections in Translation*, ed. W. G. Runciman, Cambridge: Cambridge University Press.

West, Harry G. and T. Sanders (eds) (2003) *Transparency and Conspiracy: Ethnographies of Suspicion in the New World Order*, Durham: Duke University Press.

White, L. (2008) *Speaking with Vampires: Rumour and History in Colonial Africa*, Berkeley: University of California Press.

Williams, E. (1944) *Capitalism and Slavery*, Chapel Hill: University of North Carolina Press.

Williams, R. (1976) *Keywords: a Vocabulary of Culture and Society*, London: Fontana Press.

Williams, R. (1982 [1958]) *Culture and Society: Coleridge to Orwell*, London: Hogarth Press.

Wolff, J. (1993) *The Social Production of Art*, Basingstoke: Macmillan.

Worcester, K. (1996) *C. L. R. James: a Political Biography*, Albany: State University of New York Press.

Wynter, S. (1992) 'Beyond the Categories of the Master Conception: the Counterdoctrine of the Jamesian Poesis', in *C. L. R. James' Caribbean*, ed. P. Henry and P. Buhle, Durham: Duke University Press.

Young, J. D. (1999) *The World of C. L. R. James: His Unfragmented Vision*, Glasgow: Clydeside Press.

Young, R. (1990) *White Mythologies: Writing History and the West*, London: Routledge.

Zafiri, Y. (2007) 'Chorus and Dance in the Ancient World', in *The Cambridge Companion to Greek and Roman Theatre*, ed. M. McDonald and J. M. Walton, Cambridge: Cambridge University Press.

Index

Adorno, Theodor W., 77–80, 125, 151
Aeschylus, 43, 104–5
Ambrose, Curtly, 46
American Civilization, 22, 34, 66–7, 73, 78, 91, 102, 111, 124–5
Anderson, Benedict, 147–8
Aptheker, Herbert, 61–2
Arendt, Hannah, 32, 152–5
Aristotle, 89, 100–1
Arlott, John, 128
Arnold, Matthew, 37, 52

Baldwin, James, 7
Barnes, S. F., 51–5, 72, 112
Benjamin, Walter, 57, 113
Benny, Jack, 150
Bernard, General Carey, 109, 140
Beyond a Boundary, 3, 9, 13, 21, 24–31, 33, 46, 50, 55, 84, 86, 92–3, 95–6, 102, 113, 118–19, 122, 128, 141, 147, 157
Birth of a Nation, The, 144–6
Bishop, Maurice, 9
Black Jacobins, The, 5, 9, 30, 47, 69, 72–3, 88–91
'Bodyline', 10, 71
Boggs, Grace Lee, 5, 10, 63
Bogues, Anthony, 16–17, 50, 63
Bourdieu, Pierre, 31, 38, 51, 114, 118, 140–2
Bradman, Don, 61, 85
Buhle, Paul, 80, 92, 110, 135
Bukharin, Nikolai, 74
Burke, Edmund, 92

Capitalism and Slavery, 8
Cardus, Neville, 52, 142
Carpentier, Alejo, 121
Case for West-Indian Self Government, The, 4, 110
Chaplin, Charlie, 120, 150
Cipriani, Captain A. A., 3, 108–11
Cladel, Léon, 118
Clausewitz, Carl von, 73–5
Constantine, Learie, 4, 51–4, 61–2, 95, 108, 115–20, 139, 153–4
Count of Monte Cristo, The, 78
cricket,
  history of, 20, 24, 29–30, 33, 49, 52, 71–3, 118–19, 129
  politics of, 9, 20–6, 28–31, 33–4, 44–6, 52, 95, 121–2, 129
Cudjoe, Selwyn, 50–1, 88, 135

D'Oliveira, Basil, 20–2, 31
Dhondy, Farrukh, 7, 17, 93, 111–12, 144
'Dialectical Materialism and the Fate of Humanity', 6
Dickens, Charles, 95
Donald Duck, 79
Dostoevsky, Fyodor, 56
Douglass, Fredrick, 61–3
Du Bois, W. E. B., 3–5, 41, 67–8, 138–9, 145
Dumas, Alexander, 121
Dunayevskaya, Raya, 5, 63
Durkheim, Émile, 86

Eagleton, Terry, 124
Economic and Philosophical Manuscripts of 1844, 63, 124–5
Eisenstein, Sergei, 100
Eliot, T. S., 101, 120
Ellison, Ralph, 7, 160
'Every Cook Can Govern', 111

Facing Reality, 8, 74, 80, 132
Fanon, Frantz, 4, 33, 83, 135
Flaubert, Gustave, 56
Ford, Henry, 71, 102

Garvey, Marcus, 3, 87–8
Gone With the Wind, 144–6

Gramsci, Antonio, 78–9
Griffith, D. W., 144–6
Grimshaw, Anna, 2, 22–3, 137
Guernica, 100, 156
Guha, Ramachandra, 49–50

Hall, Stuart, 73
Hamlet, 37
Hansen, Joseph, 23
Harris, Lord (George Robert Canning), 49–50, 52
Harris, Wilson, 10, 60
Hazlitt, William, 43, 115
Headley, George, 113, 126, 128–31
Hector, Tim, 43
Hegel, G. W. F., 15, 40, 68, 76, 80, 130, 149
Hemingway, Ernest, 73
History of Negro Revolt, A, 5, 87
History of the Russian Revolution, The, 148–9
Hope, Bob, 150
Howe, Darcus, 45

Invisible Man, 160

Jackson, George, 111
James, C. L. R.
  on American society, 7–8, 13, 16, 22, 27–8, 34–5, 39, 66–7, 76, 77–83, 124–5, 138
  on ancient Greece, vii, 90–1, 100–2, 104–5, 111, 148, 154–5
  on audiences, 14, 33, 37, 55, 59–60, 77, 80–1, 83–91, 100–7, 133, 139–46, 149–50
  biography, 3–10, 28, 50, 95–7, 104–5, 138
  and Black Power, 10, 14, 35
  and Bloomsbury, 5, 50, 95–7, 102, 155
  on Caribbean society, 8, 17, 30, 34, 44–7, 84, 95, 108–9, 122–3, 129
  and feminism, 15–16, 110–12
  on film, vii, 19, 57, 76–80, 100–2
  on 'genius', 41, 66, 86, 112–34, 152
  on history, 6, 41, 46–7, 62–9, 72–81, 127, 130–1, 147–9, 152–3
  and Marxism, 5–6, 15–17, 26, 35, 63–4, 34–5, 37, 63–4, 74, 77, 120, 124–6, 130, 132, 135–6, 143, 147–9
  on 'mass' or 'popular culture', 7, 13, 59–60, 65, 76–81, 91, 100–3, 116, 122–3, 124–5, 139–40, 143–5, 150–1, 160–1
  method, 103–6
  on music, 59–60, 121, 123, 150–1, 160–1
  on nationalism, 10–11, 16, 33, 87, 120–1
  on the 'Negro' question, 5–6, 35, 39, 67–8, 82–3, 87, 125–7, 139–40, 143–6
  on political organisation, 6–8, 11–13, 32–4, 46, 99–100, 106–7, 123–4, 138–9, 151–2
  on racism, 4–6, 28–9, 50, 60–2, 67, 82–3, 87, 96–7, 109, 121–2, 125–7, 139–40, 143–6
  on slavery and resistance to slavery, 30, 68, 72, 86–91, 138
  on 'spontaneity', 12, 85–6, 150–4
  and Stalinism, 2, 32–5, 61–2, 65–6, 71, 74, 101, 106–7
  on war, 73–6, 109
  on Western civilisation, 5, 9, 14, 16–17, 68–9, 71, 74–6, 88–9, 96–7, 117–18, 132, 160–1
  see also under listings by individual book title
James, Selma, *see* Weinstein, Selma
Jaspers, Karl, 106

Kanhai, Rohan, 22, 37, 60, 128, 153–7
Kant, Immanuel, 106, 150
Kermode, Frank, 158–9
King Lear, 37
King, Martin Luther, 151

L'Ouverture, Toussaint, 87–91, 111
Lamming, George, 68
Lara, Brian, 42–8
Last of the Conquerors, The, 67
Lazarus, Neil, 64, 118, 136
Lee, Grace, *see* Boggs, Grace Lee

Lenin, V. I., 68, 74, 111
Letters from London, 95–7, 102, 155
Life of Captain Cipriani, The, 4, 93, 108–11
Lincoln, Abraham, 111
Louis, Joe, 125–6
Lyrical Ballads, The, 47–8

Macherey, Pierre, 66
Maginot line, 75
Mailer, Norman, 66–7
Malcolm, Devon, 42–3, 46
Mangan, J. A., 24, 49
Mannette, Ellie, 123
Mariners, Renegades and Castaways, 58, 68–9, 78, 94
Marx, Karl, 63–4, 69, 77, 80, 87, 92, 124–6, 141
Melville, Herman, 7, 13, 34, 58, 68–9, 78, 93, 124, 130
Memmi, Albert, 125–6
Mendis, Ajantha, 160
Mighty Sparrow, 60, 121
Miller, Paul B., 90–1
Minty Alley, 4, 51, 98–9, 103, 107
Moby Dick, 10, 58–9, 68–9, 94
Modern Politics, 9, 124, 131–2
Muralitharan, Muttiah, 42
Murvin, Junior, 45
Muybridge, Eadweard, vii

Naipaul, V. S., 68
Naked and the Dead, The, 66–7
Native Son, 35, 38
Nelson (Lancashire), 4, 51–4, 108
Newbolt, Henry, 72–3
Nielsen, Aldon Lynn, 2, 18, 61
Nkrumah, Kwame, 9, 33, 111
Nobbie Stories for Children and Adults, The, 132–3
Notes on Dialectics, 6, 15, 40, 76, 143

On War, 73
Othello, 38–9, 46

Padmore, George (Malcolm Nurse), 111
Parks, Rosa, 151–2
Picasso, Pablo, 100, 156–7
Pickwick Papers, The, 95
Pinsky, Robert, 36
Pollock, Jackson, 123, 156–7
Pope, Alexander, 160
postcolonial studies, 13, 93, 151
'Preface to Criticism', 32, 59, 100

Ramchand, Kenneth, 99
Ranatunga, Arjuna, 42
Ranjitsinhji, K. S., 50
Reflections on the Revolution in France, 92
Robeson, Paul, 5, 38–9, 46, 88
Rodin, Auguste, 155
Rodney, Walter, 9, 120

Said, Edward, 10, 138
Salut au Monde, 22
Sartre, John-Paul, 83
Schwarz, Bill, 145
Searle, Chris, 42–3
Shakespeare, William, 37–9, 43, 59, 115
Shange, Ntozake, 112
Shillingsburg, Peter, 98
Simon, Spree, 123
Sitwell, Edith, 50
Smith, William Gardner, 67
Sobers, Gary, 44–8, 120–3, 133–4
Souvarine, Boris, 5
Sparrow, Mighty, 60, 121
Spengler, Oswald, 73
St. Hill, Wilton, 118–19
Stalin, Joseph, 5, 32, 111, 132
State Capitalism and World Revolution, 6, 33, 74, 77, 107
Surin, Kenneth, 69

Terkel, Studs, 104
Thackeray, W. M., 92–9, 107, 124
Thiong'o, Ngugi, 9
Thomas, J. J., 116
Thompson, Francis, 52
Tocqueville, Alexis de, 73–4, 78
Toussaint Louverture, 5, 88–91
Trotsky, Leon, 5, 12, 23, 37, 68, 73, 111, 147–9
Tubman, Harriet, 111
Turner, Victor, 126

Vanity Fair, 92–100, 107
Vitaï Lampada, 72–3

Walcott, Clyde, 121
Walcott, Derek, 130
Walsh, Courtney, 46
Waugh, Steve, 47
Webb, Constance, 3, 7–8, 11, 38, 41, 69, 105, 111, 130–1, 137, 152, 157, 160
Weber, Max, 32, 103
Webster, Margaret, 38, 46
Weinstein, Selma, 8, 111
Whitman, Walt, 22, 35, 93, 112, 125
Williams, Eric, 8, 33
Williams, Raymond, 2, 57, 113
Woolf, Leonard, 110
Woolf, Virginia, 110
Woolley, Frank, 55–7, 104, 131
Worcester, Kent, 92
Wordsworth, William, 47–8
World Revolution, 5
Worrell, Frank, 8, 25, 28–9, 40, 46, 120
Wright, Richard, 7, 35, 38, 121

Young, James, 26, 112

CPSIA information can be obtained at www.ICGtesting.com
Printed in the USA
LVOW04*2007310315

432761LV00009B/306/P

9 780230 220218